Defending the Genetic Supermarket

The law and ethics of selecting the next generation

In 1974, Robert Nozick speculated about the possibility of a 'genetic supermarket', where prospective parents could select the genetic traits of their future offspring free from state interference. In that pre-IVF era, his speculations were merely hypothetical. Advances in reproductive and genetic technologies, however, have rendered this most controversial of thought-experiments a potential reality. In particular, the technology of preimplantation genetic diagnosis, used in conjunction with in vitro fertilisation, allows prospective parents to choose between a number of 'candidate embryos', about which considerable amounts of genetic information can be known.

In the intervening decades, Nozick's idea has been attacked from left and right, by disability activists, Christian bioethicists, radical feminists, and many others. But amidst the 'designer babies' rhetoric, have any of them built a compelling case against a pro-choice model? *Defending the Genetic Supermarket* considers whether Nozick's hypothesis can in fact be faulted. Can a case be made out for state involvement in such decisions? Who stands to be harmed by a supermarket model? Are any ethical principles or societal interests threatened by it?

The central thesis of *Defending the Genetic Supermarket* is that the approach adopted by the UK Parliament, and by the Human Fertilisation and Embryology Authority, to such choices has been muddled and has taken insufficient notice of certain ethical principles that go to the core of this topic. By considering a number of individual policy decisions of the HFEA, the author hopes to show an approach informed by these principles could lead to outcomes that are both more ethically consistent, and more humane, then the Authority has so far managed. Furthermore, the author argues that many of the fears and objections levied against the notion of the genetic supermarket are internally inconsistent, philosophically unsound, or merely highly improbable.

Dr Colin Gavaghan is a lecturer in medical law and ethics at the School of Law in the University of Glasgow.

Biomedical Law and Ethics Library
Series Editor: Sheila A.M. McLean

Scientific and clinical advances, social and political developments and the impact of healthcare on our lives raise profound ethical and legal questions. Medical law and ethics have become central to our understanding of these problems, and are important tools for the analysis and resolution of problems – real or imagined.

In this series, scholars at the forefront of biomedical law and ethics contribute to the debates in this area, with accessible, thought-provoking, and sometimes controversial ideas. Each book in the series develops an independent hypothesis and argues cogently for a particular position. One of the major contributions of this series is the extent to which both law and ethics are utilised in the content of the books, and the shape of the series itself.

The books in this series are analytical, with a key target audience of lawyers, doctors, nurses, and the intelligent lay public.

Forthcoming titles:

Horsey and Biggs, *Human Fertilisation and Embryology* (2007)
McLean and Williamson, *Impairment and Disability* (2007)
Priaulx, *The Harm Paradox* (2007)
Downie and Macnaughton, *Bioethics and the Humanities* (2007)
McLean, *Assisted Dying* (2007)
Huxtable, *Euthanasia, Ethics and the Law* (2007)
Elliston, *Best Interests of the Child In Healthcare* (2007)

About the Series Editor:
Professor Sheila McLean is International Bar Association Professor of Law and Ethics in Medicine and Director of the Institute of Law and Ethics in Medicine at the University of Glasgow.

Defending the Genetic Supermarket

The law and ethics of selecting the next generation

Colin Gavaghan

Routledge·Cavendish
Taylor & Francis Group
LONDON AND NEW YORK

First published 2007
by Routledge-Cavendish
2 Park Square, Milton Park, Abingdon, Oxon OX14 4RN, UK

Simultaneously published in the USA and Canada
by Routledge-Cavendish
270 Madison Ave, New York, NY 10016

*Routledge-Cavendish is an imprint of the Taylor & Francis Group,
an informa business*

© 2007 Colin Gavaghan

Typeset in Times New Roman by
RefineCatch Limited, Bungay, Suffolk
Printed and bound in Great Britain by
MPG Books Ltd, Bodmin, Cornwall

British Library Cataloguing in Publication Data
A catalogue record for this book is available from the British Library

Library of Congress Cataloging in Publication Data
A catalog record for this book has been requested

ISBN10: 1-84472-058-6 (pbk)
ISBN10: 1-84472-059-4 (hbk)
ISBN13: 978-1-84472-058-3 (pbk)
ISBN13: 978-1-84472-059-0 (hbk)

Contents

Acknowledgements

In researching and writing this book, I have benefited enormously from assistance, encouragement and inspiration from a lot of people, but the following deserve special thanks: Avril and Jim Gavaghan, and Jessie Gavaghan, for unflagging support, emotional and financial; Sheila McLean, who put together this series, and whose encouragement and incisive suggestions contributed greatly to the research that eventually gave rise to *Defending the Genetic Supermarket*; Grace McGuire, for more help then I can remember; Derek Morgan and Lindsay Farmer, for their constructive suggestions on the PhD thesis that evolved into this book; various colleagues, friends and students for enlightening suggestions, perspectives and occasionally scathing critique (in particular, Alasdair Maclean, for hours of stimulating discussion and gallons of stimulating coffee); Maddy Langford at Routledge-Cavendish, for ushering me though the myriad complexities of getting a book into print; and of course, my partner Carol Jess for her preternatural patience and fantastic company in the face of the trials and tribulations of living with an aspiring author.

The Clark Foundation and the Wellcome Trust provided financial assistance in the early, unemployed years of study, and I am grateful to them for that.

Chapter I

The attack on the genetic supermarket

The truth is that all of us have to contend with our parents, for good or ill, but at least we can't be committed at birth to spending the rest of our lives as circus performers or bank clerks, or missionaries. We have free will, and the great thing about growing up is personal choice. What choice is there if your parents have already decided that you are going to be deaf, and that deafness will be your defining identity, just as it has been theirs? This is not the beauty of compatibility, it is genetic imperialism.[1]

Children need to be valued for themselves. They should never be used as commodities. But that's precisely what they've become through all this mucking around with human embryos. . . . Using life as a means to an end cannot be anything other than dehumanising. And indeed, children have been turned into artefacts.[2]

Whilst it is always dangerous to say 'never', most of us felt that there were many characteristics for which it would be quite inappropriate to engage genetic technology (such as embryonic selection on the grounds of myopia, or hair-colour).[3]

The excerpts are reflective of a broad contemporary consensus. Encompassing Hollywood films[4] and regulatory bodies,[5] eminent philosophers[6] and

1   Award-winning author Jeanette Winterson, writing in *The Guardian*, 9 April 2002.
2   Melanie Phillips, 'Designer baby madness', *Daily Mail*, 5 August 2002.
3   Human Genetics Commission (HGC), *Making Babies: Reproductive Decisions and Genetic Technologies*, January 2006, paragraph 1.26.
4   Andrew Niccol's 1997 film, *Gattaca*, will be the subject of further discussion in Chapter 3.
5   See HGC, op. cit., and the various reports of the HFEA considered in later chapters.
6   'It remains a horrifying prospect that a eugenic self-optimization of the species, carried out via the aggregated preferences of consumers in the genetic supermarket (and via society's capacity for forming new habits), might change the moral status of future persons . . .' Jürgen Habermas, *The Future of Human Nature*, Cambridge: Polity Press, 2003, pp 93–4.

newspaper columnists,[7] renowned conservatives[8] and disability rights campaigners,[9] this unlikely alliance brings its diverse political and ethical perspectives to a narrow confluence on one issue: a very definite 'no' to 'designer babies'.

Of course, the actual reasons why these various people and agencies take this view often differ, as do the precise technologies and outcomes with which they are concerned. For some, the predominant concern is with what they see as the inherently hubristic, sacrilegious or dehumanising connotations of a technology that allows the present generation to choose their successors.[10] For others, the concerns are more concrete, deriving from concern that people will be harmed, devalued or treated unjustly.

It is not possible to evaluate and respond to these concerns without a fuller understanding of their nature, and it is part of my purpose here to unpack and distinguish some of the more interesting species of arguments. Nonetheless, it is impossible to overlook the fact that the case I put forward in this book is likely, at least initially, to be an unpopular one. Because, unfashionable though it may be, my argument is that the best response to decisions posed by technologies of genetic selection is, as far as possible, to leave people alone to make these decisions for themselves.

This is partly because I believe that reproductive decisions are invariably intensely important to people's life plans and most important interests, so much so that we should be very cautious about taking these decisions away from them. But it also derives from my belief that many of the concerns raised about what Gregory Stock calls germinal choice technologies (GCTs)[11] could be addressed better by more rather than less choice, and less rather than more regulation and restriction.

These contentions are not only controversial, they are likely to strike many readers as counter-intuitive. To a substantial extent, our society has come to view safety as almost synonymous with restriction and regulation, invariably by the state. The Precautionary Principle, which has come to occupy a central role in most discussions of new technologies, is almost always interpreted in a way that takes state action as the default position, to be adopted even

---

7 Such views are articulated not only by conservative columnists such as Phillips; the (somewhat more specific) concerns of anti-globalisation campaigner and sometime *Guardian* columnist George Monbiot will be considered in Chapter 7.

8 Francis Fukuyama, *Our Posthuman Future: Consequences of the Biotechnology Revolution*, New York: Faber, Strauss and Giroux, 2002.

9 Tom Shakespeare, 'Back to the future? New genetics and disabled people'. *Critical Social Policy* (1995); 15 (2/3): 22–35.

10 See, for example, Bill McKibben's *Enough: Staying Human in an Engineered Age*, New York: Times Books, 2003, and Fukuyama's *Our Posthuman Future*, op. cit.

11 Gregory Stock, *Redesigning Humans: Choosing Our Children's Genes*, London: Profile Books, 2002, pp 110–11.

in the absence of clear evidence of danger.[12] In its approach to genetic testing, the UK's reproductive regulatory body has prided itself on its 'cautious' approach, allowing prospective parents to use only those tests that have been meticulously evaluated, not only for effectiveness but for ethical acceptability.[13]

Yet the notion that state regulation is invariably 'safer' than individual choice is not a self-evident, universal truth. While it would, of course, be disingenuous to use the disastrous experience of eugenics to argue against *any* kind of state regulation, it is perhaps worth keeping in mind that the worst abuses perpetrated in the name of genetics occurred when individual reproductive choice was subjected to state control and subordinated to some idea of the 'greater good'.[14] In that historical context, it is surprising that state control is so readily *assumed* to be safer than the alternative; and it is somewhat ironic to hear the fear of eugenics used in arguments for *more* limitations on reproductive autonomy.

It is important to remember, then, that there is no automatic co-relation between ever greater safety and ever greater state control. Neither, of course, can we automatically assume the opposite. As I will try to show in the next chapter, though, those who seek to restrict individual choice have an extra obstacle to overcome, an obstacle that does not confront advocates of the pro-choice position. This is because of the value widely attributed to respect for autonomy; if a particular law or regulation did not have the effect of curtailing autonomy, by preventing someone from doing as they would otherwise have done, we might ask what purpose it serves.

My approach, then, begins with a *pro tanto* statement in favour of reproductive choice. Drawing on a long philosophical and political tradition, I will try to show that before the state imposes restrictions on individual choice (especially in areas as important and intimate as reproduction), it should be required to demonstrate a plausible justification for doing so. The question of whether such justifications exist in relation to reproductive choices will be the subject of the remainder of this book.

In setting out the general nature of the proposition I intend to advance and defend, I should, perhaps, take care to avoid one potential mistaken impression. It is not in any sense my intention to argue *in favour of* the technologies discussed here, in the sense of promoting their use, either in general or for particular purposes. A truly pro-choice position with regard to GCTs must recognise that choices *not* to use these technologies at all are just as worthy of

---

12 See Dick Taverne, *The March of Unreason: Science, Democracy, and the New Fundamentalism*, Oxford: Oxford University Press, 2005, especially Chapter 7.

13 The HFEA's approach to such technologies will be discussed in more detail in Chapter 6.

14 For a detailed account of the eugenics movements in the UK and USA, see Daniel Kevles' excellent history, *In The Name Of Eugenics: Genetics and the Uses of Human Heredity*, London: Harvard University Press, 1997.

respect as choices to use them. Just as those who argue pro-choice positions in relation to abortion are sometimes caricatured as being 'pro-abortion', I am acutely aware of the danger of being misrepresented as being pro-'designer babies'.

In fact, there are certain potential uses of GCTs that I, personally, would be more than content if no one ever used: use of these technologies to determine the sex, for example, or (insofar as this proves possible) sexual orientation, of their future offspring. But there is a world of difference between decisions of which we disapprove, and decisions which we would, or should, feel justified in prohibiting. It is this distinction which lies at the heart of the approach I advocate here.

By adopting this position of neutrality, my position is at odds not only with GCT-sceptics and bio-conservatives, but with a smaller body of bio-ethical commentators who believe that there is a positive moral obligation to make use of the available technology to ensure the birth of the 'best children possible'. John Harris and Julian Savulescu are perhaps the best-known exponents of the view that prospective parents should use GCTs in this way, though it should be noted that both stop short of calling for this ethical obligation to be given legal weight. As I will attempt to show in Chapter 3, though, this approach relies on accepting certain highly questionable assumptions about the obligations we owe to future generations, and on overlooking some (perhaps uncomfortable) observations about how the choices we make impact on the *identities* of those who come after us.

My argument in this book, then, is that choices about the genetic composition of future children should, in almost all cases, be left to prospective parents. This would extend as much to those who choose to reject these technologies as to those who wish to use them; as much to those who wish to make 'unorthodox' choices as to those who wish to use it for sympathetic purposes, such as the avoidance of serious genetic disorders.

A pro-choice position, however, is not synonymous with a laissez-faire approach. As I will argue, meaningful choice involves more than liberty from state control, and a genuine concern with choice involves considering how such choice can be facilitated. This is especially important if we are to avoid the concerns advanced by writers like George Monbiot, who warns that a 'free market' approach to genetic testing could have the undesirable effect of exacerbating existing economic divisions. Genuine choice has a positive as well as a negative dimension, and concerns with both autonomy and justice count against abandoning the less affluent outside the genetic supermarket's doors.

It does not, however, follow that the only way to avoid such unjust outcomes is by abandoning the technology itself, and in Chapter 7 I consider some alternative approaches that could address concerns with both choice and justice. As will become apparent, a proper consideration of this issue cannot ignore the context in which this conversation is located. Questions about the interaction between genetics, luck and justice are fundamental to any discussion about the sort of society we wish to live in, and to leave behind us, and it may be that the concerns brought into focus by GCTs reverberate far wider than the scope of this book. My contention is that a genuine concern with fairness cannot be addressed by restricting access to GCTs, which are at worst just one manifestation of unfairness. If Monbiot's concerns are worth taking seriously – as I believe they are – they can only be addressed by a more far-reaching reappraisal of the interaction between genetics, luck and justice. But this will be equally true whether or not we have access to GCTs.

In Chapter 2, then, I will consider what it means to speak of autonomous choice in relation to access to GCTs. The principle of respect for autonomy has been expressed in different forms, and its application to germinal choices is not as straightforward as may be expected. In fact, several commentators have sought to show that respect for autonomy provides a good argument *against* a pro-choice approach to GCTs. Part of my purpose in Chapter 2 is to show that such arguments, while interesting, do not succeed in reversing the general rule that respect for autonomy is better furthered by less, rather than more, restriction on individual choices.

If I am successful in this, then we will have a persuasive case in favour of a pro-choice default position, a presumption in favour of parental choice that can only be rebutted by some relatively weighty ethical claim in the other direction. The remainder of my discussion will involve a consideration, in turn, of several of the more credible, or frequently espoused, challenges to this position. I hope to show that many of these objections are not as persuasive as they at first appear, while others are in fact wholly without substance. Other objections – such as concern for the impact of a pro-choice position on existing (or future generations of) disabled people – are considerably more tangible, and less readily dispelled. But as I will hope to show, it may be possible to redress such concerns, at least to a substantial degree, by an approach involving less rather than more regulation, and more, rather than less, parental choice. This (predictably counter-intuitive) argument will be advanced in detail in Chapter 5.

Before commencing with an evaluation of the various arguments against a pro-choice approach to genetic choice, though, it is important to be clear as to what precisely we are discussing. What sorts of germinal choices are currently available? And what choices are likely to become available in the near future?

How much 'design' is possible?

That Louise Brown was the world's first 'IVF baby' is a fact likely to be as familiar to enthusiasts of *Trivial Pursuit* as students of bioethics. The name of Chloe O'Brien has, thus far, failed to stake an analogous claim in our cultural lexicon. In 1992, Chloe became the first child in the world to be born after preimplantation genetic diagnosis (PGD). Her parents, Michelle and Paul, were both asymptomatic carriers of the cystic fibrosis gene, which meant a 1:4 chance that any child they conceived 'naturally' would be affected by the disease (and a 1:2 chance that the child would, like its parents, be an asymptomatic carrier); in fact, they had already had a son affected with the disease.

Determined to avoid having another similarly afflicted child, the O'Briens, assisted by a team of fertility specialists at Hammersmith Hospital, utilised an existing technology (in vitro fertilisation) in tandem with a new technique. This technique – PGD – was 'developed in the 1980s . . . primarily in response to requests for help from people at risk of passing on a serious genetic disorder to their children'.[15] It involves the removal of one or more cells (blastomeres) from embryos generated in vitro, at about the eight-cell stage (usually around the third day after fertilisation).[16] The DNA from the biopsied cells is then amplified, originally by the technique of polymerase chain reaction (PCR),[17] but in more recent times by fluorescence in situ hybridisation (FISH),[18] and examined before any decision will be made as to which of the various 'candidate' embryos to implant.[19] Thus, the O'Briens were able to be sure that the embryo they selected to implant – the embryo that became Chloe – did not inherit any copies of the CF gene.

As the Human Genetics Commission explains, in the United Kingdom, 'PGD is currently being offered for three major categories of disease including:

- to determine the sex of the embryo with the aim of avoiding sex-linked disorders such as Duchenne muscular dystrophy;
- to identify embryos with single gene disorders such as cystic fibrosis;
- and to identify embryos with chromosomal disorders, where a technique called fluorescence in situ hybridisation (FISH) can be used to identify or confirm abnormal chromosomal rearrangements.'[20]

At present, 12 centres in the UK are licensed to carry out PGD. Between 2001

---

15 Human Genetics Commission, *Choosing the Future: Genetics and Reproductive Decision Making*, July 2004, paragraph 3.14.

16 'Preimplantation Genetic Analysis', Robert A Kaufmann et al, *The Journal of Reproductive Medicine* (1992) 37(5); 428–36, p 428.

17 For a straightforward account of how PCR works, see Philip Kitcher's *The Lives to Come*, London: Allen Lane: The Penguin Press, 1996, p 160.

18 Karen Sermon, André Van Steirteghem, Inge Liebaers. 'Preimplantation genetic diagnosis', *The Lancet* (2004); 363(9421): 1633–41, p 1633; Dagan Wells, 'Advances in preimplantation genetic diagnosis', *European Journal of Obstetrics & Gynaecology and Reproductive Biology* (2004); Vol 115, Supplement 1: S97–S101.

19 Id.

20 Human Genetics Commission, *Choosing the Future: Genetics and Reproductive Decision Making*, July 2004, paragraph 3.16.

and 2004, the technique is believed to have brought about 45 live births in the UK,[21] while it has been claimed that over a thousand PGD births have occurred worldwide.[22]

The most straightforward, and common, type of test has involved ascertaining the sex of the embryo.[23] Certain genetic disorders are X-linked, meaning that they are only inherited by male offspring; a technique which ensured that only female embryos were implanted would similarly ensure that the unwanted condition was not passed on to the next generation.[24] The preimplantation diagnosis of single-gene defects and chromosomal disorders has, however, also been successfully accomplished.[25]

Quite evidently, PGD is only an option to those who have undergone IVF, or some other means of assisted conception which results in a number of embryos being located ex utero. The present difficulties in achieving successful pregnancies following IVF have led some commentators to the conclusion that demand for PGD will, at least in the short term, be limited to those who already know they are at risk of passing on some genetic disorder, together with those who would be making use of reproductive technologies in any event.[26] Nonetheless, the distinct possibility exists that, as the success rate of techniques such as IVF improves, and the range of genetic conditions for which screening is possible continues to expand, so too will the demand for this technology.

What should be clear from even this brief description is that the 'designer baby' tag, so beloved of the mainstream media, is simply inaccurate to children born after PGD. Chloe O'Brien was not 'designed' by her parents. Rather, she – or perhaps we should say, the embryo that became Chloe – was selected from a number of candidates, but nothing at all was done to alter her genetic composition. This fact, as it turns out, has significant implications for any ethical appraisal of the technique, and I will revisit it in Chapter 3. Furthermore, it should already be obvious that at least one kind of objection to GCTs is simply not relevant to PGD.

The notion that unrestrained access to PGD would result in a physiologically homogenous dystopia of blond-haired, blue-eyed children is, in truth, more often encountered in newspaper letters pages and radio phone-ins than

---

21 See p 6, fn 20, paragraph 3.14.
22 John A Robertson, 'PGD: New ethical challenges' *Nature Reviews Genetics* (2003); 4(1): 6.
23 C Hanson, L Hamberger and PO Janson, 'Is any form of gender selection ethical?' *Journal of Assisted Reproduction and Genetics* (2002); 19: 431–2.
24 Of course, the ability to implant only embryos of the desired sex could be utilised for 'non-therapeutic' purposes. This highly controversial possibility will be considered in due course.
25 Asangla Ao, 'Preimplantation genetic diagnosis of inherited disease', *Indian Journal of Experimental Biology* (1996) 34: 1177–82, and Hanson and Hamberger, op. cit.
26 Jiaen Liu et al, 'Cystic fibrosis, Duchenne muscular dystrophy and preimplantation genetic diagnosis'. *Human Reproduction Update* 1996, 2(6); 531–9.

in serious bioethical discourse,[27] but the spectre of eugenics – of forced sterilisation and ethnic cleansing and genocide – haunts most discussions of this topic. Whether prospective parents would, in general, want to select for such traits is questionable; most parents, it seems, want children who resemble themselves, rather than some bizarre ideal of Aryan perfection. What we can safely say is that PGD will not, for the most part, allow them to have such children. Couples without the requisite genes for blue eyes or blond hair will quite simply be unable to pass those traits on to their offspring, however many embryos they conceive.

'Designer babies' is a catchy, sensational term, but one which contributes little to the debate about PGD. It does not, however, follow that PGD does not pose important ethical challenges. Nor does it follow that the prospect of 'designer babies' is not one that should concern us. For another technology, distinct from PGD, does raise the prospect of altering the DNA of succeeding generations. Sometimes referred to as gene therapy, genetic engineering, or (my preferred term) genetic modification (the choice of terms is, I think, significant, for reasons I will explore in due course), this involves the insertion of extraneous genetic material into, or otherwise altering the genome of an existing organism. While PGD involves merely the choice of which embryo to implant, then, gene therapy/modification *does* involve, in a sense, designing an embryo, albeit that in all cases thus far recorded, this could be seen more as corrections in design flaws than as a radical reshaping.

Most of what I discuss in this book relates to PGD rather than genetic modification, simply because, while the former technique is being used on a regular basis, and has been the focus of real-life ethical and legal controversies, the questions posed by the latter remain largely (though not entirely) hypothetical. It is probably true, though, that many of the objections levied against a pro-choice approach to PGD apply at least as much to GM, and it is certainly true that many of my defences of that position would support a similar approach to GM.

Many, but not all. In at least one highly significant respect, GM poses different philosophical questions than PGD. This difference relates in large degree to my earlier comments about the difference between 'choosing' and 'creating', and it may well mean that a very different approach should be

---

27 Such fears are not uncommonly expressed in submissions to official consultations. One contributor to a recent Department of Health consultation expressed the following view: 'Any regulations imposed now will, over time, be watered down until they cease to exist, and then the medical profession will finally be free to complete the job started by Adolf Hitler, namely the production of a "Master Race". The only difference being that Hitler's "Master Race" would have been pure Ayrians [*sic*] and produced naturally using the best selected human specimens as parents, whereas the medical profession will produce "Super Humans" by unnatural, artificial means!'

adopted to regulating that technology. I will revisit these more speculative questions in the last section of the book.

I am not the first to advocate a pro-choice approach to reproductive decisions. In 1974, Robert Nozick, in what is surely one of the most intriguing footnotes in modern philosophical writing, referred in *Anarchy, State and Utopia* to the notion of a 'genetic supermarket'.[28] In keeping with the central arguments of that text, his suggestion here was that choices about what sort of people there should be[29] should be left in the hands of private individuals, and should not be determined or restricted by the state. This free market in genetic screening would meet 'the individual specifications (within certain moral limits) of prospective parents,'[30] and would possess 'the great virtue that involves no centralized decision fixing the future human type(s)'.[31] When he wrote this, the first IVF birth was yet to occur, and PGD had not even been seriously contemplated. But the use, in tandem, of these techniques, together with the early experiments with genetic modification, presents us with the very real possibility of giving effect to Nozick's vision.

My vision is somewhat different from Nozick's. Whereas for him, 'freedom' was largely synonymous with 'liberty', and 'choice' meant leaving such decisions to unrestrained market forces, my suggestion is that if we are concerned about *real* choice, we should be concerned about more than choice for those who can afford to shop at the genetic supermarket. Whether it is possible to ensure fair and equal access to PGD, without sacrificing the position of state neutrality that is central to my pro-choice stance, is a difficult question, and one that I will consider in some detail. (It may be that the only way to ensure fair access to the genetic supermarket is by ensuring a fairer society in general.)

Although I take issue with Nozick's thesis in certain important respects, though, I think he was broadly right when he argued that decisions of this sort are, almost invariably, better entrusted to prospective parents than to the state, and that will be the main argument I espouse here. Even if I am not entirely successful, though, even if the conclusion that some potential uses of GCTs should be curtailed proves unavoidable, I hope that this book succeeds in a more modest aim: as a reminder that such decisions should not *lightly* be interfered with, or, to put it another way, that it is incumbent on us to show *good reason* before we interfere with the pro-choice assumption, and take decisions about the kinds of children they will have away from prospective parents.

---

28 Robert Nozick, *Anarchy, State, and Utopia*, Basil Blackwell, 1974, 1986 edn, p 315n.
29 To slightly paraphrase Jonathan Glover's title.
30 Nozick, *Anarchy, State, and Utopia*, op. cit.
31 Id.

Chapter 2

Autonomy and germinal choice

We were not trying to replace Nicole. If we were trying to replace any-thing it was the female element that that precious child brought to our family. Parents who have both genders know exactly what we are trying to say here. Nicole brought a whole different aspect to our family. Her interaction with the boys, her interaction with myself and indeed with Louise was completely different as a female child from the experience we had with the boys. Girls are different to boys. It was just that female difference. This isn't a want. This is a need that we have.[1]

Alan and Louise Masterton's request to use PGD, it is safe to say, was never likely to be the most sympathetic application, either among regulatory agen-cies or academic commentators. Although it is impossible not to feel for their loss – their daughter, Nicole, died tragically young in an horrific accident – the nature of their subsequent campaign was sure to touch more than a few raw nerves. As the statement from Alan Masterton explains, he and Louise sought to restore 'the female element . . . to our family' by using IVF-PGD to ensure that their next (and last) child was a girl. And for many observers – even some who are sympathetic to the use of this technology in other circumstances – this was simply not acceptable.

The particular questions and objections to which sex selection gives rise will be considered in a later chapter. For the moment, though, I want to address another question, a question about how we should approach the Mastertons' desire for another daughter. Should it be incumbent on them to satisfy us that their motives are worthy, that their desire for a daughter is actually a 'need' rather than a 'want'? Or should the burden of proof, or of justification, lie elsewhere, with those who seek to restrict their access to this technology?

Although it may not be immediately apparent, the direction from which we

1 'We desperately want a girl', BBC Online, 12 November 2003. Available from: http://news. bbc.co.uk/1/hi/health/3260827.stm (accessed 19 June 2006).

approach their request is a matter of considerable importance. It was always unlikely that the Mastertons would be able to persuade the majority of their peers that their efforts at 'social sex selection' were desirable; indeed, this widespread opposition to the practice was confirmed in the survey carried out by the HFEA (and considered in Chapter 5). But should it be incumbent on them – and other couples seeking to use GCTs in unorthodox or controversial ways – to do so? Should they be prohibited from making their own choices about their future children unless they are able to present their case in a manner persuasive to most listeners?

The alternative, a 'pro-choice' default position, would hold that, *absent a convincing case to the contrary*, those who wish to use GCTs should be at liberty to do so, even if they wish to use them in unusual or unpopular ways. On such an approach, the Mastertons – and the Hashmis, the Whitakers, the infamous US 'deaf lesbians', and the other couples who will be considered throughout this book – would be permitted to make such use of these technologies as accord with their own values and priorities. They would be spared the need to convince others to share, or even empathise with, those values and priorities. And most importantly, they would be subject to restriction only if some good reason could be offered for interfering with their private choices.

As I will discuss in later chapters, this is not how the regulation of reproductive technologies in the United Kingdom actually occurs. Rather, it is not uncommonly the case that a *restrictive* starting position is adopted, with the onus lying firmly with those seeking an exception to justify that exception. This will become clear when I consider, for example, the Human Fertilisation and Embryology Authority's guidelines on the use of PGD for tissue typing, a technology that allowed Raj and Shahana Hashmi to maximise the chances of giving birth to a child that would be a viable donor for their existing child; or the Human Genetics Commission's outright rejection of selection of 'inappropriate' traits, such as myopia and hair colour.

The position I advocate in this book would constitute quite a radical departure from the manner in which such decisions are currently made in the UK. In particular, it would involve rendering prospective parents less dependent on the agreement or empathy of the committees of technicians, politicians, academics and lay people who currently are entrusted to decide the future of other peoples' families. It would involve a bold recognition that, in a complex, diverse society such as ours, some people will want to do things that most of the rest of us find odd, or unsettling, or which we cannot imagine ever wanting to do ourselves, but that, absent very good reasons to the contrary, we should not prevent them from doing so. And it would involve accepting that, if we are to tell the Mastertons, or the Hashmis, or any of the other couples or individuals who are sure to follow after them, that we have decided to thwart their most fervent and desperate wishes, then at the very least we owe them a good explanation for that.

As I will argue throughout this book, many of the explanations offered up in justification of restrictions have been far from good. Some complex ethical principles (such as the categorical imperative) have been interpreted in idiosyncratic or simplified ways, while other important philosophical insights (such as Derek Parfit's non-identity problem) have been largely ignored; flimsy evidence of risk has been exaggerated or accorded undue weight, and arbitrary distinctions have been drawn between practices that appear ethically indistinguishable, sometimes for no evident purpose than to be seen to be drawing lines (both of the latter practices are illustrated in the HFEA's response to tissue typing; see Chapter 6).

This ad hoc, inconsistent, subjective approach to regulation has been routinely justified in the name of two of our society's shibboleths, 'democracy' and 'safety'. It is right, most of us think, that potentially dangerous new technologies should not be entrusted entirely to a technocratic elite of scientists, but should be supervised and regulated to ensure they do not run 'out of control'. It is right, we surely agree, that decisions about such technologies should be made in a transparent, accountable manner that takes account of the views of society in general. Cast in such terms, it is easy to see why the restrictive approach to GCTs has proved popular.

But what does 'democracy' truly entail when the question is not who should run the country, but rather, whether a couple should be allowed to make decisions about their future children? Does it simply involve adding up 'ayes' and 'nays'? Or does it also involve recognition of areas of decision-making so personal, so integral to our individual life plans, that they should be protected from what Mill called 'the tyranny of the majority'? And what does 'safety' mean when the question is not about nuclear waste, or terrorist threats, but about risks posed to putative entities whose actual existence is dependent on the decisions we are confronting? Perhaps most troubling of all in view of the history of this area, does state intrusion into the reproductive decision-making of individuals and couples not pose certain risks of its own?

The intrinsic value of autonomy

The pro-choice approach to GCTs derives in part from a view that reproductive choices are particularly valuable and particularly vulnerable, and the particular case for specifically reproductive liberty (or autonomy; though the two concepts overlap, they are not synonymous) will be examined later in this chapter. But it is also grounded in a wider liberal, or libertarian, tradition, which regards *any* state encroachment with liberty as prima facie suspect. Many people – ethicists and otherwise – regard liberty as intrinsically valuable, or as an indispensable (though not sufficient) ingredient of autonomy, which is itself intrinsically valuable. For others, the value of liberty is derivative of other, higher values.

Tom Beauchamp and James Childress have unarguably been among the most influential voices in modern bioethics. Their 'principlist' approach[2] explicitly forswears any attempt to find a single ethical rule that underpins all others; rather, they identify four core principles, of which none is superior to or derived from any other, but which taken together form a robust and pluralistic grounding for ethical consideration. The four principles they identify – respect for autonomy, beneficence, non-maleficence and justice – do not exhaust the range of perspectives held by contemporary commentators on bioethics, nor do the definitions they offer command unanimous approval. Nonetheless, their influence is such that they provide a useful starting point for ethical evaluation of any area of bioethical controversy.

Since none of the four principles is logically prior to, or derived from, any of the others, it follows that, on this approach, each is accorded intrinsic value. That is, each principle describes something that is valuable for itself, irrespective of its ability to promote some other desirable objective. Thus, when Beauchamp and Childress list respect for autonomy as one of their principles, we must understand them to mean that the value of autonomy does not derive primarily from its tendency to promote good outcomes. In this, their approach differs from utilitarian approaches to autonomy, which I consider below.

Defining 'autonomy' is no simple task. Throughout the history of philosophy, it has been used to signify different ideas by different schools of thought, with those of the Kantian tradition meaning something very different from most contemporary ethicists. For Beauchamp and Childress, '[p]ersonal autonomy is, at a minimum, self-rule that is free from both controlling interference by others and from limitations, such as inadequate understanding, that prevent meaningful choice'.[3] Their notion of autonomy, then, comprises two distinct elements: '(1) *liberty* (independence from controlling influences) and (2) *agency* (capacity for intentional action).'[4] Beauchamp and Childress recognise, though, that autonomy is not a binary concept, either entirely present or entirely absent; rather, '[a]ctions . . . can be autonomous by degrees'.[5] Hence, when evaluating whether a decision is autonomous, we are in reality asking whether it is '*substantially* autonomous . . . not necessarily *fully* autonomous'.[6] Or to put it another way, ethicists should be concerned with whether a decision is autonomous *enough*. The significance of this recognition will become apparent later in this chapter.

For Beauchamp and Childress, then, liberty is a necessary but not sufficient

2   Tom L Beauchamp and James F Childress, *Principles of Biomedical Ethics*, fifth edn, Oxford: Oxford University Press, 2001.
3   Ibid, p 58.
4   Id.
5   Ibid, p 59.
6   Ibid, p 60.

element of an autonomous decision or act. While the satisfaction of the liberty criterion will not guarantee an autonomous decision or act, the total absence of liberty will mean that no decision can be even minimally autonomous, while substantially compromised liberty means that any ensuing decision will be negligibly autonomous. Not all forms of influencing or interfering with someone else's decision, though, constitute infringements of their liberty. Typically, attempts to persuade someone to decide a particular way may well be construed as being compatible with autonomy, depending on the form that persuasion takes, and the context in which it occurs.

For Beauchamp and Childress, the form of interference that most unambiguously undermines liberty – and hence, autonomy – is what they refer to as 'coercion', which is what occurs 'if and only if one person intentionally uses a credible and severe threat of harm of force to control another'.[7] 'The threat of force used by some police, courts, and hospitals in acts of involuntary commitment for psychiatric patients', they suggest, 'is a typical form of coercion.'[8] The essence of coercion, on this account, is a credible threat of forced compliance, or of punishment for non-compliance. It would seem clear, then, that the attachment of criminal sanctions to certain uses of GCTs would constitute coercion of those faced with those sanctions. Such sanctions are invariably directed at the clinicians and technicians involved in such practices; they are certainly being coerced, as of course is everyone confronted by a criminal prohibition of something they might want to do.

What, though, of the autonomy of the prospective parents? Since they are not likely to be fined, imprisoned or deprived of their livelihoods as a result of detection, can we say that they are being coerced? While Beauchamp and Childress do not specifically address this point, I think a plausible case can be presented that they are the victims of *indirect* coercion.

Suppose I live in a racist society (somewhat like apartheid South Africa), where marriage and sexual relationships between black and white people are criminal offences. The specifics of the criminal code, however, mean that only the black partners in such relationships are deemed to have committed that crime. As a white man, I cannot claim to be the direct victim of coercion by that law, because I face no prospect of punishment. However, although the law certainly treats black people worse then white ones, it serves to constrain the autonomy of both, at least if we assume that the law is effective in deterring those it threatens. If I find myself falling in love with a black woman, the law will make it impossible for me to act on those feelings.

The same, I think, can be said of those parents whose wish to use GCTs is constrained by law. Though they themselves are not threatened with legal

---

7   See p 14, fn 2, p 94.
8   Id.

punishment, their autonomy in this matter is wholly undermined by the law, even though they would not be the direct recipients of legal sanction. They are the victims of *indirect coercion*, because the direct coercion of another party (in this case, the class of clinicians who might have helped them) completely deprives them of the means to implement their choice.

The imposition of legal constraints on reproductive and genetic choice therefore compromises liberty, which in turn undermines autonomy, both of the clinicians who are faced with those sanctions, and (perhaps more importantly) of the prospective parents who suffer their indirect effects. Insofar as respect for autonomy is an important ethical principle, this gives us a reason to avoid such constraints without good reason. Of course, as Beauchamp and Childress make clear, respect for autonomy does not enjoy 'priority over all other principles',[9] and it is still possible that respect for autonomy in this case could be outweighed by one or more of those other principles. What we can say for now, though, is that at least one important ethical principle pulls us in the direction of more parental choice in this matter.

Autonomy and utilitarianism

The approach we have just considered views autonomy as valuable in and of itself, independent of its propensity to promote other objectives. From other ethical perspectives, though, autonomy is valuable precisely because of its tendency to promote other ends. Utilitarians, in particular, have often tended to see autonomy and liberty as useful means of bringing about good outcomes, rather than as moral axioms in their own right. 'Utilitarians', as Singer has observed, 'do not respect autonomy for its own sake.'[10]

If John Stuart Mill was not the greatest figure in utilitarian philosophy, he is certainly the best known. Yet he is probably even more renowned as a defender of liberty than as an advocate of the greatest good for the greatest number. For Mill, though, liberty and utility were not competing principles, but rather, two faces of the same philosophical coin. They could, he argued, be reconciled on the empirical grounds that, as a matter of fact, 'mankind are greater gainers by suffering each other to live as seems good to themselves, than by compelling each to live as seems good to the rest'.[11] He therefore sought to portray liberty as being the most efficient means of promoting happiness, noting first that each agent is 'the person most interested in his own well-being: the interest which any other person, except in cases of strong personal attachment, can have in it, is trifling, compared with that which he himself

---

9 See p 14, fn 2, p 57.

10 Peter Singer, *Practical Ethics*, Cambridge: Cambridge University Press, 1979, p 99.

11 John Stuart Mill, 'On Liberty', in Mary Warnock, (ed), *Utilitarianism*, Collins Fount Paperbacks, 1979, p 138.

has';[12] and secondly, that 'with respect to his own feelings and circumstances, the most ordinary man or woman has means of knowledge immeasurably surpassing those that can be possessed by any one else'.[13]

Although Mill's Benthamite language would be unlikely to appeal to modern day liberals like Joel Feinberg and Joseph Raz, the notion that the most efficient means of furthering interests is by allowing (or as the case me be, assisting) individuals to conduct their affairs and determine their priorities as they see fit may nonetheless, in many cases, be a reasonable strategy for promoting what is in their interests. And while we may agree with Gerald Dworkin that respecting liberty on the grounds that it actually *does* promote the interests of individuals 'is always a contingent question that may be returned by the evidence',[14] a presumption that this is ordinarily the case will place the onus upon those who would interfere with liberty to make out a harm-based case for doing so.

From this assumption flows the conclusion that allowing someone to make his own choices is ordinarily the best means of promoting the best consequences *for him*. It says nothing, of course, about whether this is likely to promote the best aggregate outcome for all those affected by his decision, into whose minds he can see and whose interests he cares about no more than the benevolent legislator. However, the point is precisely that the assumption of enlightened self-interest says *nothing* about the likely impact on others, while it says something *positive* about the consequences for the agent himself.

A positive that is not countered by any resulting negative leads, in utilitarian terms, to a net gain. Hence, the individual should be permitted to decide for himself in all matters *unless and until* it can be shown that his actions are likely to have detrimental effects for others. If that can be shown, then we must decide whether the detrimental effect for others outweighs, or is outweighed by, the beneficial consequences for the actor himself. Such a balancing of interests may be difficult, but the point remains that, unless some likely harm to other parties can be shown, the most likely course of action to maximise good outcomes lies in respecting liberty.

For utilitarians, then, there exists a *pro tanto* case for individual choice, albeit one that is rebuttable in individual cases. But there is, in fact, another strand of the argument in favour of a liberty presumption that has proved appealing at least to some utilitarians. This asserts that, as well as being the course of action most likely to further the agent's other interests, the very fact

---

12 See p 16, fn 11, p 206. This sentiment has been recently restated in a markedly different context, by economist Michael Albert: 'we are all the world's foremost expert in our own preferences.' 'Revolution based on reason not faith or fantasy', 18 December 2003, published on Znet at http://www.zmag.org/content/showarticle.cfm?SectionID=41&ItemID=4710.

13 Mill, 'On Liberty', op. cit., fn 11, pp 206–7.

14 Gerald Dworkin, 'Paternalism', from *Philosophy of Law*, Feinberg and Gross, (eds), Wadsworth Publishing Company, 1995, p 209.

of interfering with liberty invariably frustrates an interest in itself, specifically, the interest we each have in having our own choices respected, irrespective of the consequences that flow from those choices.

The liberty presumption may be based partly upon the 'greater likelihood of this bringing about outcomes we find satisfactory in other ways'.[15] But when we consider how much weight to attach to the principle of respect for liberty, we must also bear in mind the desire harboured by most people to make decisions for themselves. According to the philosopher Jonathan Glover, this desire for self-determination must in itself be accorded substantial weight in any utilitarian calculus: 'A desire so important to us would unavoidably be given a central role in any utilitarianism centred around people's desires and preferences.'[16]

On this view, when we deprive the reckless investor of the ability to decide how to spend his money, or when we take from the poor judge of character the freedom to choose her own relationships, we deprive them of something valuable *even if* the choices we make on their behalf lead to better returns on their money or happier relationships than the choices they would probably have made for themselves; we deprive them of the knowledge that, however good or bad their life choices, they remain *their* life choices.[17]

We therefore have (at least) three reasons for respecting liberty: first, because it is a necessary component of autonomy, which is intrinsically valuable; second, the belief that, in practice, the best means of furthering future interests and avoiding future harms in individual cases is by allowing individuals to choose for themselves; and third, the belief that there is harm inherent in any interference with liberty, regardless of the future consequences of so doing. Taken together, these beliefs give rise to a fairly strong ethical presumption in favour of respecting liberty.

Like all presumptions, this is open to rebuttal, whether by showing that the Millian presumption is untrue in a particular case, or by showing that any harm we inflict upon the individual when we interfere with his liberty is outweighed by harm avoided to (or benefit bestowed upon) other parties. But the onus of rebuttal lies squarely with those who would restrict, obstruct or criminalise, rather than with those who would avail themselves of individual choice.

The interest in reproductive liberty

While writers like Joel Feinberg and Jonathan Glover have argued that there is general interest inherent in being able to choose for oneself, others have

15 Jonathan Glover, *Causing Death and Saving Lives*, London: Penguin Books, 1990, p 80.
16 Ibid, p 81.
17 Ironically, a variant of this argument has been used to attack the pro-choice approach to genetic choice; see Chapter 3.

suggested that this is heightened further when the choices relate to matters particularly central to one's life plan. John Robertson has argued that reproductive liberty constitutes one such interest, and hence that it 'should enjoy presumptive primacy when conflicts about its exercise arise because control over whether one reproduces or not is central to personal identity, to dignity, and to the meaning of one's life'.[18] Robertson adopts a liberal approach with regard to reproductive technologies, but he does not argue that reproductive liberty should always and automatically be accorded primacy. 'Rather, it means that those who would limit procreative choice have the burden of showing that the reproductive actions at issue would create such substantial harm that they could justifiably be limited.'[19]

Does an interest in reproductive liberty encompass decisions of the sort under consideration here? Deciding to commence a pregnancy that will culminate in the birth of a severely handicapped child may well be thought to be 'central to personal identity' or 'the meaning of one's life', as would a decision to give birth to a child that will help save the life of an existing child. But can we say the same about the more 'frivolous' choices which the genetic supermarket would permit? Would a desire for a child of the preferred sex constitute such an important interest? For Robertson, whether a particular choice falls within the protected category 'depends on an evaluation of the importance of the choice to the parents and whether that choice plausibly falls within societal understandings of parental needs and choice in reproducing and raising children'.[20]

With regard to the former, Robertson maintains that '[t]he strongest case for the parents is if they persuasively asserted that they would not reproduce unless they could select that trait, and they have a plausible explanation for that position'.[21] (This bears a close resemblance to the approach of the Court of Appeal in the tissue typing case, considered in Chapter 6). While this may seem a reasonable means of gauging the subjective importance of the decision to the potential parents, it could, if adopted, allow prospective regulators to be held hostage by those who would profess a 'this or nothing' commitment to a particular application of PGD which may, in reality, constitute something of an exaggeration. Is it really advisable, from a policy perspective, to tell those like Alan and Louise Masterton, or Sharon Duchesneau and Candy McCullough,[22] that their best chance of being allowed the sort of

---

18 John A Robertson, *Children of Choice: Freedom and the New Reproductive Technologies*, Princeton: Princeton University Press, 1994, p 24.

19 Id.

20 John A Robertson, 'Extending preimplantation genetic diagnosis: medical and non-medical uses'. Comment in: *Journal of Medical Ethics* (2003); 29(4): 213–16, p 216.

21 Ibid, p 215.

22 Whose choice of sperm donor was intended to maximise the chances that their child would be genetically deaf, and whose efforts will be considered in more depth in Chapter 3.

child they want lies in an intransigent refusal to consider any other sort of child? As well as providing an incentive for exaggeration, this approach might be somewhat unfair on parents like the Hashmis and Whitakers who honestly admit that they were planning to have another child even before the possibility of a cord blood transfusion was brought to their attention;[23] would their interest in being able to have a tissue donor for Zain or Charlie be diminished just because they wished to add to their family in any event?

Robertson's second requirement, that we consider the extent to which the choice in question 'plausibly falls within societal understandings of parental needs and choice in reproducing and raising children', is also potentially problematic, in that it seems to require that the interest is one with which 'society' would empathise. While we might reasonably expect a substantial measure of public sympathy for the efforts of the Hashmis and Whitakers, it is perhaps less likely that the majority of at least the 'non-disabled' populace would have much understanding for the efforts of a deaf couple who sought a deaf child, or a couple with achondraplasia who wanted a child with that same condition.

Yet this lack of public support need not diminish the importance of those choices for those couples. The fact that their desires are not widely shared, or understood, may reflect instead the differing experiences of disabled people in a society that, as discussed in Chapter 5, is often ignorant of their experiences and perspectives. Indeed, it may be that their perseverance with a choice that risks not only exposing them to the glare of media publicity (an experience shared by all of the couples mentioned thus far, and almost guaranteed to any future parents of 'designer babies') but seeing their choice widely denounced as irresponsible, is some evidence of the importance of that choice to them, and the strength of the interests that underlie it.

While it may be that Robertson is correct to regard the interest in reproductive liberty as being among the most central and important in most people's lives, I think he is on less steady ground when he seeks to limit that interest to choices which command a degree of 'public understanding'. The lack of popular support for certain choices may be as likely to reflect a lack of understanding of the particular life circumstances and perspectives of those who wish to make them as a lack of important interests underlying such choices. Equally unconvincing is Robertson's attempt to locate the importance of reproductive liberty within some sort of socio-biological reproductive imperative, according to which:

> The more clearly an application of genetic or reproductive technology serves the basic reproductive project of haploid gene transmission – or its avoidance – and the rearing experiences that usually follow, the more

---

23 C Hall, 'Two cases have similarities and vital differences', *The Daily Telegraph*, 3 August 2002.

likely it is to fall within a coherent conception of procreative liberty deserving of special protection.... Quite simply, reproduction is an experience full of meaning and importance for the identity of an individual and her physical and social flourishing because it produces a new individual from her haploid chromosomes.[24]

This approach allows Robertson to distinguish between (a) those reproductive technologies that allow 'normal' reproduction, and which would therefore fall within the sphere of reproductive liberty, and (b) those practices – such as cloning or genetic modification for enhancement purposes, but also presumably PGD for non-pathological traits – that involve a desire 'to pass on more [than] what occurs in reproduction'. The latter are not immediately related to 'the basic reproductive project', and therefore 'seem much less deserving of special protection on that score'.[25]

From an ethical point of view, this is a non sequitur. There may be a sociobiological explanation of the interest in genetic reproduction, but this provides no obvious ethical reason why it should be privileged over other interests, e.g. of a same-sex couple or single person to have the experience of raising a child that is not genetically theirs, or even of a couple to clone a deceased child. If we accept that the naturalistic fallacy's conflation of 'ought' and 'is' is indeed a fallacy – as Robertson explicitly does[26] – then this distinction seems arbitrary.

These equivocations notwithstanding, I believe that Robertson is essentially right when he claims that decisions about whether, when and how often to reproduce are usually central to people's life plans, and to their personal identity. Less established within the pro-choice canon is the belief that *who* to reproduce merits the same status. It is impossible to read of the heart-rending attempts by Shahana and Raj Hashmi without realising that saving the life of their son Zain is entirely central to their deepest values and priorities. But can the same truthfully be said of more 'flippant' choices of offspring characteristics?

I began this chapter with the example of Louise and Alan Masterton, precisely because the choice they wanted to make is not one with which most of us would particularly empathise, or of which many of us would even particularly approve. But can anyone who has followed their gruelling struggle to be allowed to have another girl readily discount the importance of this decision to their lives? Can anyone who has viewed the opprobrium heaped upon the 'deaf lesbians', Candy McCullough and Sharon Duchesneau, glibly reject the possibility that deafness *is* a central plank of their identity, one that

---

24 'Procreative liberty in the era of genomics', *American Journal of Law and Medicine* (2003); 29(4): 439–87, p 450.
25 Ibid, p 472.
26 Ibid, pp 451–2.

they wish to transmit to their child just as surely as other couples want children of the same race?

It may well be, though, that choices of this nature will vary in the extent to which they are central to the life plans of the prospective parents in question. It is quite plausible that, as IVF and PGD become cheaper and more effective, some people will seek to use them to effect trait selection for less 'worthy' reasons, even for superficial or trivial reasons – blue eyes and long legs are the frequently advanced examples. Do such choices really merit our respect?

Perhaps it is best to view such choices as existing on a continuum of importance, with choices to avoid a 'doomed' pregnancy (i.e. one certain to end in miscarriage), or a child affected by an early-onset fatal disease, at one end, and decisions about, say, hair colour or skin complexion at the other. But then, all reproductive choices could be placed on a similar continuum. Is the desire for an abortion equally worthy of protection, regardless of whether the pregnant woman would be risking her life by carrying to term, or merely wanted to delay motherhood for a year or two until her career was more established? Pro-choice campaigners have been – rightly – sceptical of attempts to make value judgments about 'good' and 'bad' reasons for abortions, not least because they recognise that such decisions are invariably affected by factors not readily apparent to outsider observers. It may be trite to observe that no woman undertakes an abortion lightly, but it is surely worth keeping in mind that such decisions are likely to be made after a process of weighing ambitions and values and fears that only the pregnant woman herself is capable of weighing. Her inability, or unwillingness, to articulate those ambitions and values and fears in a manner that third parties will find persuasive does not lessen their importance to *her*, the party most immediately affected by the decision.[27]

The same thing, I suggest, could be said of the kinds of reproductive decisions made possible (indeed, inevitable) by genetic testing technologies. They exist on a continuum, ranging from those with which it is easy to empathise, to those which strike an outside observer as trivial or even perverse. But they can all be assumed to mean something to the person making them, to reflect her values or priorities or view of what it is that makes life important. In the same manner that abortion is unlikely to be a decision lightly undertaken, it seems unlikely that a woman would willingly submit to the discomfort and egg harvesting, and the lottery that is IVF, without good reason. Having done so, it seems even more incredible that she would reject healthy embryos on grounds that are trivial *to her*.

I cannot, of course, discount out of hand the possibility that some people, somewhere, will endure the risk, discomfort and expense without having a deep investment in the outcome. But I think such cases – if they occur at all – are likely to be rare exceptions, and that it is reasonable to attribute a presump-

---

27   The obvious retort that it is, in fact, the embryo or fetus who is most immediately affected will be considered in the next chapter.

tive importance to reproductive choice, much as we would with choice about sexual partners or religious or political affiliation. Robertson runs into difficulty when he attempts to draw lines between different *kinds* of reproductive decision, and his distinctions tend to look rather arbitrary when subjected to scrutiny. Instead, we should assume that *all* reproductive decisions are important to the people making them; whether the decision involves avoiding pregnancy (forever or for now), circumventing obstacles to infertility, or electing to have a child with particular traits, it should not be incumbent on anyone to prove, to me or to anyone else, how much these decisions matter to them.

The presumption of choice

I believe, then, that we should start out with a presumption in favour of leaving choices about whether and how to use GCTs to prospective parents. This pro-choice presumption holds true whether – like Beauchamp and Childress – we consider respect for autonomy to be intrinsically valuable, or whether – like Peter Singer – we value it as ordinarily the best means of bringing about best outcomes. It holds true whether – like John Robertson – we consider reproductive autonomy to be a distinct ethical category, worthy of particular respect, or whether we view it as part of a wider category of personal choices that are each worthy of respect.

The effect of this presumption is that it places the burden of proof firmly onto those who would constrain parental choice in this regard; it is up to them to show good reason for constraining choice. Over the next few chapters, I will consider some of the arguments that have been advanced, and principles that have been invoked, which might be thought to discharge this burden. Before doing so, though, there is another issue that I need to consider. I have argued for a presumption in favour of choice for prospective parents. But does the existence of GCTs afford real choice? Is it, in fact, possible that, far from promoting greater choice, the existence of GCTs constrains the range of choices open to prospective parents – and, in particular, to prospective mothers?

A 'silent closing'?

How could it be argued that the presence of GCTs actually limits rather than expands choice? The first challenge to the 'choice presumption' comes from those who assert that genetic counsellors and other medical professionals, far from setting out the range of options in an impartial manner, actually impose their own views regarding GCTs on their clients.[28] If such influence was shown

---

28 Angus Clarke refers to those individuals who consult genetic counsellors as 'clients' rather than 'patients', 'as the word "patient" would suggest that they were suffering from a disease, which is very often not the case'. Introduction to *Genetic Counselling: Practice and Principles*, Angus Clarke (ed), London: Routledge, 1994.

to exist, and if it was of sufficient intensity that the 'voluntariness' of the potential parents' choices was compromised, one of the essential components of an autonomous choice – independence from controlling influences – would also be compromised. Indeed, if voluntariness was undermined to a sufficient extent, we could not really speak of there being a choice at all.

Is it really the case, though, that the manner in which GCTs are presented leaves no room for choice? For this assertion to be proven, two elements must be shown to be true: that counsellors and medical professionals *do* in fact influence their clients with their own opinions; and that this influence is *sufficient* to compromise the 'voluntariness' of the clients' decisions, to an extent that would mean that choice itself was undermined.

In 1986, Barbara Katz Rothman published what was, and remains today, one of the most provocative and valuable works in the literature of reproductive technologies. *The Tentative Pregnancy* was an examination and critique of the practice of pre-natal testing, a practice, Katz Rothman argued, that often paid little heed to the views and wishes of pregnant women. In particular, she expressed scepticism about the possibility of counsellors being genuinely non-directive: 'counselors [sic] are bound to be directive sometimes – avowedly so in some circumstances, perhaps unwittingly so in others'.[29] While recognising that 'most of them do truly value nondirectiveness',[30] she argued that even the most well-intentioned of counsellors will inevitably find themselves influencing their clients with their own views: 'If the counselor thinks this woman sitting across from her is going to do something she will deeply regret for the rest of her life, how can she *not* influence her?'[31]

If Katz Rothman's views were controversial for their time, they have come to be accepted among much of the mainstream of ethical and sociological writing about reproductive technologies – not only amniocentesis, but increasingly about PGD. Those who are concerned about the influence of genetic counsellors upon their clients are effectively unanimous in their opinion that this influence will be favourably disposed towards making use of screening. Angus Clarke, for example, has expressed concerns that 'clients may be subtly encouraged to take part in a programme'.[32] This encouragement may take the form of screening being represented as 'the decision of the responsible citizen . . . reinforc[ing] the notion of "social responsibility in reproduction" '.[33] Somewhat more subtly, it may take the form of depicting screening 'as a matter of routine, with staff clearly expecting clients to participate'.[34]

29 Barbara Katz Rothman, *The Tentative Pregnancy*, Pandora, 1994 edn, p 41.
30 Ibid, p 41.
31 Ibid, p 47.
32 Introduction to *Genetic Counselling: Practice and Principles*, op. cit., fn 28, p 18.
33 Id.
34 Id.

Aside from the influence allegedly brought to bear, consciously or other-wise, by counsellors and medical staff, various references have been made to other sources of influence which may conceivably cast doubt upon the notion that the availability of GCTs enhances choice. Katz Rothman's research has, for example, revealed several instances of pressure from the husbands and families of pregnant women. It is interesting to note that, while the evidence of pressure from the medical profession suggests that it is almost entirely in favour of making use of genetic diagnosis, Katz Rothman's work concerning familial attitudes to amniocentesis reveals no such unanimity. 'Some women want the amnio,' she reveals, 'but their husbands "won't let them" have it. Others are pressured by family into having the test.'[35] Chadwick and Ngwena also speak of 'pressure from relatives to make certain reproductive decisions'.[36]

Frequent reference is also made in the literature to a source of influence which, although it lacks the immediate proximity of family, is perhaps equally powerful: prevalent attitudes within the prospective parents' (usually the con-cerns relate to the potential mothers) social environment. One American commentator has suggested that 'the cultural climate in the United States' may be such as to exert 'cultural pressures to select for . . . highly valued traits such as intelligence or thinness',[37] while British writers have referred to the fact that 'attitudes prevalent in society towards abortion and genetic disease may have an effect, as may the attitudes of religious or cultural groups to which counselees belong'.[38] The extent to which this societal influence should cause concern has been considered by Philip Kitcher. He notes that no '[i]ndi-vidual choices are . . . made in a social vacuum', but feels that present social attitudes are such as to suggest that 'many future genetic parents . . . will have to bow to social attitudes they reject and resent'.[39]

Although a handicapped neonate in the UK will not, at least in theory, be left to die due to the absence of adequate medical insurance, it has been suggested that, in a society which does not make adequate provision for the handicapped, it is misleading to speak in terms of there being a choice whether or not to make use of screening technologies. Thus it has been claimed that 'It is arguably unrealistic to suggest that people should be free to make choices about their reproductive habits, in the context of a society

35 See p 24, fn 32, p 42.
36 Ruth Chadwick and Charles Ngwena, 'The development of a normative standard in counsel-ling for genetic disease: ethics and law', *Journal of Social Welfare and Family Law* (1992) 276–95, p 284.
37 Vicki G Norton, 'Unnatural selection: nontherapeutic preimplantation genetic screening and proposed regulation', *41 UCLA Law Review* 1581 (1994), p 1602.
38 Chadwick and Ngwena, 'The development of a normative standard . . .', op. cit., p 284.
39 Philip Kitcher, *The Lives To Come*, London: Allen Lane: The Penguin Press (1996), p 199.

which places constraints on the choices available because of inadequate health and social services',[40] and that 'prenatal diagnosis cannot really be a choice when other alternatives are not available'.[41]

It is difficult to dispute the contention that having a child affected by certain conditions is likely to have a considerable impact upon the social and economic status of its parents. Certainly, it would be reasonable to expect prospective parents to have reservations about bringing a handicapped child into existence 'if there is no confidence in the willingness of society to care for their child once they are unable to do so'.[42] Whether this fact is sufficient to bear out the contention that genetic prenatal diagnosis 'cannot really be a choice'[43] is somewhat more contentious; much will depend on the nature of 'voluntariness', and the varieties of influence which can be brought to bear, and I will consider those matters later in this chapter. For the time being, however, I think we can make two observations about the 'lack of support' argument, and, in particular, about whether it renders the language of 'choice' inappropriate.

The first observation relates to the assertion levied by Abby Lippman, that '[c]ontinuing a pregnancy when the fetus has been found to have Down [sic] syndrome cannot be considered a real option when society does not truly accept children with disabilities or provide assistance for their nurturance'.[44] (Once again, although this particular argument was directed at prenatal screening by amniocentesis, I assume that the essence of Lippman's argument would be equally valid if applied to PGD.) The first, rather glib, observation in the face of such a suggestion would be that, while some women faced with a diagnosis of Down's syndrome do indeed elect to abort, many others choose to continue with the pregnancy, while at least some decide to forgo the option of amniocentesis altogether.[45] In one sense, this is surely evidence that a 'choice' exists, albeit in the crudest sense. Yet it may be that, while the prevailing societal attitudes may not be sufficiently powerful to deprive *all* women of a meaningful choice, at least *some* – perhaps those without adequate economic resources or strong networks of familial or social support – are effectively deprived of a choice.

40 Chadwick and Ngwena, 'The development of a normative standard . . .', op. cit., fn 36, p 282.
41 Abby Lippman, 'Prenatal genetic testing and screening: constructing needs and reinforcing inequalities', in Angus Clarke (ed), *Genetic Counselling: Practice and Principles*, London: Routledge, 1994, p 152.
42 Angus Clarke, 'Genetics, ethics, and audit', *The Lancet* 1990; 335: 1146.
43 Lippman, 'Prenatal genetic testing', op. cit., p 152.
44 Abby Lippman, 'The genetic construction of prenatal testing: choice, consent, or conformity for women?' from Rothenberg and Thomson, (eds), *Women and Prenatal Testing: Facing the Challenges of Genetic Technology*, Columbus: Ohio State University Press, 1994, p 19.
45 Several examples of each choice are, in fact, represented by the women whose experiences are documented by Katz Rothman in *The Tentative Pregnancy*, op. cit., fn 29.

The second observation is, perhaps, more serious for Lippman's contention. In deciding whether the availability of GCTs has widened or narrowed the degree of choice which women have in relation to reproduction, we should perhaps stop to consider what measure of choice would have been available to them had this technology never been invented. If it were really the case that those women who give birth to handicapped babies face such severe hardship that they effectively have no choice but to undergo screening, we must ask ourselves: what options would they have faced if prenatal screening (or PGD) did not exist? A woman who had already given birth to one handicapped child, or who knew from experience that a certain condition 'ran in the family', would surely be under severe, and perhaps irresistible, pressure not to reproduce at all. This is certainly the view of clinical geneticist Angus Clarke, who notes that 'many women in families with Duchenne muscular dystrophy . . . used to fear pregnancy and chose to have few children, if any, or to terminate all male fetuses'.[46]

We might also wonder whether, if Clarke, Katz Rothman et al are correct in claiming that it is genuinely impossible for counsellors to avoid influencing their clients with their own opinions, a case perhaps emerges for dispensing with the facade of non-directiveness, for stating these opinions and biases explicitly. This suggestion is taken seriously by Clarke. He considers that 'non-directiveness is unattainable, and that directiveness is acceptable as long as it is explicit; unacknowledged directiveness may be much more manipulative'.[47] A similar approach has been examined by Chadwick and Ngwena, who suggest that 'it is perhaps a matter of candidly owning up to it [the bias in favour of directive counselling] and justifying it on the grounds of non-maleficence'.[48]

While it is possible that a combination of openness, reasoned argument and sensitivity to the client's values and priorities could ensure that counsellors do not exert such influence as to undermine voluntariness or independence from controlling influences, it is of course impossible to make the same guarantees regarding other sources of influence. With the possible exception of Angus Clarke's (presumably flippant) suggestion that all prospective mothers should attend assertiveness classes,[49] it is impossible to imagine how women could be protected from familial or societal pressures which exceeded acceptable persuasion and entered the realm of manipulation, or even coercion.

It does not automatically follow, though, that these influences are sufficient to undermine the voluntariness, and therefore the autonomous nature, of the

---

46 Clarke, 'Genetics, ethics, and audit', fn 42, 1145–7, p 1145.
47 Clarke, Introduction to *Genetic Counselling: Practice and Principles*, op. cit., fn 28, p 19.
48 Chadwick and Ngwena, 'The development of a normative standard . . .', loc. cit., p 277.
49 Clarke, Introduction to *Genetic Counselling: Practice and Principles*, op. cit., fn 28, p 19.

choice in question. While there will almost certainly be circumstances in which voluntariness will be seriously compromised by manipulative or coercive influences, it may still be the case that unrestricted access to GCTs is the best available means of protecting autonomy. That this is so may become clearer if we consider the fact that a great many other choices of substantial importance are made in a similar environment.

In recent years, the view that decisions to procreate take place within an environment which portrays childbirth overwhelmingly as desirable, or even inevitable, has become increasingly accepted. Thus, it has been contended that 'the context in our culture is such that a childless woman is an unenviable social anomaly',[50] and that '[t]he ideology of obligatory fertility and the definition of women in terms of reproductive destiny and fulfilment is one of the most powerfully oppressive psychological forces bearing down on married heterosexual women of childbearing age'.[51] Indeed, the perspective of contemporary society which views it as overwhelmingly pro-natalist is becoming so widely held in some disciplines that it may even be considered the orthodox view. Does this lead inevitably to the view that *all* reproductive decisions are subject to such influence as to invalidate any purported exercise of autonomy?

In many areas of life, decisions are made in the context of a society which makes its endorsement of one set of choices rather than another quite explicit. The choice of one's sexual partner, for example, takes place within the context of a society which may be seen only fully to approve of monogamous heterosexual relationships between persons of the same race and religion.[52] Decisions concerning how we dress and what we buy, for example, may lack the dimension of moral disapproval which accompanies the other decisions mentioned so far, but there is a very real case for supposing that the influence exerted by both advertising and peer pressure is substantial.

Perhaps Katz Rothman is right when she suggests that 'what we should realise is that human beings living in society have precious little choice ever. There may really be no such thing as individual choice in a social structure,' she proposes, 'not in any absolute way. . . . Society, in its ultimate meaning, may be nothing more and nothing less than the structuring of

---

50 Paul Lauritzen, 'What Price Parenthood?', from Joseph H Howell and William Frederick Sale, (eds), *Life Choices: A Hastings Center Introduction to Bioethics*, Washington DC: Georgetown University Press, 1995.

51 Kathryn Pauly Morgan, 'Of woman born? . . .', from Christine Overall, (ed), *The Future of Human Reproduction*, Toronto: The Women's Press, 1989, p 70.

52 In many respects, it could be argued that the influence imposed by society to restrict one's sexual activities to partners of the opposite sex comes closer to Beauchamp and Childress's concept of 'coercion,' in view of the differing status of heterosexual and homosexual acts in the eyes of the criminal law.

choices'.[53] This view is closely related to that of *dialectic determinism*, the perspective which holds that 'people never act entirely voluntarily, that is, independently of societal conditions, nor entirely involuntarily, that is, totally dependently on these conditions'.[54] If this assessment is accurate, then it is not just decisions about PGD and prenatal screening which 'lead[ ] to doubts that assumptions of "free choice" ... are appropriate'.[55] Many of the most intimate and important decisions in life are, on this view, not true exercises in voluntariness at all, but responses elicited at least in part by the weight of societal pressure.

We might reasonably disagree about the extent that 'real choice' or 'voluntariness' survives this immersion in a sea of influences. What seems almost universally recognised, though, is that *some* measure of control over these decisions is retained by those making them. The alternative, it seems, would be to say that decisions about reproduction, or choices of sexual partners, are so devoid of voluntariness that it wouldn't matter if these decisions were overtly and completely taken over by someone else. It does not require any fanciful leap of imagination to anticipate that any attempt by the state to regulate the reproductive options of its citizens would meet with furious resistance.[56] While this recognition that things 'could be worse' does not constitute a resounding endorsement of the status quo, it does tend to suggest that there still exists something worth striving to protect, that some element of genuine choice remains. Similarly, in relation to GCTs, an outcry could be foreseen if geneticists were allowed to subject all in vitro embryos to whatever tests *they* deemed appropriate. Again, this seems to involve recognition that the present situation, while imperfect, allows the prospective parents/mother *some* degree of control.

We could perhaps say, then, that while some degree of influence from counsellors, and from outside sources, is likely, or even inevitable, it is less clear that such influence is greater than the influence brought to bear on many other important and intimate choices, involving choice of sexual partner or decisions whether to have children at all. Furthermore, doubts exist as to whether the influences are sufficiently controlling to rebut the presumption of choice in relation to GCTs; it is surely possible to recognise that '[w]e typically make choices in a context of competing influences, such as personal

53 Katz Rothman, *The Tentative Pregnancy*, op. cit., fn 29, p 14.
54 Theresia Degener, 'Female self-determination between feminist claims and "voluntary" eugenics, between "rights" and ethics', *Issues in Reproductive and Genetic Engineering* (1990); 3(2): 87–99, p 93.
55 Lippman, 'Prenatal genetic testing and screening: constructing needs and reinforcing inequalities', fn 41, p 152.
56 As evidenced on a yearly basis by student reactions to Hugh Lafolette's suggestion that prospective parents should be vetted by the state support this contention; 'Licensing parents' (1980); 9(2) *Philosophy and Public Affairs*, 182.

desires, familial constraints, legal obligations, and institutional pressures' but to recognise also that '[a]lthough significant, these influences need not be controlling to a substantial degree'.[57]

However, even if there were shown to be some merit in the assertion that women would in some sense have been more 'free', would have had more 'real choice' – or at least an 'easier' life[58] – had PGD and other screening technologies never been invented, it must be recognised that turning back the clock to 'uninvent' these technologies is not possible. The existence of PGD is now a technological *fait accompli*, and the hard questions it throws up are now a fact of life for many people. The choices on offer may be less than perfect, and are undoubtedly subject to certain pressures and influences. And for some women, a fatalistic acceptance of the cards dealt to them by the genetic lottery may have been preferable to the soul-searching required by the new technology.[59] But GCTs *do* exist; and since they do, the question we cannot avoid relates to who should be allowed to make the hard moral choices which accompany them.

The central tenet of the pro-choice approach holds that these choices must be made by the parents whose reproductive futures are in question. However impure or compromised the purported exercises in choice may be in the scenarios looked at here, it is difficult to see how allowing such choices to be taken over by the medical profession or by some executive body would be preferable. Whether, in retrospect, the changes brought about by GCTs should be welcomed or regretted, whether the choices to which they have given rise have improved or diminished the lives of those women touched by this technology, it is difficult to see how denying those choices to, or taking them from, individual women can really be said to enhance their control over their own lives. As Mary Anne Warren has written with particular reference to sex selection, 'it is neither necessary nor desirable to defend women's right not to be forced to use new methods of sex selection at the expense of their right to voluntarily choose to do so'.[60]

---

57 Beauchamp and Childress, *Principles of Biomedical Ethics*, 1994 edn, op. cit., fn 2, p 165.

58 Abby Lippman has argued: 'The very availability of those technologies necessarily forces every woman at least to consider if she desires genetic testing – or if she even desires that testing be available for use by other women – and merely facing this choice is itself difficult, and often painful.' 'The genetic construction of prenatal testing: choice, consent, or conformity for women?' from *Women and Prenatal Testing*, op. cit., fn 44, p 11.

59 Fern, one of the women interviewed by Katz Rothman, expressed very much this kind of sentiment when she said: 'There are times when I really curse modern technology. No one should have to make these kinds of decisions.' Katz Rothman, *The Tentative Pregnancy*, op. cit., fn 29, p 182. This kind of reaction led Katz Rothman herself to speculate whether 'Maybe there are limits to the value of knowing'. See p 24, fn 29, p 200.

60 Mary Anne Warren, *Gendercide: The Implications of Sex Selection*, New Jersey: Rowman and Allanheld, 1985, p 197.

The competitive imperative

Bill McKibben is an environmentalist writer whose books are regularly sceptical of – if not downright hostile towards – technological progress. His latest is no exception. As its title – *Enough: Staying Human in an Engineered Age* – suggests, his core argument is that biotechnology in general, and germline genetic modification in particular, are in danger of transgressing important ethical and existential boundaries. Some of McKibben's arguments are directed at the children who will result from such technologies; others rely on ideas that are closer to New Age mysticism.[61] One of his arguments, though, goes right to the heart of the choice presumption. Arguing that *'These are the most anti-choice technologies anyone's ever thought of'*,[62] McKibben sets out an argument that views the overall effect of certain GCTs as being to detract from, rather than enhance, parental choice. His argument relates specifically to genetic enhancement technologies – perhaps surprisingly, he is somewhat more ambivalent about PGD[63] – but the same critique, we might think, could be applied to screening technologies.

McKibben's vision of the future proceeds as follows. Initially, a few prospective parents will elect to use enhancement technologies to bestow competitive advantages on their children – perhaps by making them more athletic, more conventionally attractive or, should such a thing ever prove possible, more intelligent. Though the majority of prospective parents may prefer to forego such enhancements, the fact that other people are enhancing their children will make it harder and harder for the 'traditionalists' to hold to their principles. 'What choice will those parents have?', McKibben rhetorically asks. 'Only the choice to keep up with the neighbours, or the choice to put their kids behind from the start.'[64]

Although couched in his customary hyperbolic style – 'In the end,' McKibben tells us, these technologies 'will destroy forever the very possibility of meaningful choice'[65] – this argument should not be discounted out of hand. The phenomenon of one person's exercise in choice eroding the choices of others can be seen all around us. The choice of so many British people to drive their children to school has made other parents reluctant to allow their children to walk – for fear that they will be injured or killed by the numerous

---

61 'We are snipping the very last weight holding us to the ground, and when it's gone we will float silently away into the vacuum of meaninglessness.' *Enough: Staying Human in an Engineered Age*, New York: Times Books, 2003, p 47.
62 Ibid, p 190. Emphasis in original.
63 See pp 132–4.
64 Ibid, p 190.
65 Id.

cars milling around school playgrounds.[66] Sometimes that erosion of other people's choice is so serious that we may feel justified in contemplating curtailing the novel behaviour. One of the reasons sometimes given for the enforcement of bans on performance-enhancing drugs in sport is that they are unfair to those who rely on more conventional means of maximising their potential. Allowing 'doped' athletes to compete, it is claimed, would mean that an athlete who wants to have any prospect of keeping up with his pharmaceutically enhanced rivals has little choice but to assume the costs and risks of consuming EPO (erythropoietin) or nandrolone himself.[67]

Does PGD fall into the same category as enhancement modification or sports doping? In at least one obvious way, the analogy does not withstand scrutiny. As I noted in my introduction, genetic modification involves the introduction of new genetic material into an organism. Theoretically, this could mean adding genes for, say, muscle growth or oxygen uptake into an embryo that would otherwise be disposed towards an un-athletic body type. Somewhat less dramatically, POE would allow anyone's blood to carry more oxygen, but those using it would still, at some point, come up against the limitations of their own physiology; most of us could inject it every day for years, and still be nowhere close to winning the Tour de France (although there is a distinct possibility that we would do a great deal of harm to ourselves).

PGD, however, would have by far the least dramatic effects of the three technologies. As I pointed out in relation to eugenic *übermensch* fantasies, prospective parents using PGD will have their choices limited to those embryos which can in any event be created from a fusion of their respective gametes. Two people who belong to athletically mediocre families are probably unlikely to create any athletically remarkable embryos, and would therefore not have the option of selecting a future Maurice Green or Zinedine Zidane for implantation. Two people who belong to only averagely attractive families are unlikely to have the choice of implanting a future Johnny Depp or Halle Berry.

Genetic contribution to 'intelligence' is a controversial topic, not least because – unlike sporting prowess – there is no universally agreed means by which 'intelligence' can be measured. The most common measurement – Intelligence Quotient, or IQ – has been the subject of sustained assault from critics who maintain that it is, at best, a measurement of a certain *kind* of intelligence, and at worst a pseudo-scientific prop for racism and sexism.

66 This example was brought to mind by an item on the radio on the morning I wrote this section; BBC Radio 4, *Today* programme, 13 March 2006. I am quite confident that a brief perusal of tomorrow's news will reveal other examples.

67 For a thorough and thought-provoking overview of the issues posed by the use of pharmaceutical – and in particular, genetic – enhancement in sport, see Andy Miah, *Genetically modified athletes: biomedical ethics, gene doping and sport*, Abingdon: Routledge, 2004.

Nonetheless, there is wide agreement that at least *some portion* of *some kinds* of intelligence is genetically determined; the reason why humans are generally more intelligent than chimpanzees is not exclusively attributable to environment. And it is also largely beyond dispute that academic aptitude is, rightly or wrongly (I will return to the normative dimension of this later), strongly correlated with career advancement and economic security. That being so, it should come as no surprise if a significant cohort of parents chose to use GCTs to maximise their children's prospects of high academic attainment. This would – following McKibben – exert pressure on other parents to follow suit, lest their own sons and daughters be left trailing in the academic wake of their hand-picked peers. As Françoise Baylis and Jason Scott Robert put it, 'parents may well feel the need to conform just to compete'.[68]

Again, we could respond to this by pointing out that academically average parents are unlikely to produce academically excellent embryos. But the point remains that at least some of those who elect to use this technology – whether for the selection of academic, athletic or aesthetic qualities – could at very least ensure the birth of the most academically (or athletically, or aesthetically) endowed children available to *them*. While the rest of us would have to gamble on passing on the 'best' of our genes, shoppers at the genetic supermarket could be sure that they were passing on to their children the best they have to give, even if that transpires to be little better than anyone else's children receive.

Would the rest of us be compelled to follow suit? On closer inspection, this might seem less than likely. Both my partner and I are moderately athletic, naturally fit enough to participate in recreational sports to an enjoyable (non-embarrassing!) level. But we are both far from a level where we could earn a living from sport, far less earn a fortune from it. To an extent, this is probably determined by physiological limitations, which in turn are genetically determined. To perhaps a greater extent, our failure to scale the heights of sporting excellence is attributable to a lack of commitment to that path. Neither of us has dedicated our lives to the sorts of training regimes that would be needed were we to attain even modest sporting success, largely because we had other priorities and other interests.

For parents who utilise GCTs, the same prospect remains. They could, assuming their own gametes (or the donor gametes they have acquired) hold that potential, select an embryo with a genetic predisposition to a higher than average development of slow twitch muscle and VO2 max,[69] both important physiological ingredients for endurance athletes. They cannot, however,

68 Françoise Baylis and Jason Scott Robert, 'The inevitability of genetic enhancement technologies', *Bioethics* (2004); 18(1): 1–26, p 13.
69 This is a measure of the maximum amount of oxygen that a body can consume during exercise.

guarantee a child that will have the single-minded dedication to spending endless rainy nights counting off the hundreds and hundreds of miles that will be needed if she is ever to be a champion marathon runner or long-distance cyclist. Similarly, insofar as GCTs ever make it possible to select for qualities such as a good memory or perfect pitch, they seem much less likely to be able to guarantee a child who will not prefer to spend his evenings playing football, or surfing the Internet, than training to become a concert pianist.

Of course, resisting the pressures that their parents may bring to bear may be burdensome for such 'genetically elite' children, a charge that I will consider in the next chapter. For present purposes, what is significant is the extent to which McKibben's concerns about a competitive imperative match up to what we might expect in reality. PGD, at present, allows prospective parents to avoid passing on certain disadvantageous traits. At some point in the future, it may progress to a point where it allows us to select those embryos that carry the most advantageous or desirable of the genes that we already carry. Since most of us probably do not carry genes for athletic excellence or supermodel looks, the best we will be able to assure for our children is a slightly 'better' selection of fairly average traits.

Identifying the basis for complex traits like mathematical ability or good memory – to say nothing of even more 'ethereal' character traits like determination or altruism – seem likely to be even further out of reach, at least for the foreseeable future. We might wonder, then, whether many prospective parents would be willing to undertake the burdens, and possibly expense, of IVF-PGD, for a slightly higher chance of passing on traits that might – if they elect to use them in that way – bestow on their children a slight advantage in certain respects. Even assuming that a few would choose to do so, it seems unlikely that this would give their children very much of a head start, at least when the parents themselves are not already high-performance athletes or geniuses.

Some commentators suggests that advances in knowledge will mean that a genetically selected advantage today will probably be out-performed by a pharmaceutical advantage 20 years down the line. If they are right, then a greater threat to parental autonomy will come when their neighbours are dosing their toddlers with the successors to Ritalin, drugs which aid concentration or memory or balance, and which are widely touted as being on the horizon. Whether a parent will be able to hold out in the face of such skewed competition will indeed present a difficulty. But in a sense – and leaving aside any other controversies about performance-enhancing drugs – parents already face such pressures all the time. When every other child in the class has a personal computer with Internet access, it is easy to see how considerable emotional pressure is exerted on an ambitious parent to ensure their child has the same. The solution to this, egalitarians generally think, is not to ban personal computers, but to take steps to ensure that everyone has access to them, or at least to mitigate some of the disadvantages of not having one.

I am in danger of getting ahead of myself. The questions the genetic supermarket idea poses for notions of distributive justice and equality will be considered in Chapter 7. For the moment, I will note only that the advantages PGD can bestow are likely to be slight, no more than allowing a selection of the best available alleles from a rather limited range. Even assuming a society where much, much more is known about the relationship between genes and performance, those without high-performance genes will not be able to purchase them for their children – at least if they want their children to be their genetic descendants – while those *with* high-performance genes will not be able to guarantee that their children will want to follow in their illustrious footsteps, however much genetic potential they inherit. And all will risk their children being out-performed by future generations of competitors who have used much more cutting-edge enhancement technologies to make much more task-specific modifications to themselves.

Faced with such limited possibilities for skewing the playing field in their children's favour, I suspect that the lure of the 'enhancement' counter in the genetic supermarket is likely to prove quite resistible.

The Harm Principle

Most of us, I assume, would agree that democracy is preferable to other systems of government. When most people think of democracy, they tend to think of something like a system of government that allows everyone to have their say, and their vote, and which makes important decisions (such as who will run the country) based on what the majority choose. Of course, constitutional scholars will point out that the reality is nowhere near so simple. But the notion of 'majority rule' is firmly embedded in Western culture, even if it is an ideal rarely realised in practice.

Does it follow, then, that decisions about germinal choice technologies should be subject to public scrutiny – as in Slovenia, which in 2002 held a referendum on access to reproductive technologies?[70] If decisions were to be made on this basis, it is quite likely that we would arrive at a position a good deal more restrictive than the one I am advocating. Opinion polls have shown, for example, a general opposition to 'social' sex selection[71] and

---

70 This was in fact the country's first referendum as an independent state, and perhaps a somewhat surprising choice with issues such as its membership of both NATO and the European Union still to be decided.

71 A YouGov survey for the *Daily Telegraph* in August 2005 asked 2,432 adults: 'Do you agree of disagree that parents should be allowed to select the sex of their own children if they so wish?' 77% replied: 'No, they should not.'

to the sort of parental choice that the genetic supermarket model would involve.

But while this would certainly constitute a particular conception of democracy, it is not the sort of democracy with which we live, and I suspect that a little reflection might well show why not. The notion that, in certain respects, individual liberty ought to be protected, even in the face of mass opinion, can be traced back at least as far as John Stuart Mill. In probably his most renowned essay, 'On Liberty', Mill set out a position that, while purportedly flowing logically from Benthamite utilitarianism, seems to many observers to have departed substantially from it.[72] Mill used this, probably his most impassioned work, to rail against 'the tyranny of the majority',[73] claiming that 'there is a limit to the legitimate interference of collective opinion with individual independence . . .'.[74] In the essay's best known passage, Mill set out a theory with regard to the extent of this 'legitimate interference':

> the sole end for which mankind are warranted, individually or collectively, in interfering with the liberty of action of any of their number, is self-protection. That the only purpose for which power can be rightfully exercised over any member of a civilised community, against his will, is to prevent harm to others. His own good, either physical or moral, is not a sufficient warrant.[75]

Mill's argument was intellectually challenging, but it appears not to have had a great deal of impact in practice. Throughout the 19th century, and well into the 20th, laws continued to be passed on the basis of an illiberal blend of religious teachings, vested interest and popular prejudice. The next really significant milestone in the evolution and influence of the Harm Principle was the publication in 1959 of the Report of the Committee on Homosexual Offences and Prostitution, immortalised in the study of contemporary ethics as the Wolfenden Report.[76] The Report was published at a time when homosexual acts between consenting adult males were still criminal offences, often leading to prison sentences. It has been suggested that, in setting up the Commission, the government of the day was seeking more effective means of

---

72 See H L A Hart, 'Natural rights: Bentham and John Stuart Mill', in *Essays on Bentham: Jurisprudence and Political Theory*, Oxford: Clarendon Press, 1982, pp 102–3. For other contended points of departure between Mill and his utilitarian predecessors, see Neil Thornton's *The Problem of Liberalism in the Thought of John Stuart Mill*, London: Garland Publishing Inc, 1987.
73 'On Liberty', op. cit., fn 11, p 129.
74 Ibid, p 130.
75 Ibid, p 135.
76 Committee on Homosexual Offences and Prostitution, 1957. *Report of the Committee on Homosexual Offences and Prostitution*. London: Her Majesty's Stationery Office.

deterring homosexual acts, and that it had not for a moment imagined that the Report would recommend decriminalisation. Yet that is precisely what happened.

Heavily influenced by Professor H L A Hart, the Report acknowledged the existence of an area of life that should remain private, out of reach of state intrusion and legal sanction, provided that no one is harmed by the conduct in question. Hart's arguments to the Committee, subsequently popularised in his series of lectures at Stanford University and collected in *Law, Liberty and Morality*,[77] saw him adopt a stance against what he referred to as 'legal moralism' – the notion, propounded by (among others) Patrick Devlin, that an individual may be punished for conduct which, while causing no harm, transgresses against the moral norms of his society. Hart's antipathy to this doctrine is unambiguous: 'The idea that we may punish offenders against a moral code, not to prevent harm or suffering or even the repetition of the offence but simply as a means of venting or emphatically expressing moral condemnation, is uncomfortably close to human sacrifice as an expression of religious worship.'[78]

During the Second World War, Hart had worked in the British code-breaking unit at Bletchley Park, where one of his colleagues was the computer visionary Alan Turing. Turing was homosexual, and was subjected to a number of draconian measures to attempt to deter or 'cure' him of his 'deviant' inclinations, and it may be that his ordeal – which culminated in his suicide – strongly influenced Hart's antipathy towards the punishment of victimless crimes. In any event, his contribution to the Committee, and the eventual Report (which, perhaps uniquely for an official publication of this nature, sold several thousand copies within days of its release) placed the Harm Principle back in the centre of jurisprudential debate.

While the origins of the Harm Principle lie in England, in the latter part of the 20th century it assumed a more international dimension, through legal theorists Joel Feinberg and Joseph Raz. Both took Mill's basic statement as their starting point, but went on to interpret and refine the Principle in different ways. Raz, for example, sought to extend Mill's dictum so as to add harm to the actor himself as a 'justifiable ground for coercive interference with a person',[79] while Feinberg's work imported the concept of 'interests' into the notion of harm. Both, however, subscribed to the view that the prevention of harm was the only justifiable ground for state coercion.[80]

It is no easy thing to apply the Harm Principle to germinal choice technologies; as the next chapter will show, the concept of 'harm' is not as

77 H L A Hart, *Law, Liberty, and Morality*. Oxford: Oxford University Press, 1963.
78 Ibid, pp 65–6.
79 Joseph Raz, *The Morality of Freedom*, Oxford: Clarendon Press, 1986, p 413.
80 See Raz, Chapter 15, particularly pp 400, 413, 419, and Feinberg pp 11–12 and 15.

straightforward as Mill or Hart perhaps assumed, and it is especially problematic in relation to 'genesis questions', that is, decisions about who should be born. But the Principle has at least one clear application to the subject of this book, and that is that individual liberty should not be subject to the whims and tastes of the majority. Hart, and those on the Wolfenden Committee who supported him, realised that in proposing decriminalisation of consensual homosexual relations, they were swimming against the tide of popular opinion. That fact alone, though, was not sufficient reason to use the criminal law to persecute people like Alan Turing, people whose private conduct harmed no one.

If the analogy between gay rights and the genetic supermarket seems somewhat strained, the principle underlying both my position and Hart's should be more obvious. In some areas of our lives, we must be free to do as we please, without seeking the approval of our peers and neighbours. Not so long ago, in the west of Scotland, 'mixed marriages' between Catholics and Protestants were frowned upon by a great many people. In other places, the same would have been true of inter-racial relationships, or couples who lived together without being married. Had such couples been subject to opinion poll rule, it is likely that, at certain times and in certain places, they would have been forbidden to be with the person they loved.

We live in a society where we are routinely invited to submit our opinions to myriad television, radio or newspaper surveys, on issues both great and trivial. Following the death of Princess Diana, British newspapers were highly critical of the Queen because her grief was apparently not as ostentatious as the British public demanded. When Prince Charles's relationship with Camilla Parker-Bowles became common knowledge, public opinion was widely sought as to whether or not they should marry. And 'reality television' shows like *Big Brother* encourage us to scrutinise the mundane minutiae of people's daily lives, with a view to punishing – by voting out – those whose conduct or manner displeases us.

In that context, making the case that, sometimes, the choices other people make just aren't our business is a hard line to sell. I have no doubt that a television show that required the Mastertons or the Hashmis to appeal to the viewing public, with their fates being subject to a mass viewers' vote at the end of the show, would be immensely popular. To some people, it may even be the most 'democratic' way to make such decisions. But the Mastertons and the Hashmis are not like the contestants on *Big Brother*. They did not volunteer to have the details of their lives paraded before the nation, but wanted only to be left alone to make decisions for themselves and their families. Furthermore, viewers of reality television shows are not required to explain their votes; their reasons may be sincere and considered, they may be mischievous or driven by bitterness or bigotry, they may even be the result of a post-pub whim. This may be a reasonable way to run light entertainment. It is not, I would suggest, such a good way to determine other people's reproductive futures.

Prospective parents are not game show contestants. The choices they make are likely to matter deeply to them, and we should not lightly interfere with them. If we are to deny them reproductive autonomy, then we must be able to give them a good reason, grounded in widely shared and clearly understood ethical principles. Just as moral squeamishness and widespread prejudice were not good enough reasons to carry on persecuting people like Alan Turing, neither are they good enough reasons to interfere with the sorts of choices the genetic supermarket will offer.

Conclusion

The principle of respect for autonomy, then, provides us with a reason to respect individual choice in relation to GCTs. Not, admittedly, a definitive reason – there are other ethical considerations yet to be considered that may outweigh the case for choice – but nonetheless, an initial presumption that it is incumbent on opponents of choice to rebut. Josephine Quintavalle, a high-profile campaigner against GCTs, has criticised the Human Fertilisation and Embryology Authority for being 'influenced by the fashion of the week but predominately in the direction of the people who ask them "Please can I do this?" ' rather than being 'influenced in general by society'.[81] If we are serious about our respect for autonomy, though, we must recognise that, in certain decisions that are central to our lives, and which have no important implications for other people, 'society' should not be afforded a veto. That most people don't approve of my choices, or are made uneasy by them, is not reason enough to take these choices away from me. Respect for autonomy means precisely *not* having to ask 'Please can I do this?'

---

81 'Fertility law review could make dads redundant', *Daily Mail*, 17 August 2005.

Chapter 3

Children of the genetic supermarket

The question we must ask, then, is whether any coherent reason can be given for denying choice to prospective parents. If respect for autonomy does not succeed as a convincing argument against choice, then we must consider, in turn, the other ethical rules that might be infringed. Contemporary bioethics, as we have seen, typically lists a number of core principles that must be weighed in evaluating controversial actions. The influential 'pluralist' approach espoused by Beauchamp and Childress was concerned with, respectively, respect for autonomy, beneficence, non-maleficence, and justice. Considerable weight is also still accorded, in some circles, to the so-called categorical imperative, broadly construed as respecting persons as ends in themselves, rather than as mere means to some other end. As we will see, ethicists differ on the question of which of these broad principles is most important, and even those philosophers who agree that, say, justice matters most can disagree greatly about what exactly that concept involves, or how it should be applied in particular cases.

Is anyone likely to be harmed by the choices prospective parents make? Will anyone's rights be infringed? Will they perpetuate injustice? If we have no reason to suppose that any of these adverse outcomes is likely, then we have no business foisting our tastes and values onto those who do not share them.

I intend to turn first to the question of non-maleficence – or, in everyday terms, harm. The literature on PGD contains no shortage of suggested harms and wrongs that could follow from its practice. Probably the most obvious of the parties that we might consider to be at risk, though, are the potential children whose futures hang in the balance when their (potential) parents make such decisions. We live in a society that (at least purportedly) prioritises the safety and well-being of children, that regards their interests as paramount. No evaluation of GCTs, then, can proceed without a detailed consideration of how the technique will impact on those interests. As will become clear, determining where those interests lie is not always a straightforward matter. Before addressing that question, though, we need to consider two more general questions. Who precisely are we talking about when we speak of the 'children of the genetic supermarket'? And just what, exactly, do we mean by 'harm'?

The nature of harm

We saw in the previous chapter how 'liberal' philosophers like Mill and Hart viewed the threat of harm as the only – or at least, one of the very few – legitimate reasons for interfering with individual liberty. It is not only adherents to the Harm Principle, though, who are concerned with questions of harm. In fact, it has come to occupy a very central place in evaluation and regulation of GCTs.

Perhaps most obviously, this can be seen in the legislation which governs reproductive technologies and use of embryos, the Human Fertilisation and Embryology Act 1990, s 13(5) of which stipulates: 'A woman shall not be provided with treatment services unless account has been taken of the welfare of any child who may be born as a result of the treatment (including the need of that child for a father), and of any other child who may be affected by the birth.' While 'welfare' is not synonymous with 'harm', it is, I think, difficult to conceive of any calculation of welfare that does not take account of harm, even as it sets out to balance these against potential benefits. We can see this in the interpretation of 'welfare' adopted by the Human Fertil-isation and Embryology Authority (HFEA), and its Ethics Committee (con-sidered in more detail in Chapter 6). In its recent review of 'welfare of the child' assessments, the HFEA made clear and specific reference to the risk of harm to the child as a possible reason for denying access to reproductive technologies:

> There should be a presumption to provide treatment to all those who request it, unless there is evidence that the child to be born would face a risk of serious medical, physical or psychological harm.[1]

As I will argue in Chapter 6, the HFEA's use of the concept of harm is far from unproblematic, but it is clear that it is a concept that features promin-ently in its reasoning. One recent example – of the Authority's concern with harm, and perhaps also of its confusion over the concept – can be found in its decision to license PGD for those who wish to use it only for 'tissue typing'. The specifics of those decisions will be considered later, but for the time being it is sufficient to note that the Authority's Press Release couched

---

1   *Tomorrow's children. Report of the policy review of welfare of the child assessments in licensed assisted conception clinics*, November 2005, available at http://www.hfea.gov.uk/ AboutHFEA/HFEAPolicy/TomorrowsChildren-ReviewoftheHFEAsguidanceonWelfareof theChild (accessed: 19 June 2006).

its change of policy in the language of one particular conception of harm – 'harm as damage' – its initial unwillingness to permit this use being attributed to 'a concern about a potential risk of damaging the embryo'.[2]

It is interesting to note that, at the time of the Authority's initial decision about tissue typing, no significance was attached, either by the Authority itself or its Ethics Committee whose advice (on this matter) it ignored, to any such danger arising from the procedure itself. However, the Ethics Committee's approach was, once again, clearly informed by considerations of welfare, of which an evaluation of potential harm clearly played an important part:

> the Ethics Committee had in fact identified the 'putative child's actual moral, psychological, social and physical welfare' as an issue of great significance.[3]
>
> Its Report considered a fairly traditional formulation of the 'welfare principle', asking 'whether the outcome of the technique adversely shifts the balance of benefit and harm'.[4]

There is evidence, also, that consideration of harm informs parliamentary debates surrounding reproductive and genetic technologies, and PGD in particular. A recent series of interviews conducted by the House of Commons Science and Technology Committee provides some evidence that concerns about harm remain a prominent consideration of the Committee's deliberations, as the following questions asked by members of the Committee suggest:

> If a proper social research study found that gender selection caused no harm, would you support it?[5]
>
> Would you support it [sex selection] if it was found there was no harm caused?[6]
>
> May I ask what evidence there is in the scientific literature that there is

---

2   'HFEA agrees to extend policy on tissue typing', 21 June 2004, at http://www.hfea.gov.uk/ PressOffice/Archive/1090427358 (accessed: 19 June 2006).
3   Ethics Committee of the Human Fertilisation and Embryology Authority, *Ethical Issues in the Creation and Selection of Preimplantation Embryos to Produce Tissue Donors*, 22 November 2001, paragraph 3.2.
4   Ibid, paragraph 2.14.
5   Question asked by Robert Key during Oral Evidence Taken before the Science and Technology Committee, on Wednesday 23 June 2004, at http://www.publications.parliament.uk/ cgi-bin/ukparl_hl?DB=ukparl&STEMMER=en&WORDS=fertilis+harm+&COLOUR= Red&STYLE=s&URL=/pa/cm200304/cmselect/cmsctech/uc599-ii/uc59902.htm#muscat _highlighter_first_match (accessed: 18 July 2004).
6   Id.

harm to donor-conceived children from not being able to trace their genetic parent?[7]

In your evidence you do mention that you feel gender selection inflicts no harm on the child, family or society. If there were any research which indicated that this was not the case, would it change your views?[8]

While the views and concerns of the Select Committee are not necessarily reflective of those of the wider legislature, it would perhaps be surprising if they were entirely divorced from them.

Although not directly related to the legislative or regulatory processes, the views of major professional and other prestigious bodies on such matters display a concern with potential harmful consequences. In its submission to the Select Committee on the subject of tissue typing, the British Medical Association noted as a 'key concern . . . the possibility of psychological harm resulting to the child who would be selected and born to be a donor', though it also acknowledged that 'these hypothetical risks of harm needed to be balanced against other harms, primarily the real harm to the sibling who would suffer or die without this treatment'.[9] In addition, the Royal Society of Edinburgh considered the potentially pivotal effect of evidence of harm to the embryo if PGD were employed:

It is not clear, however, on what basis there should be restrictions of PGD to only serious clinical conditions, although there may be practical reasons for wishing to do so. If there are clinical reasons for undertaking PGD at all – and given that the consultation document itself notes in paragraph 26 that few people are likely to choose it – there appears to be little logic in limiting its use to certain conditions. Of course, this balance might change if it became clear that PGD caused significant harm in large numbers of cases. The balance would then perhaps shift towards

---

7   Question asked by Evan Harris during Oral Evidence Taken before the Science and Technology Committee, on Wednesday 23 June 2004, at http://www.publications.parliament.uk/cgi-bin/ukparl_hl?DB=ukparl&STEMMER=en&WORDS=fertilis+harm+&COLOUR=Red&STYLE=s&URL=/pa/cm200304/cmselect/cmsctech/uc599-ii/uc59902.htm#muscat_highlighter_first_match (accessed: 18 July 2004).

8   Question asked by Geraldine Smith, recorded in Minutes of Evidence Taken Before Science and Technology Committee, Wednesday 30 June 2004, at http://www.publications.parliament.uk/cgi-bin/ukparl_hl?DB=ukparl&STEMMER=en&WORDS=fertilis+harm+&COLOUR=Red&STYLE=s&URL=/pa/cm200304/cmselect/cmsctech/uc599-iii/uc59902.htm#muscat_highlighter_first_match (accessed: 18 July 2004).

9   Memorandum from the British Medical Association to the House of Commons Science and Technology Committee, May 2004, available at http://www.publications.parliament.uk/cgi-bin/ukparl_hl?DB=ukparl&STEMMER=en&WORDS=fertilis+harm+&COLOUR=Red&STYLE=s&URL=/pa/cm200304/cmselect/cmsctech/599/599we13.htm#muscat_highlighter_first_match, paragraph 33 (accessed: 18 July 2004).

not permitting it in 'minor' clinical conditions because of the greater harm caused by using it – namely the additional damage to, or destruction of, the embryo.[10]

In the realm of bioethical literature, concern with the avoidance of harm has a long tradition. As Beauchamp and Childress explain, the 'obligation not to inflict harm on others' is '[o]ften proclaimed the fundamental principle in the Hippocratic tradition of medical ethics', yet its precise origins are somewhat uncertain; the Hippocratic Oath certainly does not accord a prominent role to this principle.[11] Nonetheless, the maxim *primum non nocere* appears to be widely accepted as a core tenet of medical ethics.

Within the contemporary literature of bioethics, concern about the avoidance of harm is widespread, occupying some role in a variety of ethical traditions. Most obviously, as we have seen, adherents to the Harm Principle regard harm as *the* necessary prerequisite of any legal intervention with individual liberty. This view is perhaps less popular than once it was, having been supplanted to some extent by pluralist, utilitarian and rights-based approaches, but nonetheless, a small but respected body of bioethical literature persists which advocates just such a view. Max Charlesworth, Emeritus Professor of Philosophy at Deakin University, has based his consideration of bioethical issues around a decidedly Millian approach:

> In a liberal society people should as far as possible be allowed to make their own moral decisions for themselves and it is not the business of the law to enforce a common code of morality. The law should be brought in, so to speak, only when other people are likely to be harmed in some obvious way.[12]

Heta Häyry has expressed her approach in somewhat different terms, and in particular does not couch it in the language of harm, but there are clear similarities between her 'liberal utilitarianism' and the harm-based approach adopted by Charlesworth: 'Individuals should be left free to make their own choices, provided that the consequences of their decisions are not likely to have a negative effect on the basic need-satisfaction of others.'[13] Whether Häyry would agree to applying the term 'harm' to having 'a negative effect on

10 Memorandum from the Royal Society of Edinburgh to the House of Commons Science and Technology Committee, May 2004, at http://www.royalsoced.org.uk/govt_responses/2004/reproduction.htm (accessed: 19 June 2006).
11 Tom L Beauchamp and James F Childress, *Principles of Medical Ethics*, fifth edn, New York: Oxford University Press, 2001, p 113.
12 Max Charlesworth, *Bioethics in a Liberal Society*, Cambridge: Cambridge University Press, 1993, p 74. See also p 86, in relation to surrogacy.
13 Heta Häyry, *Individual Liberty and Medical Control*. Aldershot: Ashgate, 1998, p 99.

the basic need-satisfaction of others' is a moot point, but it is clear that her approach shares the liberal presumption of adherents to the Harm Principle, and shares also their view that that presumption can be rebutted *only* to avoid adverse consequences for others.

For Charlesworth and Häyry, then, the presence of harm (or adverse consequences) to others is the only legitimate basis for state interference with individual liberty. More commonly, harm features as an element of a less narrowly focused approach to ethics. For ethical pluralists like Beauchamp and Childress, the obligation to avoid the infliction of harm – expressed as the principle of 'non-maleficence' – is one of the four core ethical principles,[14] not derived from, nor either superior or inferior to, the others. Furthermore, the notion of 'harm' with which Beauchamp and Childress are concerned is remarkably similar to that adopted by 'harm theorists' like Joel Feinberg; thus, they 'construe harm exclusively in the second and nonnormative sense of thwarting, defeating, or setting back some party's interests'.[15]

As distinct from some of the utilitarian commentators, who question the distinction between acts and omissions, Beauchamp and Childress reject the idea that non-maleficence (avoiding harm) and beneficence (the conferring of benefit) should be incorporated into one principle.[16] However, they also reject the assumption implicit in the *primum non nocere* principle that the former obligation should automatically take precedence over the latter:

> In general, if in a particular case the injury inflicted is very minor . . . but the benefit provided by rescue is major . . . then we tend to think that the obligation of beneficence takes priority over the obligation of nonmaleficence.[17]

In this, they are closer to those utilitarian commentators who are also concerned with balancing benefit and harm. John Harris has explicitly rejected the idea of the Harm Principle:

> The decision to 'criminalize' conduct is surely principally a question of the utility of so doing. The issue is most sensibly decided by weighing up the social, political, and moral consequences of using the apparatus of the criminal law and of imposing the stigma and social consequences of

14 Together with respect for autonomy, beneficence and justice.
15 Beauchamp and Childress, *Principles of Medical Ethics*, op. cit., fn 11, p 116.
16 'In our view, conflating nonmaleficence and beneficence into a single principle obscured relevant distinctions.' Ibid, p 114.
17 Id.

criminality on offenders. We should not predetermine this issue by deciding in advance that if conduct is not harmful it is not criminal.[18]

It is not overly far-fetched to suggest that Harris's concern with 'the social, political, and moral consequences' of criminalisation could, at least to a large extent, be rephrased in terms of the language of harms and benefits, a contention that may to some extent be borne out by the fact that the remaining 11 pages of the chapter in which Harris makes this claim are given over almost entirely to defining the concept of 'harm'.

'Harm' defined

How, though, are we to understand 'harm'? In common parlance, the verb 'to harm' is often used as a synonym for 'to damage'; it is, for example, both commonplace and intelligible to enquire 'will this weedkiller harm my lawn?' Whether a notion of harm can be extended to beings or objects which possess no awareness of being harmed is an important decision, as will be seen when we consider whether embryos are harmed when they are destroyed. For, in much the same way as herbicide may 'harm' a lawn by killing it outright or retarding its growth, so too might the destruction of embryos, or the prevention of their development such as by cryopreserving them, be thought to 'harm' an embryo.

Joel Feinberg, whose work has been so influential in exploring the notion of harm, is quick to distinguish, and dismiss from his consideration, this notion of harm in its 'derivative or extended sense', that is, 'the sense in which we can say that any kind of thing at all can be "harmed" '.[19] This is the sense in which harms can be attributed to asentient, and possibly even inanimate objects, such as when we say 'frost does harm to crops'.[20] As Feinberg explains, 'this is harm in a transferred sense; we don't feel aggrieved on behalf of the windows or the tomatoes, nor are they objects of our sympathies. Rather our reference to their "harm" is elliptical for the harm done to those who have interests in the . . . crops'.[21] For in the absence of an interest in growing or developing, how are we to conceive of a change in the status of the lawn or the crops as being welcome or unwelcome? Certainly, being sprayed with herbicide may well retard the growth of a field of grass, but relative to what ethical principle are we to judge this retardation problematic? For Feinberg, it is a straightforward matter to exclude these suggested instances of 'harm', since the purported victims do not possess a quality that

---

18 John Harris, *Wonderwoman and Superman: The Ethics of Human Biotechnology*, Oxford: Oxford University Press, 1992, p 86.
19 Joel Feinberg, *Harm to Others*, Oxford: Oxford University Press, 1994, p 32.
20 Id.
21 Id.

he regards as a prerequisite of being 'harmed': the capacity to be a bearer of interests.[22]

On Feinberg's conception, what distinguishes 'harm' from other ways in which we can affect an object – such as 'damage' or 'break' – lies in the requirement that the victim of 'harm' must possess interests. Harm, therefore, consists of 'the thwarting, setting back, or defeating of an interest'.[23] What, then, is an interest?

It is perhaps useful to locate Feinberg's seminal contribution to legal theory within the context of the evolution of consequentialist thought. The tradition of evaluating actions in terms of their effects upon people was already long established before the notion of harms and interests (arguably) became the dominant concepts in consequentialist thought. In the essay entitled 'Utilitarianism', Mill contended that

> ... pleasure, and freedom from pain, are the only things desirable as ends; and that all desirable things (which are as numerous in the utilitarian as in any other scheme) are desirable either for the pleasure inherent in themselves, or as means to the promotion of pleasure and the prevention of pain.[24]

Although, at the outset of *Harm to Others*, Feinberg openly acknowledged his intellectual debt to Mill, he completely rejected this notion of 'mental state' utilitarianism, the view that the aim of morality is to promote some kind of subjectively pleasurable states of mind.[25] Rather, Feinberg's approach added and relied upon the concept of 'interests', closely related to, but distinct from, 'wants' or 'desires'. (Feinberg had earlier explained the relationship as being of the nature that 'desires or wants are the materials interests are made of'.[26]) 'A person has an interest in Y,' he claimed, 'when he has a *stake* in Y, that is, when he stands to gain or lose depending on the condition or outcome of Y.'[27] If this definition is accepted, then the connection with wants becomes apparent. It may, after all, be difficult to see how a person could be said to 'gain' or 'lose' save by making reference to what he actually wants.

Feinberg certainly accepted this in relation to what he refers to as 'ulterior'

---

22 For a contrary view, according to which a certain variety of interests can meaningfully be attributed to inanimate objects, see Tom Regan, 'Feinberg on What Sorts of Beings Can Have Rights', *The Southern Journal of Philosophy* (1976); 14: 485–98.

23 Ibid, p 33.

24 J S Mill, 'Utilitarianism', in Warnock, (ed), *Utilitarianism*, op. cit., p 257.

25 Feinberg, *Harm to Others*, op. cit., fn 19, p 85.

26 Feinberg, 'Rights of Animals and Unborn Generations', in *Rights, Justice, and the Bounds of Liberty*, Princeton University Press, 1980, p 169.

27 Feinberg, *Rights, Justice, and the Bounds of Liberty*, op. cit., p 45.

interests.[28] However, he did not hold this to be true for that class of interests which he called 'welfare' interests, that is, that class of minimum interests such as 'health, economic sufficiency, emotional stability [and] political liberty',[29] the fulfilment of which are necessary for the fulfilment of all other interests.[30] As regards these welfare interests, Feinberg took the view that 'what promotes them is good for a person *in any case*, whatever his beliefs or wants may be'.[31]

It is difficult to disagree with the claim that a certain minimum standard of health is likely to be a prerequisite of most other interests; someone may not care very much about his health for its own sake, but will require to be in moderately good health if he is to act on his desire to visit Paris or make a parachute jump. This would be an example of an interest which is linked to wants, but at one remove; the person does not want X for itself, but will require to have X if he is to achieve Y, which he *does* want. More generally, it may be that health can be seen as a desire in itself; as Ruth Chadwick has commented, 'it might be possible to construe all claims for medical help in terms of a desire, e.g. the desire to be well'.[32]

For the time being, I think we can say that, while almost all persons may be supposed to have interests which are bound up to some extent with health, for example, this interest is not entirely independent of their wants. Certainly, some scepticism must be expressed as to the claim that *anything* could be said to be in the interest of all persons in all circumstances.

Taking an interest and *having* an interest

There are, though, undoubtedly circumstances in which individuals may be said to have interests which do not correspond exactly with wants. An

---

28 '[I]t is difficult at best to explain how a person could have a direct stake in certain developments without recourse to his wants and goals,' *Harm to Others*, op. cit., fn 19, p 42.

29 Ibid, p 41.

30 The concept of 'welfare interests' has also been postulated by Goodin. He defines them as 'that set of generalized resources that will be necessary for people to have before pursuing any of the more particular preferences that they might happen to have' – Goodin lists '[h]ealth, money, shelter [and] sustenance' as examples. The essence of welfare utilitarianism, according to Goodin, lies in a recognition of the fact that the majority of preferences are formed in circumstances far removed from what he refers to as an 'ideal choice situation', that is to say, a situation 'characterized by perfect information, strong will, settled preferences, and such like'. This being so, a number of those preferences expressed by persons will have failed to take account of their welfare interests; in such a situation, 'welfare utilitarianism would suppress short-sighted preference satisfaction in favour of protecting people's long-term welfare interests'. Robert E Goodin, 'Utility and the good', in Peter Singer, (ed), *A Companion to Ethics*, Oxford: Blackwell, 1991, p 244.

31 Feinberg, *Harm to Others*, op. cit., fn 19, p 42.

32 Ruth Chadwick, 'Having children: Introduction' from her collection *Ethics, Reproduction and Genetic Control*, London: Routledge, 1990, p 18.

obvious example occurs when someone is unaware of the existence of certain factors which will have a significant bearing upon certain wants which he does harbour, or where he is unaware of the relationship of these factors to his wants.

Anton is going about his daily business, blissfully unaware of the fact that Leon has been offered a substantial sum of money to kill him. Leon, although he is desperate for the money, is wracked with indecision about whether or not to carry out the contract; as well as *wanting* the money, he also *wants* to comply with his moral beliefs, which tell him that killing is wrong, at least in circumstances such as these, and he also *wants* to be free from the feelings of guilt which he suspects may trouble him if he kills Anton. In view of the fact that Anton is not aware of Leon's existence, still less of the moral quandary with which he is faced, one could not truthfully say that Anton *wants* or *desires* or *would prefer* Leon to choose not to kill him. Quite simply, he has no view on the subject at all. But Anton has a whole range of wants and desires which will be frustrated if Leon kills him before he has a chance to fulfil them. There are friends he wants to see again, books he wants to read, and myriad other ambitions, great and small, which he will be denied the opportunity to achieve if his life is ended now. It would therefore be completely wrong to say that the outcome of Leon's decision is of no consequence to Anton.[33]

In situations such as these, where the likelihood of someone's desires being satisfied is affected by decisions or action about which he knows nothing, a person may be said to have an interest in that decision, even though he has no desires or preferences corresponding directly to it. As Mary Anne Warren has said:

> Non-self-aware beings may not consciously *take* an interest in their own survival, but it does not follow that they cannot *have* such an interest. Having an interest in something does not require a conscious desire for it, but only the potential to experience some benefit from it.[34]

This idea of having an interest could, therefore, be extended to beings that are unaware even of the *concept* of interests, as in Warren's example:

> Thus, it seems plausible that if a spider has an interest in anything, then it has an interest in not being smashed flat – even if the process is quite painless. Because continued life is necessary for the spider's future

---

33 James Griffin has illustrated the same thing with a slightly more prosaic example: 'If you cheat me out of an inheritance that I never expected, I might not know but still be the worse off for it.' 'A sophisticated version of the desire account', in Jonathan Glover, (ed), *Utilitarianism and its Critics*, New York: Macmillan, 1990, p 72.

34 Mary Anne Warren, *Moral Status: obligations to persons and other living things*, Oxford: Oxford University Press, 1997, p 80.

enjoyment of whatever pleasures it has enjoyed in the past, it seems obvious that it has an interest in survival.[35]

Certainly, a spider is unlikely to possess the requisite reflective capacities to enable it to *take* an interest in its continued survival – existential musing almost certainly requires a more sophisticated brain. But implicit in Warren's contention is that the spider possesses *some* interests, even if it is not consciously aware of possessing them. Were it not capable even of enjoying basic sensual pleasures, it is difficult to see what interests would be frustrated or thwarted by its painless demise. This question of the attribution of interests to beings that are not aware, in any reflective sense, of *having* interest is of obvious relevance to the question of whether embryos can be harmed.

Harms and wrongs

Feinberg's approach does not hold that any harmful conduct can justifiably be curtailed by the criminal law. For one thing, he recognises an important *de minimis* restriction, according to which trivial harms should not be prevented by disproportionately intrusive restrictions. But it is also true that some non-trivially harmful conduct cannot, on Feinberg's conception, be constrained by law. He has argued, for example, that 'no plausibly interpreted harm principle' would justify the prohibition of, for example, 'setbacks to interest incurred in legitimate competition or harms to the risk of which the "victim" freely consented'. Rather, 'only setbacks of interests that are wrongs . . . are to count as harms in the appropriate sense'.[36]

What does Feinberg mean by a 'wrong'? This he explains by reference to 'established priority rankings' of potentially competing interests:

> The interests of different persons are constantly and unavoidably in conflict, so that any legal system determined to 'minimize harm' must incorporate judgments of the comparative importance of interests of different kinds so that it can pronounce 'unjustified' the invasion of one person's interest of high priority done to protect another person's interest of low priority. Legal wrongs then will be invasions of interests which violate established priority rankings.[37]

Criminal prohibition, then, is only justified when the conduct in question interferes with an interest deemed in advance to be of high priority. In the previous chapter I explained that, to some people, the interest in reproductive

---

35 See fn 34.
36 Feinberg, *Harm to Others*, op. cit., fn 19, p 36.
37 Ibid, p 35.

liberty should be accorded just such a status, and it is probably true that interferences with it will usually, on Feinberg's analysis, constitute both harms and wrongs.

Although Feinberg's work is probably the most influential in the ethics of harm and interests, his definitions and explanations have not gone unchallenged. Bioethicist John Harris has proposed an alternative account of 'harms' and 'wrongs', and of the relationship between them. Harris begins by seeking to identify the common ground he shares with Feinberg: 'A condition that is harmful, Feinberg and I would agree, is one in which the individual is disabled or suffering in some way or in which his interests or rights are frustrated.'[38] However, even this early in his commentary, Harris has created difficulties for himself, or at least for his readers, by virtue of some uncharacteristically careless use of language. First, this does not seem entirely to accord with Feinberg's definition of a *harmful*, as opposed to a *harmed*, condition. For Feinberg, a harmful condition is one likely to give rise to further, future harms:

> A *harmed* condition of a person may or may not also be a *harmful* condition, depending on whether it has itself the tendency to generate further harm. A blistered finger may be to some small degree a harmed condition, but unless the finger is on the hand of a concert pianist or a baseball pitcher, it may not be at all harmful.[39]

Secondly, Harris is equally careless in his use of language when he claims that Feinberg would agree that a harmful (or harmed) condition is one in which the individual's 'interests *or rights* are frustrated'. A situation which sees someone's rights frustrated – perhaps 'infringed' or 'violated' are more apt verbs – would for Feinberg, constitute a 'wrong', but need not involve a harm; indeed, he specifically acknowledges the possibility of 'harmless wronging'.[40]

In large part, the essence of Harris's disagreement with Feinberg lies in his contention that is possible to be harmed without being rendered worse off. He offers this example:

> When in the First World War soldiers deliberately shot themselves in the foot, or injured themselves in some other way so as to get what was called a 'Blighty Wound', one that would get them sent home to 'Blighty', and out of the fighting, they were guilty of an act of deliberate self-harming. Indeed were it not an act of self-harming, which may have disabled or handicapped the individual to some extent, it would not have secured the

---

38 John Harris, *Wonderwoman and Superman*, op. cit., fn 18, p 88.
39 Feinberg, *Harm to Others*, op. cit., fn 19, p 31.
40 Feinberg, *Harmless Wrongdoing*, New York: Oxford University Press, 1988.

desired effect. . . . Insistence on tying harm to the idea of being made 'worse off' deprives us of the ability to characterise what is going on here as a self-interested act of harming. It is surely clearer and more consistent with what we wish to say in such cases to describe the acts of these soldiers as acts of self-harming but by which they did not wrong themselves.[41]

In a sense, Harris is undoubtedly right when he claims that the soldiers 'harmed' themselves; there is no question that they did indeed set back some of their own interests, interests in avoiding extreme pain and possible disability, and perhaps interests in being suspected of, or even executed for, cowardice. However, if any act that sets back *any* interests whatever were to be regarded as a harm for the purposes of the Harm Principle, then it would seem that the range of justifiably prohibited behaviours would be very wide indeed; it is possible to find in almost any act an interest somewhere, however trivial, that is thwarted or frustrated. Most troublingly, acts that clearly benefit an individual by promoting some of his most important interests in important ways will often involve the setting back of some other of his interests. (To take an obvious example, life-saving heart surgery on someone who wants desperately to avoid death would be universally considered a benefit, but there is no question that such surgery sets back that person's interests in avoiding pain and a prolonged period of infirmity while he or she recovers.)

By claiming that the soldiers *harmed*, but did not *wrong*, themselves, it seems perhaps as if Harris's principal disagreement with Feinberg is not in his definition of 'harm', but rather his definition of 'wrong'. For Harris, it would seem, a wrong occurs when someone sustains a balance of harms over benefits. Thus, the soldiers are not wronged because their more important interests in avoiding early death are furthered, but are nonetheless harmed because their (relatively unimportant) interests in avoiding pain and disability are set back.

As I will explain later, this distinction is particularly important when considering GCTs, particularly in relation to what has become known as the Non-Identity Problem. For the moment, it will suffice to say that a distinction can be drawn between harms per se and harms *on balance*. Such a distinction would allow us to say, with Harris, that a soldier harmed himself when he shot himself in the foot, but that in so doing he sustained a *net balance* of benefits over harms. Assuming the wound has the desired effect, and he does not end up succumbing to gangrene or a firing squad, in the overall reckoning, he was made better off than he would have been but for the injury; thus, he is not harmed on balance.

There are still numerous controversies surrounding the concept of harm, but if we accept for the moment the rough description of 'harm' as a set-back

41 Harris, *Wonderwoman and Superman*, op. cit., fn 18, p 92.

to interests, and 'interests' as things that are related to, though not identical with, what we happen to want in or from our lives, it is possible at least to begin a consideration of when or whether GCTs are likely to cause harm. Let us begin with probably the most obvious category of potential 'victims' – the discarded embryos.

Potential lives or discarded cells?

When Michelle and Paul O'Brien chose to implant the embryo that would develop into Chloe, they also decided *not* to implant several other embryos. The same choice is made by any prospective parents utilising PGD. The respective fates awaiting the two groups could not be more different. For those which are selected, the possibility[42] that they will one day be born into an environment where they are much wanted beckons, while for the 'unsuccessful' candidates, the future holds only the prospect of destruction, perhaps after being the subjects of experimentation. In view of this situation, the conclusion that the embryos have some interest in what is decided, and therefore stand to be harmed by it, might seem an obvious one.

For a number of reasons, though, determining whether embryos qualify as interested parties is problematic. Certainly, any decision will have an *effect* upon the embryos; but this is not the same as saying that the embryos have interests bound up with the outcomes of those decisions. Any attempt to make a determination as to whether the interests of the cryopreserved embryos should enter into an evaluation of the potential harm caused by PGD will of course depend upon the answer to the question as to whether embryos are the kinds of beings which are capable of having interests at all.

Earlier, I suggested that the sort of interests the frustration of which give rise to harms are those which relate, albeit not always directly, to wants. There, I argued that while it is not unknown to hear people ask whether a particular weedkiller might harm their lawn, this was not harm in the normative sense; we do not feel any sympathy for, nor empathy with, the lawn, do not feel that it has sustained any loss that is meaningful to *it*. It is widely recognised in bioethical literature that the question as to whether a being is the bearer of interests (or the type of interests with which ethics is properly concerned) depends upon the possession of *consciousness*; for interests to be meaningfully attributed to any person, that person must be, or at some point have been,[43] conscious. Thus, it has been observed that:

---

42 It must of course be remembered that this *is* only a possibility; the majority of embryos implanted after IVF will not result in a successful pregnancy. See *The Patients' Guide to DI and IVF Clinics*, 3rd edn (1997), published by the Human Fertilisation and Embryology Authority.

43 The question of whether interests can survive the being who harboured those interests is philosophically contentious, and will be considered again later in this chapter.

it is both a necessary and sufficient condition for having interests, in the sense that is relevant to the question of moral status, that one be conscious in the minimal sense of that term,[44]

and that:

[i]t makes no sense to suppose that something has interest of *its own* – as distinct from its being important what happens to it – unless it has, or has had, some form of consciousness: some mental as well as physical life.[45]

The question of when precisely a human being attains a level of consciousness sufficient for us to attribute to it even the most basic of interests has still not been answered to the satisfaction of all, but although this is of great importance in any consideration of the ethics of abortion, for example, ascertaining the precise timing of the onset of consciousness does not present a problem when talking about PGD. For while doubt may exist as to when consciousness is first present in a human being, no one would seriously seek to attribute that quality to an eight-cell embryo.

The reason for this certainty lies in recognition of the fact that, in order for consciousness to be possible, a being must fulfil certain physiological criteria.[46] As Burgess and Tawia have commented,

(mental) facts about human consciousness are supervenient on (physical) facts about the human central nervous system – more specifically, they are (at least largely) supervenient on facts about the cerebral cortex,[47]

that is, 'the folded sheet of gray matter . . . that covers the surface of the cerebral hemispheres'.[48]

When precisely an adequate neural substrate for sentience can be assumed to be present is the subject of some dispute. A review of the literature does suggest, however, that there is no serious doubt that the possibility of sentience does not exist until a relatively advanced stage of the pregnancy. Thus it has been claimed that:

---

44 J A Burgess and S A Tawia, 'When did you first begin to feel it? – Locating the beginning of human consciousness', *Bioethics* (1996); 10(1):1, p 25.

45 Ronald Dworkin, *Life's Dominion*, p 16.

46 'An interest, however the concept is finally to be analyzed, presupposes at least rudimentary cognitive equipment. Interests are compounded out of *desires* and *aims*, both of which presuppose something like . . . cognitive awareness.' Joel Feinberg, 'The rights of animals and unborn generations', from *Rights, Justice, and the Bounds of Liberty*, op. cit., fn 26, p 168.

47 Burgess and Tawia, 'When did you first begin to feel it?', loc. cit., p 2.

48 Rodrigo O Kuljis, 'Development of the human brain: the emergence of the neural substrate for pain perception and conscious experience', from *The Beginning of Human Life*, Beller and Weir, (eds), Dordrecht: Kluwer Academic Publishers, 1994, p 50.

it appears unlikely that the neural apparatus with which the foetus is endowed is capable of much more than unconscious reflex activity until at least midgestation and perhaps much later.[49]

The Royal College of Obstetricians and Gynaecologists Working Party were somewhat more specific, observing that 'thalamocortical connections are first observed penetrating the frontal cortical plate at 26–34 weeks' gestation' and stating that 'before that time there is no sensory input to the cortex'.[50]

Indeed, so widely shared is this view among embryologists and neurologists that to describe it as the orthodox view is something of an understatement – as Bonnie Steinbock has said,

> there is complete agreement that the very early embryo cannot be sentient, because it has not yet developed the rudimentary structures of a nervous system.[51]

Even Elizabeth Peacock of the UK Parliamentary Pro-Life Group has tacitly conceded that the capacity for pain cannot exist before ten weeks' gestation.[52] Thus, embryos do not and can not in any sense be said to care about what happens to them, or indeed care about anything at all: '[w]hether they are preserved or destroyed, cherished or neglected is of no concern to them.'[53]

This does not necessarily lead us to conclude that what happens to an embryo is a matter of moral indifference; other individuals may have interests bound up with the fate of the embryos, and other ethical principles may be violated if they are treated in certain ways.[54] Nonetheless, it is as well to be clear at this point that, if it is possible to treat an embryo in ways that may be said to be 'wrong', it is not because the embryo itself is being harmed in any subjectively meaningful sense: 'a being without interests has no "behalf" to act in, and no "sake" to act for.'[55] In short, it cannot be harmed.

What could be argued, however, is that embryos possess the *potential* to

---

49 See fn 48, p 55.
50 RCOG Report, p 16. See also Grobstein, *Science and the Unborn: Choosing Human Futures*, New York: Basic Books, 1988, p 55.
51 Bonnie Steinbock, 'The moral status of extracorporeal embryos', from Dyson and Harris, (eds), *Ethics and Biotechnology*, London: Routledge, 1994, p 84.
52 *The Guardian*, 22 July 1996.
53 Steinbock, 'The moral status of extracorporeal embryos', above, p 81.
54 Steinbock draws an illuminating parallel with the issue of flag burning in the USA.
55 Joel Feinberg, 'The rights of animals and unborn generations', from *Rights, Justice, and the Bounds of Liberty*, op. cit., fn 26, p 167. A rare opposition to this view can be found in Francis Fukuyama's *Our Posthuman Future: Consequences of the Biotechnology Revolution*, New York: Faber, Strauss and Giroux, 2002. Fukuyama claims that 'embryos are routinely harmed by in vitro fertilization clinics when they are discarded' (p 91), but makes no attempt to situate this assertion within the context of the debate as to whether embryos are the sort of beings that can be harmed.

become beings with interests. Establishing that there exists no reason to be concerned about the interests of the embryos – quite simply, they have none – doesn't address the question of whether we ought to care about the future interests of the persons[56] those embryos have the potential to become. For many people who think that embryos are of moral significance, it is this potential which renders those lives valuable. There are, however, persuasive reasons to reject that argument. As John Harris has pointed out,

> the fact that an entity can undergo changes that will make it significantly different does not constitute a reason for treating it as if it had already undergone those changes,[57]

adding somewhat flippantly that '[w]e are all potentially dead, but no one supposes that this fact constitutes a reason for treating us as if we were already dead'.[58]

Furthermore, many ethicists have drawn attention to the fact that, were a duty 'to protect and actualize all human potential'[59] held to exist, it would logically extend beyond a duty to refrain from killing embryos. As Harris has stated,

> it is not only the fertilised egg, the embryo, that is potentially a fully-fledged adult. The egg and the sperm taken together but as yet un-united have the same potential as the fertilized egg. For something (or some-things) has the potential to become a fertilised egg, and whatever has the potential to become an embryo has whatever potential the embryo has.[60]

Following the same logic, Peter Singer has noted that the potentiality argument 'does not provide any means for thinking abortion worse than any other means of population control',[61] including

> contraception, whether by 'artificial' means or by 'natural' means such as abstinence on days when the woman is likely to be fertile; and also celibacy.[62]

---

56 For the purposes of this thesis, the term 'person' may be taken to denote any being to which interests can meaningfully be attributed. In so saying, it is acknowledged that many writers in this field have set the threshold for personhood considerably higher. For example, in *Wonderwoman and Superman*, John Harris defines a person as 'a creature capable of valuing its own existence' (p 68).
57 Harris, *Wonderwoman and Superman*, op. cit., fn 18, p 34.
58 Id.
59 Id.
60 Id.
61 Peter Singer, *Practical Ethics*, Cambridge: Cambridge University Press, 1993, p 155.
62 Id. See also Ronald Dworkin, *Life's Dominion*, op. cit., fn 45, p 16.

If the 'argument from potentiality' is flawed when applied to abortion, it runs into even trickier difficulties when applied to extracorporeal embryos. Bonnie Steinbock has pointed out that the potentiality argument depends upon the view that:

> fertilization marks the beginning of an ongoing process which, if it is not deliberately interrupted, has a pretty good chance of resulting in the birth of a baby.[63]

This may form a good description of the ordinary pregnancy, but it can in no way be seen as applicable to IVF. As Steinbock says, there is no possibility of the *ex utero* embryo developing into anything else '[u]nless someone intervenes, and transfers the embryo into a uterus'.[64]

At this point, we should perhaps note that the foregoing applies specifically to *experiential* interests, i.e., those interests that relate to the subjective experiences of the being in question. In recent years, a trend has emerged in bioethics towards respect for another form of interests, which do not rely on the present subjective mind-state of the interest-bearer. Ronald Dworkin has dubbed these *critical* interests,

> Interests that it does make their life genuinely better to satisfy, interests they would be mistaken, and genuinely worse off, if they did not recognize. Convictions about what helps to make a life good on the whole are convictions about those more important interests. They represent critical judgments rather than just experiential preferences. Most people enjoy and want close friendships because they believe that such friendships are good, that people *should* want them.[65]

If the critical interest thesis is accepted, this might lend ethical credence to the widely held belief that the wishes of the deceased, the permanently unconscious or the senile should be respected even once they cease to be aware of such wishes. Many people, it seems, care deeply that their bodies are treated in a 'dignified' manner after their death, despite the realisation that, at that time, they will have neither awareness of nor concern with such matters. The notion of critical interests adds both coherence and ethical force to such feelings.

Could presentient embryos be said to possess something akin to critical interests, vesting them with an interest in, for example, not being turned

---

63 Steinbock, 'The Moral Status of Extracorporeal Embryos', fn 51, p 85.
64 Id.
65 Dworkin, *Life's Dominion*, op. cit., fn 45, pp 201–2. In his more recent work, Dworkin has rephrased this distinction in terms of critical and volitional well-being: *Sovereign Virtue: The Theory and Practice of Equality*, London: Harvard University Press, 2000, p 242.

into earrings?[66] A closer examination of the concept of critical interests suggests that their application to preimplantation embryos may be somewhat problematic. In each of the scenarios I looked at in the preceding paragraphs, the party to whom the critical interests were attributed, although now no longer aware of their existence, at one time harboured beliefs, values and preferences from which these interests can be said to derive. If the vegetative patient can be said to possess a critical interest in not being used as a side-board,[67] this, we might think, is because he once harboured values that would be offended by such treatment of his body. And if the deceased person has a critical interest in being remembered in a particular fashion, this is because, when alive, she wished to be remembered in that fashion.

The attribution of continuing interests to those who are no longer aware of them is problematic in itself, especially when we come to consider whether any harm would result if those interests were frustrated (who, after all, would sustain the harm?), and turn to the vexed question of how such interests should be weighed against the contemporaneous, experiential interests of the incompetent individual who now exists. But for present purposes, we can say that the extension of critical interests to that class of beings that do not possess, and have *never possessed*, experiential interests, would involve extending the thesis onto even more treacherous ground.

While the nature of the critical interests which we may want to attribute to the deceased can be derived from the interests they harboured while alive, it is difficult to see how we might arrive at a similar body of critical interests for the embryo. Critical interests, as conceived by Dworkin, 'represent critical *judgments* rather than just experiential preferences',[68] while he goes on to add that '[m]ost people enjoy and want close friendships because they *believe* that such friendships are good'.[69] Preimplantation embryos being capable of neither forming judgments nor holding beliefs, it isn't at all obvious how critical interests, at least as Dworkin describes them, can be attributed to them.

Indeed, it is difficult to see how any interests attributed to the embryo could be any more than projections of our own views and preferences, or perhaps of those that we might assume the embryo would one day possess if it survived until sentience. Whether any weight should be accorded to such presumed future interests is a question I have yet to address. For now, it is sufficient to note that, even if such interests can be attributed to the potential future person that the embryo might some day become, they cannot be attributed to the embryo itself.

66 Matti Häyry and Heta Häyry, 'The bizarre case of the human earrings', *Philosophy Today* 7, 1991, 1–3. Reprinted in: *Bioethics News* no. 4, 1991, 23–4.
67 To borrow John Keown's *reductio ad absurdum*; 'Restoring moral and intellectual shape to the law after *Bland*', *The Law Quarterly Review* (1997); 113: 481–503, p 494.
68 Dworkin, *Life's Dominion*, op. cit., fn 45, p 202, emphasis added.
69 Id., emphasis added.

'Withering on the vine': those who might have been

The fact that the embryos have the potential to become morally valuable beings, or interest bearers, if some other party intervenes and treats them in a particular way, then, does not provide a reason to accord value to the embryos themselves. Does it necessarily follow, though, that no value should be accorded to the potential future persons which could have existed? In deciding not to implant a particular embryo, do we harm the potential future person who that embryo could have become? Should we be concerned about those potential lives that, as one participant in a discussion group once put it, are left to 'wither on the vine'?[70]

A recent proponent of this kind of harm is Francis Fukuyama. In *Our Posthuman Future*, Fukuyama addresses the perceived excesses of bio-technology. In the context of a discussion of preimplantation gender selection, he makes the following claim:

> In many Asian cultures, having a son confers clear-cut advantages to the parents in terms of social prestige and security for old age. But it clearly harms the girls who then fail to be born.[71]

There are certainly particular problems raised by the prospect of gender preselection, but for present purposes, what is interesting about Fukuyama's claim is the tacit assumption that a being which has never existed can be the subject of harm.

The problem with this assumption should become clear when we remember the relationship between harms and interests. Following Feinberg, I showed that a harm occurs when an interest is thwarted or frustrated. The concept of 'interest' was somewhat complicated when consideration was given to Ronald Dworkin's controversial notion of critical interests, but not even Dworkin would dispute that interests can only meaningfully be attributed to beings which exist, or have existed.

To argue that a potential future person has an interest in being brought to existence is problematic for at least two reasons. First, this claim would seem to fly in the face of the earlier suggestion that interests are a product of awareness. Embryos, I argued, have no interests, because they lack even a basic awareness of their surroundings, and have not even the most rudimentary preferences. If this is true of embryos, then it is surely at least as true of the ethereal class of 'potential persons', which at the time of the implantation decision, exist more as hypothetical concepts than as actual entities.

A second objection to Fukuyama's attribution of harm to 'those who might have been' arises when we consider the question of numbers. How

---

70 Cited in Colin Gavaghan, 'Off-the-peg offspring', *Philosophy Now*, Winter 1998–1999.
71 Francis Fukuyama, *Our Posthuman Future*, op. cit., fn 55, p 97.

many such potential future persons are harmed? It is a straightforward matter to count the number of embryos discarded in a fertility clinic. But since we are concerned not with embryos per se, but with potential persons who might have lived but for our decisions, then we cannot confine the calculation to that setting. What of the potential persons who might have lived had the prospective parents harvested more ova and created more embryos?[72] And those who might have lived but for the availability of contraception? Or for lifestyle choices like celibacy, voluntary childlessness or deferring reproduction until later life? The potential future girl who might have lived in Fukuyama's hypothetical scenario has no more actual existence, and no more *right* to existence, than the potential future children who might have lived but for any of the other choices that limit the number of children brought into the world.

The sort of conceptual confusion underlying Fukuyama's contention can also be found in an argument advanced almost 30 years before by R M Hare. In an article entitled 'Abortion and the Golden Rule', Hare sought to develop an argument along the lines that, if an individual is now glad to be alive, then being born was clearly a benefit to him; and if this is so, then it follows that an act – such as abortion – that prevented his being born would have constituted a harm to him. 'If it would have been good for him to exist,' Hare argued, 'surely it was a harm to him not to exist.'[73]

This sort of harm–benefit symmetry is problematic in many other settings. Michael Bayles has claimed that, while an act may confer benefit on someone – giving him $500, for example – it doesn't follow that omitting to do so harms him. In arguing otherwise, Bayles maintains, Hare 'has collapsed the distinction between harm and nonbenefit'.[74] The Hare–Bayles dispute raises a serious question for the ethics of harm, specifically: if I have it within my power to benefit someone, and I elect not to do so, does it immediately follow that I have harmed him?

This is an important and complex question for the ethics of harm, but fortunately, it needn't detain us further here. Whether or not Hare's claim is true with regard to gratuitous donations of money, it is almost certainly not true with regard to the present question. 'Genesis questions' – questions about which beings should come into existence – have certain distinct characteristics that render Hare's claim particularly problematic. The fact that a person is relieved that his parents brought him into existence does not

---

72 In practice, there is a limit imposed on the number of embryos that can be implanted in each cycle of IVF; a policy was framed without apparent concern for the potential future lives sacrificed by this limit.

73 R M Hare, 'Abortion and the Golden Rule', *Philosophy and Public Affairs* (1975); 4(3): 208, p 221.

74 Michael D Bayles, 'Harm to the unconceived', *Philosophy and Public Affairs* (1976); 5(3): 292–304, p 298.

support the conclusion that he had such interests when they made their decision about whether to abort or continue with the pregnancy.

In Bayles' hypothetical scenario, Smith may not harm Jones when he declines to give him the $500, but it is at least coherent to speak of Jones having interests that are affected by Smith's decision. If, though, the alleged harm that Smith had visited upon Jones took the form of a decision not to implant the embryo that would some day have become Jones, then it appears that Jones had no interests bound up in the outcome of Smith's decision at the time Smith made it. Furthermore, the nature of Smith's decision is such that he ensures that Jones will never acquire any interests that are affected by Smith's earlier decision.

Thus, Derek Parfit, while sharing Hare's view that causing someone to exist may indeed confer a benefit upon him,[75] does not accept Hare's purportedly symmetrical conclusion that preventing him from existing inflicts a harm. 'Causing someone to exist,' Parfit contends,

> is a special case because the alternative would not have been worse for this person. . . . When we claim that it was good for someone that he was caused to exist, we do not imply that, if he had not been caused to exist, this would have been bad for him. . . . We are not claiming that it is bad for possible people if they do not become actual.[76]

Similarly, Harris asserts that:

> to cause someone to exist is to benefit that person, but to cause someone not to exist by failing to bring them into existence harms no one; for the simple and sufficient reason that there is no one who suffers this misfortune.[77]

If harm is inextricably linked to interests, and non-existent people have no interests, then it is meaningless to speak in terms of causing them harm. To seek to attribute interests, in existence or anything else, to those who never existed seems to require a belief in some sort of extracorporeal waiting room, a 'a strange never-never land from which phantom beings are dragged

---

75 Derek Parfit, *Reasons and Persons*, Oxford: Clarendon Press, 1984, p 489.

76 Id.

77 Harris, *Wonderwoman and Superman*, op. cit., fn 18, p 55. See also Melinda Roberts, *Child versus Childmaker*, Maryland: Rowman and Littlefield, 1998, p 11: 'We cannot wrong those who we refrain from ever bringing into existence'; Joel Feinberg, *The Moral Limits of the Criminal Law, Vol 1: Harm to others*, New York, Oxford: Oxford University Press, 1984, pp 96–7; Hans S Reinders, *The Future of the Disabled in Liberal Society: An Ethical Analysis*, Notre Dame: University of Notre Dame Press, 2000, p 40.

struggling and kicking into their mother's wombs and thence into existence as persons in the real world.'[78]

Potential persons: those actually born

So concern for the people they might have become gives us no reason to be concerned about harming embryos. But this doesn't necessarily mean that potential future persons are outwith the sphere of legitimate ethical concern. We might all agree that potential harms to 'actually existing people' should be considered in evaluating GCTs. And it might be equally clear that those potential persons who might have existed, but who will now never exist, can't be said to be harmed. But what of that class of persons, about whom we might say that they either *will* or *might* come to exist at some point in the future?

We might, of course, avoid all such worries by regarding non-maleficence as requiring us to be concerned only about harms to presently existing people. But this would require us to reach some conclusions that, I think, few people would find satisfactory, as in this example from Derek Parfit:

> Suppose that I leave broken glass in the undergrowth of a wood. A hundred years later this glass wounds a child. My act harms this child. If I had safely buried the glass, this child would have walked through the wood unharmed. Does it make a moral difference that the child whom I harm does not now exist?[79]

Anyone who thinks it would be wrong to abandon the glass would seem to be sharing Parfit's view that 'Remoteness in time has, in itself, no more significance than remoteness in space',[80] a view he shares with Glover,[81] Feinberg,[82] and many other bioethicists.[83] Thus, it would be wrong to bury radioactive

---

78 Joel Feinberg, *Harm to Others*, op. cit., fn 77, p 101. Jonathan Glover has also rejected this 'immigration-queue' model of potential children. *Choosing Children: The Ethical Dilemmas of Genetic Intervention*, Oxford: Clarendon Press, 2006, p 54.

79 Parfit, *Reasons and Persons*, op. cit., fn 75, p 356.

80 Ibid, p 357.

81 'Why should a bias in favour of people living *now* be any more defensible than a space bias in favour of people living *here*?' Glover, op. cit., p 66.

82 'We can tell, sometimes, that shadowy forms in the spatial distance belong to human beings, though we know not who or how many they are; and this imposes a duty on us not to throw bombs, for example, in their direction. In like manner, the vagueness of the human future does not weaken its claim on us in light of the nearly certain knowledge that it will, after all, be human.' Joel Feinberg, 'The rights of animals and unborn generations', in Feinberg, *Rights, Justice, and the Bounds of Liberty*, Princeton University Press, 1980, p 181.

83 See, for example, Roberts, *Child Versus Childmaker*, op. cit., fn 77, pp 15–18, Singer, *Practical Ethics*, op. cit., fn 61, p 268, and Harris, *Wonderwoman and Superman*, op. cit., fn 18, p 178.

material in such a way that it will be rendered safe for only 200 years, despite the fact that no one alive today is likely to suffer as a consequence.[84]

But if we are to regard abandoning the broken glass, or burying the radioactive waste, as harmful acts, a question inevitably arises about the identity of the subject of that harm. After all, at the time I abandon the glass, the party who is eventually cut by it doesn't exist. Indeed, following Parfit's example, no harm is caused by my carelessness until long after my own probable death. Does it follow that these future people are in the same class as the 'potential future people' who could have been born but for the use of GCTs? And does it therefore follow that, at the time of leaving the broken glass, I have done nothing wrong?

Fortunately, the interests-based approach to non-maleficence need not lead us to that conclusion. Although my act inflicts no harm *at that time*, it sets in motion a chain of events that will eventually result in harm to an actual, existing person. In fact, the same could be said if the eventual victim is presently existing, but is currently playing in the meadow and has not yet entered the woods. If that child injures herself on the glass in six months', or five minutes', time, I could not reasonably claim that I had no responsibility for her injury. The extent of culpability that should attach to me will depend on various factors, including the foreseeability of the harm, and any contributory carelessness on the part of the child or its parents. But the fact that time has passed between my negligence and the eventual harm doesn't present a particular problem.

Neither is there an insurmountable problem with the fact that my victim's actual identity is unknown (and unknowable) to me. As long as it can be predicted with reasonable certainty that the affected areas will be inhabited by some human or other sentient life, it would be wrong to act in a way likely to frustrate the interests which those beings are likely to possess.

What significance does this acknowledgement have for GCTs? This, I fear, is a far from straightforward matter. For the moment, though, it is enough to note that we can meaningfully speak about harming people who don't presently exist, provided we know or have strong reason to suspect that they will exist at some time in the future. Unlike 'those who will never be', the subjects of the harm in this case will develop interests, and it makes sense to consider whether our actions now will lead to those interests, in time, being thwarted or frustrated. I don't need to know their names in order to predict that they will have interests in not being cut by broken glass, or avoiding premature and unpleasant death from radiation poisoning. I should therefore avoid harmful acts, even though the harms they cause may not eventuate for many years. Furthermore, legislators may – in terms of the Harm Principle – be justified in intervening to prevent me from so acting.

---

84 This famous example was postulated by Derek Parfit; see *Reasons and Persons*, op. cit, fn 75.

Possible harms to future people

What kind of harms might we expect the genetic supermarket to inflict on the future people who emerge from its doors? The literature is replete with suggestions, but these appear to fall into two broad categories:

- Children of the genetic supermarket could suffer psychologically and emotionally as a result of unusual relations with their parents.
- Those children may be harmed by the particular traits chosen by parents.

To deal first with the former of these concerns, there are several ways in which future children might be thought to be harmed by their parents' use of PGD. This may be because they will be burdened with unrealistic expectations. Perhaps their parents will believe that the genotype they have selected will guarantee success in a particular field, or a particular kind of character, and will exert unfair pressure on the child to conform to their own ambitions. For present purposes, this can be deemed the *Parental Pressure Problem*.

Andrew Niccol's 1997 film *Gattaca* postulates a dystopian future where the use of PGD is so widespread, and its consequences for employment so significant, that it has become effectively compulsory. (The suggestion that such pressure can be brought to bear on prospective parents was considered in the previous chapter.) Much of the film's attention is focused on Vincent Freeman, one of the few remaining 'faith babies' (those whose parents entrusted their genotype to chance rather than science), whose ambition to go into space is thwarted by the genetic flaws which his parents did not eliminate. However, equally interesting, and perhaps more tragic, is the character of Jerome Eugene Morrow, a man so haunted by his failure to live up to the quality of his premier-quality genome that he several times attempts, ultimately successfully, to take his own life. Although to most people's eyes a successful athlete, Jerome never quite attained the supremacy that his parents expected – a failure powerfully (if unsubtly) symbolised by the silver medal which he places around his neck before his final act of self-immolation.

Another recent artistic depiction of the Parental Pressure Problem can be found in Margaret Atwood's 2003 novel, *Oryx and Crake*. This deeply techno-pessimist tale is set in a world devastated by a genetically modified plague, but alludes in a series of flashbacks to other 21st-century developments. In one such recollection, the protagonist, Jimmy/Snowman, recalls a conversation with his step-mother:

> Ramona would write him chatty, dutiful messages: no baby brother for him yet, she'd say, but they were still 'working on it'. He did not wish to visualize the hormone-sodden, potion-ridden, gel-slathered details of such work. If nothing 'natural' happened soon, she said, they'd try

'something else' from one of the agencies – Infantade, Foetility, Per-
fectababe, one of those . . . Terrific, thought Jimmy. They'd have a few
trial runs, and if the kids from those didn't measure up they'd recycle
them for the parts, until at last they got something that fit all their specs –
perfect in every way, not only a math whiz but beautiful as the dawn.
Then they'd load this hypothetical wonderkid up with their bloated
expectations until the poor tyke burst under the strain. Jimmy didn't
envy him. (He envied him.)[85]

Is it plausible that parents who use PGD will see this as a guarantee that their
children will grow up according to their expectations? Such an assumption
would display a startling degree of ignorance about the interaction between
genes and environment, and a naïve faith in genetic determinism. It might
be hoped that counselling would dispel many such errors. Yet the possibility
that such pressures might be brought to bear on children of the genetic
supermarket cannot readily be discounted.

Whether such problems would be unique to such children is, of course, a
different question. Both literature and real life are replete with accounts
of children who have been unable to conform to their parents' Willie
Loman-esque expectations. Even Bill McKibben, whose polemical *Enough*
rails against attempts to modify future children, concedes such attempts are
already routinely made:

> We all know people whose lives have been blighted trying to meet the
> expectations of their parents. We've all seen the crazed devotion to get-
> ting kids into the right schools, the right professions, the right income
> brackets. . . . No dictator anywhere has ever tried to rule his subjects with
> as much attention to detail as the average modern parent.[86]

For McKibben, though, attempts to plot our children's futures on a genetic
level are even more objectionable, because they are more likely to be
successful:

> Such parents would not be calling up their children on the phone at
> annoyingly frequent intervals to suggest that it's time to get a real job;
> instead . . . they would be inserting genes that produced proteins that
> would make their child behave in certain ways throughout his life. You
> cannot rebel against the production of that protein. Perhaps you can still
> do everything in your power to defeat the wishes of your parents, but

85 Margaret Atwood, *Oryx and Crake*, London: Bloomsbury, 2003, p 250.
86 Bill McKibben, *Enough: Staying Human in an Engineered Age*, New York: Times Books,
    2003, p 56.

that protein will nonetheless be pumped relentlessly into your system, defining who you are.[87]

The notion that social conditioning is easier to escape than genetic 'programming' is also proposed by Jürgen Habermas, who worries that such children may feel 'bound by the chains of the previous generation's genetic decisions'.[88] In espousing such concerns, though, both may be skirting close to the borders of what Ted Peters calls 'puppet determinism',[89] the notion that our genes do not merely shape us, but control our every thought and action. To most people, it seems, such a view is bleak indeed. Typically, we prefer to think that how our lives progress is, at least substantially, a matter of our own choices; the notion that, from conception, our destinies are already genetically pre-ordained is impossible to reconcile with notions like autonomy and responsibility.

Wishing it so, of course, does not make it so, and the view that what we think of as 'free will' is in reality just a psychological coping strategy favoured by evolution cannot be discounted out of hand. If free will was merely an illusion, and we were in reality pre-programmed automatons, this would of course have enormous implications for how we think about morality. It might, after all, seem unfair to attribute blame and credit, punishment and reward, for behaviour over which people have no control. Indeed, I will argue later that GCTs leave us with little choice but to confront some of the injustices inherent in how resources and status are allocated in capitalist societies, and this conclusion follows without accepting anything remotely as radical as puppet determinism.

Questions of free will and determinism have confounded philosophers for millennia, and it is a relief to note that responding to McKibben and Habermas doesn't require me to resolve them here. For it seems that, whatever position we occupy in that debate, GCTs make little difference to the situation in which future children will find themselves. If it really is true that our genes control our lives in a manner incompatible with free will, then that will be true whether those genes were selected by parents or by 'natural selection' or God or pure, blind luck. In no case have they been chosen by the children themselves – indeed, we could create an interesting paradox by enquiring how it might be possible to choose our own initial dispositions! It seems, then, that insofar as future children will be 'slaves to their genes', this will be no more and no less true than it was of all the generations that preceded them. There is no reason to suppose that GCTs will deprive them

---

87 See fn 86, pp 58–9.

88 Jürgen Habermas, *The Future of Human Nature*, Cambridge: Polity Press, 2003, p 92.

89 According to puppet determinism, the DNA defines who we are, and the genes, like the puppeteer, pull the strings that make us dance. Ted Peters, *Playing God? Genetic Determinism and Human Freedom*, second edn, London: Routledge, 2003, p 8.

of any degree of authorship of their lives that they would otherwise have possessed.

In choosing their children's genes, then, parents do not diminish the control those children would have had over their lives. If free will is compatible with genetic predispositions, that will be true for the children of the genetic supermarket just as surely as it is true for the rest of us. If our genes 'enslave' us, then we are all already slaves.

Is it possible, nonetheless, that those children might be resentful of the very fact that their parents made choices about their genetic composition?[90] While accepting the inevitability of the genetic lottery is one thing, the knowledge that one's parents had made such choices could be altogether more problematic:

> Even if an individual is no more locked in by the effects of a parental choice than he or she would have been by unmodified nature, most of us might feel differently about accepting the results of a natural lottery versus the imposed values of our parents. The force of feeling locked in may well be different.[91]

A degree of expertise in the complex psychology of parent–child relationships would be required to stand any realistic prospect of evaluating this claim, and even then the evaluation would be highly speculative. But we can, I think, see why there may be unique problems in the knowledge that one's life has been pre-determined to a significant extent by another. For present purposes, this can be referred to (following Josh Parsons[92]) as the *Resentment Problem*.[93]

Nor does the realisation that such children will carry no greater genetic shackles address the warning from Niccol and Atwood that their origins will

90 'Parents have significant control over the social and physical environment of the child, but no control over their own genetic influences. The question that is emerging is whether it is desirable to permit parents social, environmental, *and* biologic control over children. The issue is one of independence and individuality in their deepest senses. Such control may have a powerful psychological effect. . . . We must be seriously concerned about the psychological implications for both children and parents of the knowledge (or fear) that we were carefully selected or even made to be the way we are. While there might be satisfaction all around for a child well made, there may also be a loss of full authorship in victory, and broader grounds for resentment in failure.' Jeffrey Botkin, 'Fetal privacy and confidentiality', *Hastings Center Report* (1995); 25(5): 32–9, p 35.
91 Allen Buchanan, Dan W Brock, Norman Daniels, Daniel Wikler, *From Chance to Choice: Genetics and Justice*, New York: Cambridge University Press, 2000, pp 177–8.
92 Josh Parsons, 'Why the handicapped child case is hard', *Philosophical Studies*, 15 October 2002.
93 The question of the likely impact of parental genetic choices on parent–child relationships is also considered by Jeffrey Botkin, in 'Prenatal diagnosis and the selection of children', *Florida State University Law Review* (2003); 30: 265–93, p 292.

see them subjected to greater *environmental* pressures. It is all but impossible to read a popular account of biotechnology or neuropharmacology without encountering some reference to *Brave New World*. Sometimes overlooked, though, is the importance of early environmental conditioning in Huxley's dystopia. The Social Predestination Room, where embryos were physically altered to fit given social roles ('The lower the caste . . . the shorter the oxygen'), operated in tandem with the Neo-Pavlovian Conditioning Room, where lower-caste infants were given aversion therapy to curb their interest in books and flowers.[94] That anyone would administer electric shocks to curious babies may seem barbaric and far-fetched. But can we readily discount the possibility that parents who have paid to select embryos with genetic dispositions for academic or athletic excellence will not be more demanding, more overbearing, less willing to accept that their children may have different interests and priorities?

There may be unique and unforeseeable burdens associated with being a 'designer baby'; the technology is still too new to be certain. Equally, though, it is foreseeable that there would be unique burdens associated with being born into a family with a history of criminality, or a history of notable achievement. There have always been unrealistic parental expectations, and some of these have even had genetics at their core, albeit a more unsophisticated genetics that simply assumed that talent would be passed through blood.[95] As Julian Savulescu has noted,

> parents inevitably have hopes and expectations for their children which are deflated every day. . . . Some parents want their children to be great musicians. Sometimes this desire becomes overbearing, as depicted in the film *Shine*. But the answer is not to ban music schools. The solution is to help parents to be more tolerant and accepting.[96]

Even if this is unduly optimistic, though, there is another reason why this concern should not be fatal to a pro-choice approach to GCTs, a reason that doesn't require us to discredit or reject either the *Parental Pressure Problem* or the *Resentment Problem* on empirical, psychological grounds. Rather, a more sweeping and less empirically contingent counter-argument can be raised against both claims.

---

94 *Brave New World*, originally published 1932, HarperPerennial ModernClassics, 2004, p 28.
95 See, for instance, the tale of Beethoven's son, as recounted in *Immortal Beloved*, Columbia/ Tristar Studios, 1994.
96 Julian Savulescu, 'Sex selection: the case for', *Medical Journal of Australia* (1999); 171(7): 373–5, p 373.

Chapter 4

Impossible alternatives: Derek Parfit and the Non-Identity Principle

In his seminal work of consequentialist philosophy, *Reasons and Persons*, Derek Parfit offered up the now famous hypothetical example of the 14-year-old girl. The imagined facts are these:

> This girl chooses to have a child. Because she is so young, she gives her child a bad start in life. Though this will have bad effects throughout the child's life, his life will, predictably, be worth living. If this girl had waited for several years, she would have had a different child, to whom she would have given a better start in life.[1]

Parfit invites us to leave aside scepticism about the accuracy of any such prediction about the child's future, and to turn instead to what might seem an easier question: has the 14-year-old girl made the wrong decision? The obvious answer, it seems, is that she has indeed decided badly. After all, just waiting a few years would mean that her child would be better off. Surely opting to have the child now is selfish, maybe even unfair to the child.

As Parfit famously demonstrated, though, the question is not so simple. The girl's decision might, at first glance, *seem* wrong. But who – with the possible exception of herself – has she harmed by it? To whom has she been unfair? In fact, if anything is wrong with her decision to have a child now, it cannot be due to any harm which has been done either to the child which she actually had, or to the child which she could have had several years from now.

When they first encounter it, this strikes many people (myself included) as an odd claim, but closer examination makes it hard to refute. The child she could have had later is an example of a never-existing potential future person, and, as shown earlier, may be discounted from the array of potential subjects of harm. It never possessed, nor will it ever possess, any interests to be taken into account, and to speak in terms of its having an interest in being allowed to have interests seems circular and ultimately nonsensical.

---

1 Derek Parfit, *Reasons and Persons*, Oxford: Oxford University Press, 1984, p 358.

What, though, of the child which the 14-year-old girl actually goes on to have? As a being that will have interests, it is meaningful, and arguably morally obligatory, to take these interests into account when we act, even though the harms we may cause will not eventuate for some months or years. To speak, then, of harming the future child is not incoherent. As Parfit demonstrated, though, greater difficulties are encountered when we ask what form these harms may take.

As Parfit showed, even if its life did in fact transpire to be poorer due to its bad start in life, this is not sufficient to draw the conclusion that the girl's decision caused it harm. This becomes clear when we consider that the difficulties that the child will face were an inevitable and indispensable consequence of *that* child coming to exist at all. For *that* child, the option of being born to a more adult mother, or into a more secure environment, was simply not available. 'If she had waited,' Parfit explains, 'this particular child would never have existed.'[2]

The question, then, must be whether the child of the 14-year-old girl is likely to be born into a life so wretched that it would have been preferable for that child – from its own, subjective point of view – never to have been born. As Parfit suggests, 'We should ask, "If someone lives a life that is worth living, is it worse for this person than if he had never existed?" '[3] concluding that inevitably 'Our answer must be "No" '.[4] This is the famous Non-Identity Problem with which his work has become closely associated.

This is a powerful claim, and many people find it deeply counter-intuitive. It relies on a recognition that an embryo produced by this girl at a different time, resulting as it invariably would from the fusion of different gametes, would develop into a different person.[5] This notion has been referred to by Bernard Williams as the *Zygotic Principle*. Williams describes this as holding that:

> the identity of human beings, as of other sexually reproducing creatures, lies in the union of two given gametes: if either the sperm or the ovum

---

2   See fn 1, p 359.
3   Id.
4   Id.
5   Parfit, interestingly, seems to require that *both* gametes be different before we can speak of a wholly different person. This is implicit in his statement that '[i]f any particular person had not been conceived within a month of the time when he was in fact conceived, he would in fact never have existed' (*Reasons and Persons*, op. cit., fn 1, p 372), the implication being that both sperm and ovum must be different. This seems to beg the question as to how much genetic difference is required before we can speak of a 'different person'. Would a child conceived of the same ovum but a different sperm be sufficiently similar to constitute, in some sense, the same person as the child that would have been conceived a few hours or days earlier? Issues relating to the constitution of identity will be revisited at the end of this book.

or both had been different, a different human being would have been formed and born.[6]

The extent to which our genes determine 'who we are' is a question every bit as profound and perplexing as the question of how much they determine what we do. Is my DNA more constitutive of my identity than my upbringing, or my memories? How much of my genome would need to be changed before it was no longer reasonable to speak of 'me with different genes', but rather, a different person altogether?

These are difficult and profound questions, and the latter at least raises awkward issues for proponents of genetic modification. With regard to PGD, though, it seems impossible to deny that the various candidate embryos are each different potential people, genetically related but also genetically unique.[7] After all, to say otherwise would mean that a decision to implant two of those embryos would raise the possibility of giving birth not to siblings, but to the same person twice!

The Zygotic Principle, then, means that an embryo conceived of different gametes will become a different person. This being so, it seems that no harms – present or future – may be said to be caused by the 14-year-old girl's decision. That this conclusion has serious implications for the study of PGD becomes clear when we return to the question of the *Parental Pressure Problem* and the *Resentment Problem*. In both cases, to conclude that the children in question had, on balance, been harmed, we would need to conclude that these problems were so severe that the very fact of their existences constituted net harms.

Parfit's Non-Identity approach succeeds, then, in rebutting the claim that the children of the genetic supermarket themselves will be subjects of harm – at least in the sort of circumstances considered thus far. Referring to the Non-Identity Problem, however, may be seen as somewhat question-begging. It seems implicit in this terminology that this approach is unsatisfactory, in need of resolution or refinement. (For Parfit, the contradiction between this conclusion and the intuitive sense that the 14-year-old girl should delay procreation is indeed unsatisfying, although he has admitted being unable to find a way around this without abandoning the Person-Affecting Principle that I will consider later.[8])

It seems to me, though, that there is nothing inherently problematic in this approach or the conclusion to which it leads, save that it is difficult to

6 Bernard Williams, 'Who might I have been?', in *Human Genetic Information: Science, Law and Ethics*, Ciba Foundation Symposium 149, Chichester: John Wiley & Sons, 1990, p 169.
7 The issue of clones, of course, raises particular problems in this regard!
8 Parfit, *Reasons and Persons*, op. cit., fn 1, p 443.

reconcile with some of our less-considered intuitions.[9] For that reason, I will refer instead to a Non-Identity Principle (NIP). I concede that this Principle might sometimes lead to conclusions that are counter-intuitive or unappealing. This, though, is no more than could be said for the Harm Principle, the principle of respect for autonomy, or indeed any other ethical principle when applied in 'hard cases'. The Non-Identity Principle is the direct offspring of the marriage of the Harm Principle and the Zygotic Principle; acceptance of those parent principles leaves us no option but to accept the NIP.

'Harmful' choices

The Non-Identity Principle, then, provides a response to both the *Parental Pressure* and *Resentment Problems*. But does it allow us to refute the second category of purported harms that were mentioned above, the harms that would derive from the actual choices prospective parents made, rather than the mere fact of making those choices?

At first glance, the prospect of parents making such choices might seem unlikely; Fukuyama's view that '[w]e can further presume that parents will not seek to deliberately harm their children, but rather will try to maximise their happiness'[10] surely seems more plausible than a scenario where parents deliberately choose traits that could be deemed harmful. Difficulties arise, however, when we note the inherent ambiguities in the concepts of 'harm' and 'benefit' as invoked in this context. The well-publicised attempts by Sharon Duchesneau and Candy McCullough to ensure their child was deaf (although not actually relying on GCTs to give effect to their choices) illustrates the controversies surrounding these concepts.[11]

Much of the commentary on Duchesneau's and McCullough's attempts have concentrated on the couple's claim that deafness, and more specifically membership of the Deaf community, is in fact properly regarded as a minority

---

9 Philip G Peters, Jr, for example, asserts that the Non-Identity conclusion 'assaults our common sense' and 'simply do[es] not pass a moral gut test'. 'Harming future persons: Obligations to the children of reproductive technology', *Southern California Interdisciplinary Law Journal* (1999) 8: 375–400, at pp 384–5.

10 Francis Fukuyama, *Our Posthuman Future: Consequences of the Biotechnology Revolution*, New York: Faber, Strauss and Giroux, 2002, p 92. See also: 'Presumably all parents, if given a choice, would wish their children to have the level of intelligence and other skills that we now regard as normal, or even that we now believe superior' (Ronald Dworkin, *Sovereign Virtue: The Theory and Practice of Equality*, Cambridge, London: Harvard University Press, 2000, p 441); 'I suspect that most parents would make the safe choices and avoid the ragged uncertainties at the edges of human possibility' (Gregory Stock, *Redesigning Humans: Choosing Our Children's Genes*, London: Profile Books, 2002, p 112).

11 M Spriggs, 'Lesbian couple creates a child whom is deaf like them', *Journal of Medical Ethics*, Online eCurrent Controversies, 2 May 2002.

status, akin to membership of a racial minority, rather than a disability.[12] K W Anstey, for example, gives serious attention to the claim that the harms experienced by deaf children are at least in part socially constructed rather than inherent to the condition of deafness.[13] What is interesting for the present discussion, though, is the assumption implicit in Anstey's analysis that the child in question will indeed be harmed by being born deaf. While prepared to concede the prospective parents' contention 'that it is not wrong to have a child when the harms they will experience are socially imposed',[14] he at no point considers the possibility that the child is not a subject of harm at all.

Yet that is precisely the conclusion to which the Non-Identity Principle commits us. Duchesneau and McCullough have not taken an existing baby and rendered it deaf (although as I discuss later, that in itself would be a scenario that poses interesting questions for the Non-Identity Principle). Rather, they have brought into existence a little boy – Gauvin – for whom deafness is an indispensable prerequisite of existing at all. Had they not sought out the sperm of a deaf man, *Gauvin* would never have existed at all, but rather would have been replaced by a different, perhaps hearing child (or, of course, by no child at all).

If we assume that deafness is not so limiting a condition, or one which imposes so much suffering, as to render a life intolerable, then it is difficult to conclude that Gauvin was harmed by the act which, in giving him deafness, also gave him existence. Sharon Duchesneau and Candy McCullough sought to make a deaf baby, not to make a baby deaf. If there is anything objectionable about their attempt, it doesn't lie with any harm done to Gauvin himself.

How far, though, does this assessment of the Duchesneau–McCullough case answer the broader question of 'harmful choices'? The reliance on the example of deafness, after all, might be thought to be taking an easy option, given the controversy at the heart of this case as to whether deafness is in fact a disability. The choice of a deaf child would indeed be unproblematic if we accepted that deafness is unlikely to impact deleteriously on the child's quality of life – but what of more uncontroversially deleterious conditions? It may be straying into the realm of horror fantasy to suggest that a parent would deliberately choose to have a child affected by cystic fibrosis, for example. But with suggestions of genetic predispositions toward aggression, or certain

---

12 K W Anstey, 'Are attempts to have impaired children justifiable?' *Journal of Medical Ethics*, 2002; 28: 286–8.

13 'The limitation of opportunity here [in the case of deafness] is not inherent in the sense of residing solely in the impairment: to be understood as a limitation of opportunity, there must be a social expectation that the activity that is limited ought to be performed.' Ibid, p 286.

14 Ibid, p 287.

sexual preferences,[15] it is perhaps prudent to imagine future disputes about what constitutes saddling a child with a harmful condition.

My argument here, though, doesn't rely on any particular position as to the effects of deafness, or aggression, or sexual preferences, on a child's life. Although there are certain to be controversies at the margins of defining harmful conditions, it is not at all implausible that there are some genetic traits that will have a predictably positive or negative impact on the quality of life of those affected by them. Buchanan, Brock, et al refer to 'natural primary goods', capacities such as sight that are 'useful or valuable in carrying out nearly any plan of life'.[16] Irrespective of the provisions society made to allow blind people to function and interact with a minimum of danger and inconvenience, there are no – or almost no – imaginable societies in which being blind would be anything other than a disadvantage.[17]

Yet the Non-Identity Principle doesn't require a comparison between life with sight and blind life, but rather, between blind life and no life at all. Whatever the disadvantages and frustrations of blindness, the possibility of sighted life was never available for the child which is chosen to be blind. The only way in which such a child could be said to be harmed would be if we concluded that being born without sight was worse than never being born at all. As Melinda Roberts reminds us, the 'sole means of saving the baby from the effect of the disorder . . . is to refrain from bringing the baby into existence to begin with'.[18]

The Non-Identity Principle renders it meaningless to speak in terms of harming a future child where:

- the 'harmful' act is an indispensable condition of the child's coming into existence at all – a so-called 'genesis act'; and
- the child has a minimally worthwhile quality of life.

It leaves open, however, the possibility that a child could be harmed by a 'genesis act' where that minimal standard of quality of life is not met. This possible exception, and the implications for the law arising from it, will be considered later in this chapter.

15 See, for example, the theories expounded in Dean Hamer and Peter Copeland's *Living With Our Genes*, London: Pan Books, 2000.

16 Allen Buchanan, Dan W Brock, Norman Daniels, Daniel Wikler, *From Chance to Choice: Genetics and Justice*, New York: Cambridge University Press, 2000, at pp 167–8.

17 In a somewhat similar vein, Joel Feinberg has written of 'The Child's Right to an Open Future'; in Aitken and LaFollette, (eds), *Whose Child? Children's Rights, Parental Authority, and State Power*, New Jersey: Rowman and Littlefield, 1980.

18 Melinda Roberts, 'Present duties and future persons: When are existence-inducing acts wrong?', *Law and Philosophy* (1995); 14(3/4): 297–327, p 316.

Voices of dissent: Person-Affecting objections

Following the Non-Identity Principle, then, only those children born into lives so wretched that non-existence would be preferable – those which Glover describes as falling below the 'zero line'[19] – have a complaint against those who brought them into existence. Where a handicapped but worthwhile life was the only life available to that child, it simply cannot claim to have been harmed by the acts that bestowed that life upon it.

In fact, the majority of opponents of the pro-choice or genetic supermarket approaches to PGD accept the Non-Identity Principle. They do not direct their objections at alleged harms to the children actually born, but instead, their opposition generally derives either from Non-Person-Affecting concerns, or from perceived negative externalities. Before going on to look at those objections, though, there are a couple of perspectives from which the pro-choice position could be criticised, and objections like the *Parental Pressure, Resentment* and *Harmful Choice Problems* salvaged, without abandoning the Person-Affecting Principle.

The 'No Trade Offs' view

James Woodward has taken issue with the idea that gains and losses can be offset in the manner implicit in the Non-Identity Principle. While conceding that cases exist where the benefits of existence can be said to outweigh any harms, he questions whether this is sufficient justification for such harms. Interests, Woodward argues, are not fungibles that can be traded off against one another, or factored into a single calculation of 'overall well-being'. Rather, he maintains,

> people have relatively specific interests (e.g., in having promises kept, in avoiding bodily injury, in getting their fair share) that are not simply reducible to some general interest in maintaining a high overall level of well-being and . . . many moral requirements function so as to protect against violations of such specific interests. That an action will cause an increase in someone's overall level of well-being is not always an adequate response to the claim that such a specific interest has been violated.[20]

By way of illustration, Woodward offers the following hypothetical example:

> Suppose that Smith, who is black, attempts to buy a ticket on a certain airline flight and that the airline refuses to sell it to him because it discriminates racially. Shortly after, that very flight crashes, killing all

---

19 Jonathan Glover, *Choosing Children: The Ethical Dilemmas of Genetic Intervention*, Oxford: Clarendon Press, 2006, p 58.
20 James Woodward, 'The Non-Identity Problem', *Ethics* (1986); 96: 804–31, p 809.

aboard. There is a clear sense in which the airline's action has the result that Smith is better off than he otherwise would be, and if selling or not selling Smith the ticket are the only relevant actions which the airline can perform, not selling leaves him better off than any other possible action the airline might have performed. Nonetheless, it seems quite natural to say that the airline's action wrongs Smith.[21]

For Woodward, then, I may wrong someone by an action that leaves him better off than he would have otherwise been, or indeed 'better off than any other action one might have taken',[22] if I have breached a particular obligation that I owed to him.

> We resist the temptation to think just in terms of some single dimension of moral assessment (how well off overall a person is) and to think that if an action affects a person negatively in some respect but has other effects such that the net result is an overall gain (or no total loss) in well-being: moral assessment ought to focus just on this overall outcome.[23]

When applied to Parfit's hypothetical 14-year-old girl, this approach allows Woodward to conclude that she will in fact wrong her future child by the very fact of bringing it into existence. Designating the girl 'Alma', Woodward contends that:

> Alma knows that if she has a child she will incur certain duties and obligations which she would not otherwise have and which she is very unlikely to meet adequately. I contend that the failure to fulfil these duties and obligations constitutes an important reason . . . for Alma *not* to have a child. If Alma has her child and fails to meet the duties and obligations she owes to her child, the child has a complaint against her, based on a wrong done to the child.[24]

There are two counter-arguments that can be levied against Woodward's contention that Alma has acted wrongly. The first doesn't involve rejecting Woodward's central premise – that rights and interests (he seems to use the terms interchangeably) are distinct and that their breach or frustration cannot be offset against other gains – but questions precisely which interest or right has been breached in such cases. This counter-argument begins by asking precisely what duties and obligations Alma actually owes to her future

---

21 See fn 20, at pp 809–10.
22 Ibid, p 812.
23 Ibid, p 818.
24 Ibid, p 815.

child that she is overwhelmingly likely to breach by virtue of her immaturity. We might answer this by reference to any number of obligations that a parent might be thought to owe her children: emotional stability and a minimum standard of economic security being but two. The fact that Alma will foreseeably be unable to meet these obligations would, for Woodward, provide a reason for her to refrain from creating those obligations in the first place.

But what exactly is the nature of the obligation owed by Alma to her future offspring? In particular, is the standard of emotional stability or economic security that she is obliged to provide an absolute or a relative standard? On an absolute standard, it might be argued that she must provide X amount of stability (however we might quantify this) and Y of economic security. Any parent who failed to provide these quantities would derogate from their duties, and the mere fact that they *could not* fulfil them is to be no excuse, for the preferable option in such circumstances would be to refrain from procreating at all.

Yet it is unlikely that many of us regard parental obligations in such terms. Is it Woodward's contention that the 800 million of the world's population who live on less than $1(US) per day act wrongly whenever they procreate? For it is not unreasonable to suppose that a mature woman living in an area beset by famine, war, disease or abject poverty will be worse placed than a 14-year-old girl living in the UK or USA to provide emotional stability and economic security for her children. Indeed, the situation is worse for such women, because unlike Alma, they are not merely being required to delay procreation for a few years, but indefinitely.[25]

One way of avoiding this conclusion is to gauge the extent to which parents meet their parental obligations against the extent that it was possible for them to do so. On that relativist analysis, we would judge the extent to which Alma (or the grossly malnourished woman living in abject conditions) fulfilled her duties relative to what it was possible for *her* to have done. Provided the child's life is not of the worse-than-nothing variety, then, we might say that she has breached no obligation to it provided *she does her best* to provide the child with emotional stability and economic security, even if she is, by virtue of her tender years, incapable of providing these things in the same quantities as an older parent might.

A further conception of the duty she owes to her child might say that what she is obliged to provide for her future offspring is as good a life as was possible *for that child*. The Non-Identity Principle holds that, for this child, the only alternative to a life of relative instability and insecurity was no life at

---

25 In fairness, Woodward does claim that Alma's obligations might be different if it were likely to be the case that she would never be able to meet these obligations. But why should this be so? If the obligations owed to the child are absolute and not relative to Alma's circumstances, then what difference does it make whether she would be better equipped to provide for a different child in the future?

all. If Alma's obligation is to provide the best that this child could possibly have, then she might satisfy this even by providing less stability and security than a different child, born to an older Alma, might have enjoyed.

An obligation to provide one's children with as optimal an environment as that child could possibly have enjoyed is actually a very onerous obligation indeed, and we may need to balance this against Alma's other obligations, and indeed her own interests. But again, it becomes clear that it is possible to reconcile Woodward's claim about the specificity of interests or duties with the claim that Alma does no wrong, simply by defining those specific interests and duties in a different way.

The No Trade-Offs view only leads to Woodward's conclusion, then, if we adopt a particular view of the duties Alma owes her child, a view that takes no account of what was possible for Alma, or for this child. This view, as well as being somewhat arbitrary in its selection of duties, might be thought unappealing because it appears to have the consequence of requiring the majority of the world's population to refrain from procreation.

Woodward's objection to the Non-Identity Problem was actually anticipated by Derek Parfit, who proposed a different counter-argument. Interestingly, Parfit didn't take issue with Woodward's claim that the breach of a particular obligation cannot just be set off against overall benefit. Nor did he dispute that breaching a duty might be wrong even when it is an indispensable pre-condition of existence itself, conceding that 'The objector might reply: "It is wrong to cause someone to exist if we know that this person will have a right that cannot be fulfilled." '[26] What Parfit does point out is that rights are the sorts of thing that can be waived.

> Suppose that I have a right to privacy. I ask you to marry me. If you accept, you are not acting wrongly, by violating my right to privacy. Since I am glad that you act as you do, with respect to you I *waive* this right. . . . This would have undermined our objection to his mother's act.[27]

Since rights can be waived contemporaneously, it makes sense to assume that they can be waived retrospectively; and since, if people like Alma's child 'knew the facts, they would not regret that we acted as we did', they 'might waive their rights'.[28] With characteristic intellectual candour, Parfit conceded that this is merely an assumption, and that it is possible that some future people will not regard the violation of their rights as a price worth paying for their existence. For that reason he regarded this as only a partial response to the No Trade-Offs view.

---

26 Parfit, *Reasons and Persons*, op. cit., fn 1, p 364.
27 Id.
28 Ibid, p 365.

It seems to me that Parfit is being unduly tentative here. It is by no means certain that the wrongness of an act should be judged with the benefit of hindsight, according to the subjective perception of another party. For a consequentialist like Parfit, an act that turns out to produce bad consequences may be a source of regret, but whether it should be a source of guilt or shame or moral opprobrium – whether it could be described as a *morally wrong act* – depends largely on the intent with which it was carried out. If it is reasonably foreseeable that you will regard the violation of your right as a price worth paying for some benefit you accrue (as Parfit puts it, that you will retrospectively waive your right) then it would be unusual to regard that violation as wrongful.

Or think of it another way. Almost any conception of rights will include some variation of a right to bodily integrity. Yet even among the most ardent proponent of rights, there are few who would claim that I act wrongly when I push you out of the way of the swerving bus. In so doing, I have clearly violated one of your rights, but the anticipated benefit for you – survival or the avoidance of serious injury – is foreseeably great enough to justify my act, in the eyes of almost all ethicists, and indeed of UK law. This will be equally true if, for some reason, you subsequently take exception to my push, claiming that you would have preferred to take your chances with the bus. My act does not become wrongful in retrospect, with the occurrence of some unforeseeable event or eccentric views.[29]

By the same token, while it is (as Parfit acknowledges) theoretically possible that Alma's child might not regard the violation of its rights as a price worth paying for a life that is on balance worthwhile, we might well conclude that this is a turn of events so unlikely as to lie outwith the realm of reasonable foreseeability. Alma is justified in infringing her child's rights to emotional stability and economic security (or, to be more accurate, acting in a way that ensures those rights will one day be infringed) because of her reasonable belief that the child will one day regard that infringement as a price worth paying, just as surely, and for exactly the same reason, as she

---

29 It does not, however, follow that my competent refusal can be disregarded by a well-meaning surgeon because of his firm conviction that I will subsequently regard his actions with gratitude. As I explained in Chapter 2, the express wishes of a competent person are, in the ordinary case, assumed to be the best indication of what is best for that person. If it were somehow possible to ask Alma's future child its opinion of the trade-off between rights and benefits, then that opinion should guide her action. Since it is not, she has no option but to rely on foreseeable outcomes and probabilities. In this respect, her position is closer to the surgeon who operates on me without my consent when I am unconscious. His invasion of my bodily integrity is deemed justifiable if it was foreseeably in my best interests, and does not subsequently become wrongful if I subsequently respond with unforeseeable hostility to his actions.

would be justified in infringing her child's right to bodily integrity by pushing it out of the way of a swerving bus.[30]

The 'Generic Child' view

Robert M Green is another writer who has sought to challenge the 'No Difference' conclusion without straying from the realm of Person-Affecting Principles. Green's argument rests on two premises that, if accepted, seem to allow us to conclude that someone is harmed by Alma's decision to become pregnant now:

• the rejection of the comparison between the life her child actually has and the only alternative for it (i.e. non-existence) with a comparison with 'the *reasonably expected health status of others in the child's birth cohort*';[31]
• the attribution of interests to a 'generic' child, a sort of composite of all the possible children our hypothetical prospective parent might have had.

Green's argument relies on the (uncontested) realisation that, prior to conception, the 'potential future child' of whom prospective parents speak is not a discrete entity at all, but rather, an amalgam of myriad possibilities:

> before conception (for most people) and even following conception during early pregnancy (for many others), lives are in a sense 'fungible'; they are interchangeable generic units, rather than identifiable and unique. Parents intending to have a child do not imagine the identifiable child 'Mary' who they come to know in the years following her birth, but a 'generic' child with qualities like those of most other children being born in its cohort. It is this imagined child whom they usually have in mind in choosing to have a child in the first place, and against whom they and others measure the actual condition of the real child when it is born.[32]

If it is intelligible to speak of a single 'generic child', then it is perhaps intelligible to attribute to that child a unitary set of interests; and it may be

---

30 Habermas has recently expressed a roughly analogous view with regard to genetic modifications, according to which 'Only in the negative case of the prevention of extreme and highly generalized evils may we have good reasons to assume that the person concerned would consent to the eugenic goal'. *The Future of Human Nature*, op. cit., chapter 2, fn 88, p 63.

31 Robert M Green, 'Parental autonomy and the obligation not to harm one's child genetically', *Journal of Law, Medicine & Ethics* 25 (1997): 5–15, p 8.

32 Id. For a similar argument, see Simo Vehmas, 'Is it wrong to deliberately conceive or give birth to a child with mental retardation?' *Journal of Medicine and Philosophy* (2002); 27(1): 47–63, at pp 52–3.

intelligible to include among those interests something like an 'interest in being born in the best possible genetic health', or perhaps an 'interest in being born with a minimum standard of genetic health'.

For Green, the required standard would fall between these two poles. He goes considerably further than those like Parfit, who argue only that a prospective parent should stop short of bringing a child into existence who would have a worse-than-nothing life. Rather, Green thinks that 'we should compare the status of the actual child born with that of the average child in its birth cohort',[33] acting so as to avoid:

> 'significantly greater' suffering or disability than others in the child's birth cohort. . . . As a practical measure, we can determine whether harm is significant by asking whether, as a generality, children (or, later, adults) with a specific condition would prefer to have lived their lives free of their specific congenital disorder or disability.[34]

Some of Green's argument seems to rely heavily on the presumed linguistic slackness and conceptual confusion of others. 'This is the appropriate benchmark,' he argues,

> . . . because it is the one that most parents are likely to use in deciding whether to have a child in the first place, and it is also the benchmark that the child and those around it are likely to use in assessing the quality of its start in life.[35]

It is worth noting that although his suggestion derives from an empirical rather than philosophical premise – we should adopt this benchmark because most people do in fact think this way – he offers no sociological evidence to support this. Even assuming the accuracy of his contention, though, it might be thought somewhat illiberal to use the fact that 'most parents' think this way as a justification for forcing the few dissenters whom he goes on to discuss to comply. In the absence of some argument proving the superiority of the majority view, this might be thought little more than an example of gratuitous reproductive totalitarianism, forcing a particular view of reproduction on a minority for no other reason than that theirs is not a common view.

Yet not only does Green fail to demonstrate the superiority of his view, he actually concedes, quite explicitly, its paucity of intellectual rigour. In discussing the claim 'If my mother had only waited a few months until after

33 Green, 'Parental autonomy and the obligation not to harm one's child genetically', op. cit., fn 31, p 8.
34 Ibid, p 9.
35 Ibid, p 8.

the rubella epidemic had passed to conceive me, "I" would never have been born with this deformity', he concedes that 'Taken strictly, this statement is nonsense: the child who could have been conceived and born after a delay of some months is not the same child as the one who was conceived and born earlier.'[36] The only way to circumvent the absurdity of this position is by

> think[ing] of ourselves before conception or birth as an imaginary fungible intended child of our parents, who could come into being with roughly the same physical and mental attributes as other children, this statement makes perfect sense.[37]

These two statements, taken together, reveal that Green's argument is weakened by reliance on what he acknowledges to be a fantasy, in which interests are projected onto an 'imaginary' child, in an attempt to prop up a belief that its chief proponent admits is 'nonsense'. It may well be that disabled children or adults from time to time engage in the sort of speculation he suggests, about how much better 'their' lives would have been had their parents delayed conception. Many of us have daydreamed of alternative lives in alternative times or places that we might have lived. But, as even Green acknowledges, these alternative lives of which we dream would not have been 'our' lives at all.

Of course, jurisprudential and philosophical reasoning have long and respected traditions of reliance on imagined entities, from Hobbes' Leviathan to Nozick's Utility Monsters. Green's reference to a 'generic' child and 'an imaginary fungible intended child of our parents' bears some superficial similarities to one such fantastic entity: John Rawls' ideal lawmaker, peering out through the 'veil of ignorance'.[38] In this famous thought experiment, Rawls imagined a lawmaker passing laws from a position of ignorance about which position he would occupy in the world.[39] If he didn't know whether he would be a prince or a pauper, then his decisions as to what the law should be were unlikely to be unfairly skewed in the interests of either princes or paupers, but would be designed so as to produce the best outcome for the lawmaker irrespective of the role he is allocated. (For Rawls, in fact, the logical lawmaker would act so as to level out the inequalities in society, thereby ensuring that whatever role he was allocated would not be intolerably bad.)

It is possible that Green had something of this nature in mind when he thought of the 'generic child', which is also a sort of pre-existence entity that could view all of the possible lives into which it could be born. However,

---

36 See fn 33.

37 Id.

38 John Rawls, *A Theory of Justice. Revised Edition*, Oxford: Oxford University Press, 1999.

39 The lawmaker would, of course, be able to suppose that he would not fall into that category of beings who are unable to consider the very question that s/he is presently considering. To paraphrase Descartes, 'I think, therefore I am, at a minimum, the kind of being that can think.'

unlike Green, Rawls never seriously sought to argue that such an entity actually existed; rather, this was an imagined ideal to which the just lawmaker ought to aspire. If the lawmaker transpired to be less than just, Rawls at no time argued that this would be bad for the being that exists behind the veil of ignorance. His decisions would be bad because they were bad for others, or bad because they were unjust. The imagined veil of ignorance serves as a useful device insofar as it provides us with a mechanism to make sure we act fairly. Unlike Green's generic child, though, the pre-existence lawmaker who dwells behind it has no interests of its own, and no intrinsic worth beyond its value as a decision-making device.

Person-Affecting objections: summary

The arguments I have considered thus far would appear to give no reason whatever for preferring to implant Embryo X rather than Embryo Y. This is so because, despite the fact that Person X is likely to have a much higher quality of life than Person Y, the decision to bring about the existence of the latter cannot be shown to be contrary to the interests of a particular person. Person Y, after all, has 'a life that is better than no life at all',[40] and the only alternative for him would have been non-existence; the 'sole means of saving the baby from the effect of the disorder . . . is to refrain from bringing the baby into existence to begin with'.[41] As I discussed above, we have no duty to bring Person Y into existence. Having done so, however, we have no alternative but to consider the effect of that act on Person Y by reference to the whole package of harms and benefits that life brings him.

Person X, meanwhile, has no interests and never will have any interests to be frustrated since, in this scenario, she will never exist. Those who accept David Heyd's 'generocentric' version of the utilitarian moral axiom[42] may find this conclusion quite acceptable; if concern in ethical matters should be restricted to the interests of 'actual' persons, present or future, then the failure to create a more rather than less worthwhile life may be seen to be of no consequence. On such a view, the only interests to be weighed up[43] in deciding how GCTs should be regulated are those of the prospective mother and those third party interests which will be considered later.

But for those who find this perceived moral neutrality of the woman's choice to be unsatisfying, it would seem that some argument must be advanced for the implantation of Embryo X rather than Embryo Y which relies on

40 Dan Brock, 'The Non-Identity Problem and genetic harms – the case of wrongful handicaps', *Bioethics* (1995) 9(3/4): 269.
41 Roberts, 'Present duties and future persons', op. cit., fn 18, p 316.
42 David Heyd, *Genethics: moral issues in the creation of people*, Berkeley: University of California Press, 1992.
43 Assuming that no embryo exists which would lead to a person with a life worse than non-existence.

something other than frustrating the interests of particular persons, an argument which rejects the claim that a 'wrong act must be bad for someone'.[44]

Non-Person-Affecting objections

I have argued, then, that the Non-Identity Principle means we can speak of harming a potential future child by a genesis act only in those rare cases where its life is foreseeably so awful as to constitute a harm in itself. Does this, then, conclude the question of future children? For the majority of commentators in this area, the matter cannot be left there; the conclusion that implanting a disabled embryo rather than a healthy one is a matter of ethical indifference – what Parfit called the 'No Difference' conclusion – is just too odd, too seemingly wrong, to be accepted. However, the majority of commentators also accept the Non-Identity Principle, which presents them with the problem of identifying who precisely is the subject of harm.[45]

For such writers, the only way to establish a harm resulting from such choices is by moving away from Person-Affecting approaches and seeking to ground their arguments in Non-Person-Affecting (NPA) concepts of harm. This was what Parfit attempted by his *Same Number Claim*, or Q.[46] He explained this in the following way: 'If in either of two possible outcomes the same number of people would live, it would be worse if those who lived are worse off, or have a lower quality of life, than those who would have lived.'[47]

Similar NPA principles have been suggested by Joel Feinberg,[48] Buchanan, Brock, et al,[49] and by Julian Savulescu.[50] As Buchanan et al explain,

44 Brock, 'The Non-Identity Problem and genetic harms', op. cit., fn 40.

45 Buchanan, Brock, Daniels, Wikler, *From Chance to Choice*, op. cit., fn 16, p 225; Peters, 'Harming future persons', op. cit., fn 9, p 399; Julian Savulescu, 'Procreative beneficence: Why we should select the best children', *Bioethics* (2001) 15 (5/6): 413–26, p 418.

46 Parfit, *Reasons and Persons*, op. cit., fn 1, p 360.

47 Id.

48 'The wrongdoer in the example must be blamed for wantonly introducing a certain evil into the world, not for inflicting harm on a person.' Feinberg, *Harm to Others*, op. cit., chapter 3, fn 19, p 103.

49 Their version of an NPA principle is referred to as 'N', and states that: 'Individuals are morally required not to let any child or other dependent person for whose welfare they are responsible experience serious suffering or limited opportunity or serious loss of happiness or good, if they can act so that, without affecting the number of persons who will exist and without imposing substantial burdens or costs or loss of benefits on themselves or others, no child or other dependent person for whose welfare they are responsible will experience serious suffering or limited opportunity or serious loss of happiness or good.' *From Chance to Choice*, op. cit., fn 16, p 249.

50 Savulescu has argued for a Principle of Procreative Beneficence, which would maintain that: 'couples (or single reproducers) should select the child, of the possible children they could have, who is expected to have the best life, or at least as good a life as the others, based on the relevant, available information.' Julian Savulescu, 'Procreative beneficence: Why we should select the best children', *Bioethics* (2001) 15 (5/6): 413–26, p 415.

this principle for the prevention of suffering applies not to distinct individuals, so that the prevention of suffering must make a distinct individual better off than he or she would have been . . . but to the classes of individuals who will exist if the suffering is or is not prevented . . .'[51]

While it would still, then, be true that no distinct individual is harmed if the disabled embryo is implanted, the subject of harm can be seen as 'the classes of all persons who will exist in each of two or more alternative courses of action will be a non-person-affecting principle'.[52]

This view might seem very close to that espoused by Robert Green, and considered (and ultimately rejected) in the preceding section. The NPA approach, though, differs from Green's in several important respects. Green, for example, sought to keep his argument within the confines of the Person-Affecting Principle, by speaking of one Generic Child, an amalgam of all the possible future children that the prospective parents might have. The person to whom the harm might be done, then, is this fungible, composite Generic Child.

The NPA approach is somewhat different. Instead of attempting to iden-tify a particular person (notional or otherwise) who is the subject of harm, it relies on the purportedly shared interests of that group of potential future persons. As such, it is not subject to the criticism that was levied at Green; namely, that he relied upon an admittedly fictitious entity for a subject of harm. There clearly *are* a number of potential future children who could arise from the parents' use of PGD, and to speak of them as a 'class' is not obviously nonsensical in the manner of Green's Generic Child.

Nonetheless, I think the NPA objections to the pro-choice position are themselves ultimately unsatisfactory, for at least two distinct reasons. First, doubts may be expressed about the NPA's reliance upon a notional class of potential beings with a collective pool of interests. There are, of course, myriad circumstances in which it is quite accurate to refer to classes of indi-viduals having collective interests. A footballer may resent being substituted in an important match, but his manager may justify this as being in the interests of the team. If the player accepts this, it is because he identifies his own interests with the team's ultimate success; his individual interest in staying on the pitch coexists with the collective team interest, of which others of his individual interests form a part.

There is nothing linguistically or logically incoherent about referring to X and Y as belonging to the class of potential future beings. What is problem-atic is seeking to attribute to that class a pool of shared interests, analogous with that of a football team, which can be furthered or frustrated by the implantation choice. Quite simply, only one of the rivals for implantation will

51 Buchanan, Brock, Daniels, Wikler, *From Chance to Choice*, op. cit., fn 16, p 249.
52 Id.

ever attain any interests whatever – a fact that Buchanan et al specifically acknowledge.[53] The choice between X and Y is simply a choice between which of two different sets of interests we will bring into existence. To speak of the two as having a shared pool of interests flies in the face of this reality. The notion that we can owe duties to the class of possible children we might have is tempting only in the linguistic sense, relying as it does on the false aggregation of interests which cannot co-exist.

A rather different conception of the NPA principle has been advanced by writers such as Harris and Feinberg. While explicitly recognising that the disabled child will, in all but the rarest scenarios, have no cause for complaint, both agree that the mother who chooses a disabled over an able-bodied child still acts wrongly. For Feinberg, the wrong lies in 'wantonly introducing a certain evil *into the world*, not for inflicting harm on a person',[54] while in almost identical terms, Harris speaks of 'the wrong of bringing avoidable suffering into the world, of choosing deliberately to increase unnecessarily the amount of harm or suffering in the world or of choosing a world with more suffering rather than one with less'.[55]

On the face of it, an ethical principle that imposes impersonal duties to *the world* is tempting for those who are dissatisfied by the No Difference conclusion, as it obviates the need to identify a particular person – actual, potential or notional – who is the subject of the harm. It would allow us to conclude that the 14-year-old girl, as well as Candy McCullough and Sharon Duschesneau, acted wrongly, even though the children that they brought into the world have no grievance against them.

On closer examination, though, it seems that the 'duty to the world' approach presents its own problems. Such a duty – at least in the vaguely utilitarian sense advanced by Harris and Feinberg – must take one of two forms. The first involves a duty to minimise the amount of suffering in the world, regardless of any offset against happiness (referred to here as the *No Suffering* view. There is a suggestion, perhaps, that this is what Harris is thinking of when he refers to the wrong of 'choosing a world with more suffering rather than one with less'.[56])

If the duty took this form, then it would make sense to say that the mother of the disabled child does wrong when she goes ahead with the pregnancy, because the child she has – although benefited overall – will live a life containing more suffering than the alternative child that she could have had. Thus, her choice causes more rather than less suffering in the world. This view, however, poses a problem. If our obligation is simply to minimise suffering,

---

53 See fn 51, p 236.
54 Feinberg, *Harm to Others*, op. cit., chapter 3, fn 19, p 103, emphasis added.
55 John Harris, *Wonderwoman and Superman: The Ethics of Human Biotechnology*, Oxford: Oxford University Press, 1992, p 90.
56 Id.

then this means that *anyone* would do wrong when they bring *any child* into existence. Every life involves some degree of suffering, and while we ordinarily regard this as being offset by the happiness/enjoyment/satisfied desires in those lives, the *No Suffering* view appears not to allow us any such trade-off.[57]

The ethical imperative to minimise the amount of suffering in the world, then, could best be achieved by having no children at all, and anyone who chooses to have a child in the knowledge that its life will contain some degree of suffering seems to violate this imperative.[58]

Alternatively, we may recognise a duty to the world that is slightly more complex than the *No Suffering* view, requiring instead that we do indeed offset the suffering we introduce into the world against the happiness we introduce. A duty to maximise the amount of happiness-over-misery in the world – what we might call the *Aggregate* approach – would provide us with a reason to say that the actions of the 14-year-old girl and Duschesneau and McCullough are wrong *only if* there was an alternative course of action open to them that would have produced a greater aggregate of happiness-over-misery in the world.

Since, in Parfit's scenario, the 14-year-old girl has the option to delay pregnancy until such time as she can give her child a better start in life, and since Duschesneau and McCullough could certainly have had a child that was not (or had a much lower likelihood of being) deaf, they acted wrongly when they elected to act as they did. But had those children been the only children they could possibly have had, then – assuming the lives of those children contain *some* balance of happiness over misery – they have not offended the *Aggregate* principle.

It is easy to imagine how this version of the NPA principle might seem more moderate, and hence more appealing, than the *No Suffering* view. Yet on reflection, it seems that it too offers conclusions that are implausible or unappealing. What distinguishes the *No Suffering* view from the *Aggregate* view is that it contains not only an obligation to minimise suffering in the world, but a symbiotic obligation to maximise happiness (perhaps conceived of in terms of satisfied interests). This is quite different from an obligation to satisfy existing interests. Instead, the obligation implicit in this version of the ethical axiom is to create satisfiable interests *ab initio*, in order that they might be satisfied.

What would this mean in practice? It would regard as ethically wrong not only the decision to create a less-than-optimally-happy baby, but would also regard as wrong the decision to refrain from having a child at all. After all,

57 A point eloquently expressed by S D Edwards in 'Prevention of disability on grounds of suffering', *Journal of Medical Ethics* (2001); 27: 380–2, p 380.
58 It is also, perhaps, interesting to note that the *No Suffering* conception of the NPA principle would seemingly find no objection to the deliberate creation of an anencephalic or otherwise asentient child.

someone who elects to remain childless when the option of having a reasonably happy child was open has failed in her duty to maximise the amount of happiness-over-suffering in the world.

To say otherwise would be to adopt the rather strange position of denying that a woman is subject to any kind of moral obligation to increase the overall 'happiness' by reproducing, but that having voluntarily elected so to do, she suddenly becomes subject to a more onerous obligation to increase the overall happiness *to as great a degree as possible* by having a particular kind of child. This is a bit like arguing that, while no one is obliged to donate money to charity at all, those who voluntarily elect to give a little will be forced to give as much as possible.

In fact, the *Aggregate Principle* seems to require each of us to reproduce to the optimum degree, or at least up to the point where each additional child would cease to yield a marginal gain to 'the world' in terms of happiness. There may, of course, come a point where poverty or overcrowding meant that the birth of an extra child would actually decrease the happiness balance, because its life would be of a low quality, while its birth would impact detrimentally on the lives of its siblings. But until that point is reached, and while the birth of each successive child contributes positively to the happiness-over-misery balance sheets, it is difficult to see how the reproductive imperative can be avoided.

Several writers have attempted to avoid this conclusion by claiming that the effect upon the quality of lives of those coerced into having unwanted children would be so severe as to render this argument redundant,[59] while others have argued that the act of procreation constitutes an inefficient use of resources which could, from a utilitarian view, be better spent improving the lives of existing persons – the so called Argument From Transfer.[60] Neither argument, though, is entirely convincing. The claim that forcing reluctant parents to procreate would cause more harm than good seems dubious; if the reluctant parents still have worthwhile, albeit diminished, lives, it is difficult

---

59 See, eg, Glover, *Causing Death and Saving Lives*, London: Penguin Books, 1990, p 70.
60 Christian Munthe, 'The argument from transfer', *Bioethics* (1996) 10(1); 26–42. It should be noted that Munthe's argument does not rely upon a belief that concern should be restricted to actual persons, nor indeed does it require a belief that the interests of actual persons be accorded priority over those of potential future persons. Rather, his claim is based upon the reasoning that, while creating a worthwhile life involves an improvement in overall utility of +1, there are in existence a considerable number of persons whose lives are in fact so bad as to be subjectively worse than non-existence, and to whom we could accord a utility rating of −1. Obviously, if it were possible to render these existing lives subjectively valuable by using the resources which would have been spent on a new person, this would be the better course of action, since the improvement from −1 to +1 is greater than the improvement from 0 to +1. His argument, of course, depends for its success upon the assumptions that (a) there are in existence significant numbers of persons whose lives are worse than non-existence, and (b) that these lives could be made worthwhile by the deployment of the resources which would otherwise have been spent upon procreation.

to see how their loss could outweigh the gain in overall utility brought about by the creation of another worthwhile life.[61]

The Argument From Transfer, meanwhile, seems only to discharge from the duty to procreate those who redirect that time and effort which would have been spent on the new child to improving the lot of those leading the most miserably unfulfilled lives. There is nothing logically wrong with this view, though the burden it imposes may strike some people as unduly oner- ous. Perhaps, though, it is right that we should accord a higher priority to the most wretchedly disadvantaged people in the world. Perhaps it is right that those of us with comfortable lives should be made to account for our failure to help the starving and the desperate. Certainly, philosophers like Peter Singer have argued very persuasively along these lines.

The problem with the Argument From Transfer (AFT), I think, is not that it imposes obligations to help the needy, but rather that it allows us to discharge those obligations by making a contribution elsewhere in the pool of happiness. It draws on a particular impersonal form of utilitarianism that is concerned only with the *quantity* of happiness in the world, but which isn't concerned at all with how it is distributed. It would, for example, give us no reason to object to Nozick's Utility Monsters – hypothetical utilitarian ogres who derived enormous pleasure from the suffering of others. If indulging the Utility Mon- sters was the most efficient means of increasing the aggregate of happiness, then that is what the AFT would have us do, regardless of the fact that their happiness was bought at the expense of suffering of a great many others.

More obviously, we might object to the AFT on the grounds that creating interests simply in order to satisfy them is not morally equivalent to satisfying existing interests, because we have obligations to actually existing people that we do not owe to potentially existing people. The duty of beneficence, we might think, is a duty that is owed to people, not to some impersonal felicific calculus. When we fail in our duties to our fellow persons, they have com- plaints against us; but it isn't obvious who I owe an apology to when I fail to make 'the world' a better place.

The AFT, then, is unappealing to those of us who regard Person-Affecting obligations as being more important than any impersonal obligations; who think helping *people* is what matters rather than racking up points on a felicific calculator; who are sceptical of the claim that having enough happy babies discharges us of obligations to the starving or homeless. On the other hand, we should not expect it to appeal much to those who resent being told that every waking hour spent not working for Oxfam should be dedicated to procreation. Overall, I think it is a brave, but ultimately unsuccessful defence of the *Aggregate Principle*.

The application of Non-Person-Affecting principles, of the type advocated

---

61 See Stuart Rachels, 'Is it good to make happy people?', *Bioethics*, (1998) 12(2); p 109.

by Harris and Feinberg, to GCTs seems destined to be acceptable only if we concede either (a) that all potential parents can be subject to a duty to reproduce, and continue reproducing up the point where their own or the children's lives would be miserably wretched, or (b) that all potential parents should refrain from reproducing at all, since every life contains *some* degree of suffering. Since it seems safe to assume that both of these conclusions would be ridiculous or repugnant to most people, I would suggest that NPA principles are unsatisfactory, and that instead, we should concentrate on the effect of GCTs on actual people, current or future.

'Worse Than Non-existence' lives

The Non-Identity Principle, then, makes it impossible to argue that a child was harmed on balance by a decision on which its very existence was contingent – with one possible exception: those cases where the child's life is so awful that we can actually deem it worse than non-existence, or worse than nothing (WTN). Such a judgment could be made where the child's most important interests are doomed from the outset – such as its interest in avoiding intolerable suffering – while at the same time no corresponding interests could be furthered.

Since predictable future interests constitute a valid, indeed unavoidable, cause for concern, we could say that, in electing to implant a 'doomed embryo', a course of events is set in motion which will result in a predictable future harm, just as surely as when the broken glass is carelessly discarded in the woods. The harm in question, though, will not be a cut foot, but rather a life of such wretched quality that, from the subjective perspective of the child itself, it would have been better never to have been born.

Examples would almost certainly be rare, but we might plausibly consider that the lives of those affected by genetic disorders that guarantee brief, severely cognitively impaired and pain-filled lives might be so considered. Consider, for example, Philip Kitcher's description of the progress of Lesch-Nyhan syndrome:

> an allele on their single X chromosome causes boys to suffer mental retardation and extreme physical pains of the type associated with gout. Yet perhaps the most disturbing feature of the condition is an apparently irresistible urge to self-mutilation – the boys chew their lips and the tips of their fingers until they are raw and bleeding. At present, doctors can relieve some of the gouty symptoms, but they are unable to prevent the mental retardation and can only block the compulsive mutilation by applying bandages to hands and lips.[62]

---

62 Philip Kitcher, *The Lives to Come*, London: Allen Lane: The Penguin Press 1996, p 82.

There is, we might think, a strong argument for concluding that such lives are 'worth not living'; they contain constant pain which cannot be entirely relieved, a compulsion to self-mutilate which can only be controlled by restraining the child, and – in view of the severe retardation, behavioural disorders and short life expectancy – no real opportunity for compensatory pleasures or satisfied interests of any sort. 'There is nothing to be done,' Kitcher observes, 'except to alleviate pain and discomfort, no aspirations we can expect to foster, no plans, however humble, to bring to fruition.'[63]

UK law adopts a somewhat ambivalent attitude to the prospect of WTN lives. In the context of non-treatment decisions involving infants, the courts have been willing to recognise that a child's life can be so subjectively unpleasant that life-prolonging treatment would not be justified. In *Re B (a minor) (wardship: medical treatment)*,[64] Lord Templeman was willing to confront this issue head on. It was the duty of the court, he stated,

> to decide whether the life of this child is demonstrably so awful that in effect the child must be condemned to die or whether the life of this child is still so imponderable that it would be wrong for her to be condemned to die.[65]

In this particular case, the court concluded that the child's condition was not of that awful quality; life-sustaining treatment could achieve more than the prolongation of suffering. However, Lord Templeman went on to make it quite clear that there may be other circumstances where 'the future [of the child] is so certain and where the life of the child is so bound to be full of pain and suffering that the court might be driven to a different conclusion'.

In several later cases, the courts *did* in fact reach different conclusions about the requirement to prolong life, and in each of those the principle that, occasionally, life can be a burden rather than a benefit was restated. In *Re J (a minor) (wardship: medical treatment)*,[66] Lord Donaldson MR acknowledged the 'very strong presumption in favour of a course of action which will prolong life', but added that this presumption 'is not irrebuttable'. On the contrary,

> account has to be taken of the pain and suffering and quality of life which the child will experience if life is prolonged . . . In the end there will be cases in which the answer must be that it is not in the interests of the child to subject it to treatment which will cause increased suffering and produce no commensurate benefit.[67]

---

63 See fn 62, p 288.
64 (1981) 3 All ER 927.
65 Ibid, per Lord Templeman, p 929.
66 [1991] Fam 33.
67 Ibid, p 46.

At least one lower court judge has been willing to recognise a positive interest held by an infant in being allowed to die. In the much-publicised conjoined twins case,[68] Johnston J claimed that:

> the few months of Mary's life if not separated from her twin would not simply be worth nothing to her, they would be hurtful. . . . To prolong Mary's life for these few months would in my judgment be very seriously to her disadvantage.[69]

The courts have, though, displayed a marked reluctance to require such evaluations to be made prospectively. 'Wrongful life' actions are a peculiar class of law suit. Although such claims are raised on behalf of handicapped children, they do not allege that the handicaps are the fault of the other party. Instead, they rely on the claim that, but for the negligence of the other party, the child would not be alive to suffer the bad effects of the handicap. Such actions have arisen after botched prenatal screening, or unsuccessful abortions. They have not, however, tended to be well received by the courts.

In the one and only 'wrongful life' case to be heard in the UK, *McKay v Essex Area Health Authority*,[70] the Court of Appeal refused to attempt a comparison between a particular quality of life and non-existence, Stephenson LJ expressing this reluctance in the following terms:

> The only loss for which those who have not injured the child can be held liable to compensate the child is the difference between its condition as a result of their allowing it to be born alive and injured and its condition if its embryonic life had been ended before its life in the world had begun.[71]

It is interesting to note that the Lords of Appeal seem to have enjoyed a firmer grasp of the Non-Identity Principle than the members of the HFEA showed when discussing PGD or tissue typing.[72] Stephenson LJ continued:

---

68 *Re A (children) (conjoined twins: surgical separation)* [2001] 57 BMLR 1.
69 Ibid, p 10. The claim that Mary's life would be 'hurtful' to her might, however, be thought difficult to reconcile with Johnston J's comment on the preceding page that: 'There is no way that could remotely be described as reliable by which those tending Mary can know even now whether she is hurting or in pain.'
70 [1982] QB 1166.
71 Ibid, p 1181.
72 Even clearer evidence of this understanding can be found on p 1182, per Stephenson LJ: 'If a court had to decide whether it were better to enter into life maimed or halt than not to enter it at all, it would, I think, be bound to say it was better in all cases of mental and physical disability, except possibly those extreme cases already mentioned . . . but certainly not excepting such a case as the present.' See also Ackner, LJ, p 1189.

But how can a court of law evaluate that second condition and so measure the loss to the child? Even if a court were competent to decide between the conflicting views of theologians and philosophers and to assume an 'after life' or non-existence as the basis for comparison, how can a judge put a value on the one or the other, compare either alternative with the injured child's life in this world and determine that the child has lost anything, without the means of knowing what, if anything, it has gained?[73]

In a similar vein, Ackner LJ asked:

> But how can a court begin to evaluate non-existence, 'the undiscovered country from whose bourn no traveller returns?' No comparison is possible and therefore no damage can be established which a court could recognise.[74]

This is a curious contention, and, perhaps, an even more curious choice of quotation with which to illustrate it. The reference to the 'undiscovered country' comes from Hamlet's soliloquy on contemplating suicide, and its context makes it entirely clear that it refers to *death* and not to non-existence:

> Who would fardels bear, to grunt and sweat under a weary life,
> But that the dread of something after death,
> The undiscover'd country from whose bourn no traveller returns . . .[75]

Can it really be Ackner LJ's contention that no meaningful comparison can be attempted between death and life? This would certainly fly in the face of the rationale of the non-treatment cases considered above. The only way to make sense of non-treatment decisions (and of the damages awarded for '[l]oss of expectation of life' referred to by Stephenson LJ[76]) is by demonstrating that wrongful life claims are asking the courts to consider, in non-existence, something that is not only *different* from death, but somehow more difficult to quantify or compare. In this, it may be seen the Lords of Appeal were less than wholly convincing. Certainly, Stephenson LJ's claim that

> In measuring the loss caused by shortened life, courts are dealing with a thing, human life, of which they have some experience; [in the wrongful

73 See fn 70, p 1181, per Stephenson LJ.
74 Ibid, p 1189.
75 *Hamlet*, Act 3, Scene 1.
76 [1982] QB 1166, p 1181.

life case] the court is being asked to deal with the consequences of death for the dead, a thing of which it has none[77]

appears to offer scant support for the distinction. It simply isn't true that wrongful death cases involve only a knowledge of life, nor that wrongful life cases involve only a knowledge of 'the consequence of death for the dead'. Rather, both – and we may also involve non-treatment decisions in this – involve comparisons *between* existence and non-existence.

To award damages on the basis that someone has lost out by being deprived of life necessarily involves some tacit assumptions about what death involves, and those assumptions seem to be that death is, ordinarily, worse than further life. It is obviously true that neither judges nor anyone else has personal knowledge of what that 'undiscover'd country' involves, but no decision about whether to allow a handicapped neonate to die could be meaningful without some means to effect a comparison between the alternatives on offer. If such assumptions, unsubstantiated by evidence, are possible in relation to non-existence states after death, there is no obvious reason why similar assumptions could not be possible in relation to non-existence states prior to birth.

It may, indeed, be true that – as Stephenson LJ suggested[78] – in many cases, an accurate prediction of the future child's state will be extremely difficult in advance of its birth. This, though, is an evidentiary problem, and if it were shown that the extent of the child's suffering was not foreseeable at the time of the implantation decision, then this would presumably constitute a defence against either a criminal charge under s 13(5), or a civil suit for wrongful life. However, this difficulty provides no principled basis to distinguish the task before the court in a wrongful life suit from the equally galling tasks it faces in non-treatment and other decisions;[79] in both cases, assumptions must be made about the subjective experiential existence of an entity that will sometimes have no means of communicating its feelings.

Attaching a notional value to non-existence is undeniably problematic, but it is as necessary for any comparison between life and death (which courts make on a regular basis) as it is for a comparison between life and never existing (which the Court of Appeal steadfastly refused to undertake). While Stephenson LJ was almost certainly right to rule that it could not be suggested of the child in *McKay* that 'the quality of her life is such that she is

---

77   See fn 76.

78   Ibid, p 1180.

79   A point made by Robert Lee in 'To be or not to be: is that the question? The claim of wrongful life', in Lee and Morgan, (eds), *Birthrights: Law and Ethics at the Beginnings of Life*, London: Routledge, 1989, p 177.

certainly better dead',[80] even this observation seemed to sit uncomfortably with his contention that no such comparison was possible.

Even less easy to reconcile is the judicial reluctance to attempt such comparisons, and the willingness of Parliament to impose a duty on providers of reproductive technologies to do exactly this. Section 13(5) of the 1990 Act specifically requires a consideration of the welfare of the future child prior to the provision of such services. Since it is presumably unlikely that parliamentary intent was that such a consideration should have no bearing on the decision whether to provide treatment, it seems obvious that the intention was that certain welfare considerations would lead to the refusal of such treatment.

Implicit in such a provision is the assumption that, in certain circumstances, it is foreseeably in the interests of a potential future child to be spared existence, or that the life of such a child, were it to be created, would contain such a balance of harms over benefits that its life would constitute a 'harm on balance'.[81] Thus, a burden has been placed on infertility clinics that the Court of Appeal deemed too onerous to assume for itself.[82]

What, then, would constitute a proportionate and consistent approach to WTN lives? Given the predictability of the phenotypical manifestations of certain genetic conditions, it may be that the judges in *McKay* were unduly reticent about attempting a comparison between a life of *any* quality and non-existence. Indeed, we may well be sceptical about the disanalogy between death and non-existence, upon which the distinction between non-treatment and wrongful life cases rests.

Perhaps more compelling is John Harris's observation that wrongful life actions, even if successful, do not extinguish the harm of a WTN life. After all, he observes, if monetary compensation raises the quality of life, from the

80 See fn 70, p 1180. The child was deaf and partially blind as a result of contact with the rubella virus.
81 Lee and Morgan have claimed that, by avoiding mention 'of any requirement that the welfare of that child be considered as paramount', Parliament 'at least saved the workings of the section from a philosophical appreciation of existence against non-existence'. Robert G Lee and Derek Morgan, *Human Fertilisation and Embryology: Regulating the Reproductive Revolution*. London: Blackstone Press Limited, 2001, p 164. Although the absence of such a paramountcy requirement may have some significance in tissue typing cases – see Chapter 6 – it is unclear how this obviates the need for such a comparison, or with confronting the NIP. Considering the welfare of the future child before providing treatment services can only be a meaningful requirement if it is envisioned that, in some cases, this will lead to a decision – motivated by concern for that child's welfare – not to provide such services. This, I suggest, inevitably involves a comparison between the child's likely welfare if born, and the alternative for that child, ie, non-existence.
82 Though, as Lee and Morgan note, 'there seems to have been relatively little overt resistance from doctors disclaiming the capacity to make the social assessments required by s 13(5)', this does not detract from the inconsistency of requiring them to do what the Court of Appeal has effectively ruled impossible. Ibid, p 165.

child's subjective perspective, above the threshold of a life worth living (or at least a life *not* worth *not* living; an anencephalic neonate, for example, we might consider to have no interest in whether it lives or not) then their lives were 'only contingently worth not living',[83] i.e. it was their economic circumstances as well as their genetic condition that rendered their lives so wretched.

This seems a valid observation, but it is also possible that a wrongful life payment, while perhaps not raising the life in question above the threshold, will raise it *to an extent*, rendering it slightly less intolerable for the child concerned. If WTN can be counted as 'less than nothing', then there is no reason why we cannot designate some as further below Glover's 'zero line' than others. Nonetheless, provided even a successful wrongful life action would leave the child in the WTN category, it is difficult to disagree with Harris's conclusion that, in such cases, the appropriate remedy would be euthanasia.[84] Since UK law continues to uphold its (almost) absolute prohibition on active killing, even in cases where this may be thought to be in the individual's interests,[85] euthanasia will not be a practical solution. However, in those cases where the WTN infant requires life-sustaining medical treatment (which we might assume will all but invariably be the case) the judgments in *Re B* et al will allow for a decision that will expedite the child's death. (Although the recent European Court decision in *Glass v UK*[86] recognises the familial right to be consulted, it would not allow the parents of a WTN child to demand that its life be prolonged when this was manifestly contrary to the child's interests.)

From a harm-avoidance or non-maleficence perspective, though, the ethically preferable outcome is that such lives should not come into existence at all, or should not develop to the point of acquiring sentience; preventing suffering, surely, is preferable to ending it once it has begun. A requirement that prospective parents avoid creating such lives would impact significantly on their interests in reproductive liberty, as discussed in Chapter 2, and would harm those (presumably very few) who either wished to create such children,[87] those who sought to forego screening altogether, and those who merely feel

---

83 Harris, *Wonderwoman and Superman*, op. cit., fn 55, p 96.
84 Id. See also Patricia M A Beaumont, 'Wrongful life and wrongful birth', from Sheila A M McLean, (ed), *Contemporary Issues in Law, Medicine and Ethics*, Aldershot: Dartmouth, 1996, p 112.
85 *R v Director of Public Prosecutions, Secretary of State for the Home Department, ex parte Diane Pretty* [2002] 1 AC 800.
86 *Glass v United Kingdom* (61827/00) [2004] 1 FLR 1019.
87 This presumes that, unlike Feinberg, we do not exclude from our ethical considerations those interests which he deems inherently immoral, such as the sadist's interest in torturing others. As well as the danger of arbitrariness – it requires no great imagination to foresee such a limiting rule being used to designate as inherently immoral interests in, for example, forming same-sex relationships – such a designation, of course, requires appeal to some extraneous ethical axiom, and for adherents to the Harm Principle, this may seem to bring them perilously close to legal moralism.

aggrieved at the curtailment of what they believe should be exclusively their choice. But it may be legitimate to regard such a harm as outweighed by the harms sustained during its brief sentient existence by a child affected by a WTN life.

This, in view of the Non-Identity Principle, would be the one intelligible, child-oriented application of s 13(5). A narrow construction of the welfare test would require fertility clinics to refuse treatment only in those cases where it is foreseeable that the life of the resulting child would be subjectively WTN. Since many genetic conditions vary in terms of penetrance, meaning that it is often impossible in individual cases to make an accurate pronouncement on the quality of a life until the child is born (and perhaps not until some time thereafter), it might be anticipated that the range of conditions to which s 13(5) would actually apply would be narrow indeed. Certainly, it could not meaningfully be interpreted as including such matters as 'the child's need for a father', a 'need' that, were it not met, would be vastly unlikely to render a child's life WTN.

An approach which saw a small range of the most severe genetic disorders regarded both as suitable cases for prospective prohibition on implantation of such embryos under s 13(5), and for retrospective wrongful life actions raised on behalf of the children affected where negligence, malice or indifference saw the s 13(5) requirement ignored, would not provide a panacea to all the problems that bedevil this area, but it would lend a degree of coherence and consistency to an area that at present lacks both.

Children of the genetic supermarket: an overview

What can I conclude, then, about the children of the genetic supermarket? First, being deselected/destroyed is harmful neither to the embryos themselves, nor the persons they might one day have become. In contrast, the potential future persons who will, or might, one day exist have (potential, future) interests that will one day be actualised, and these interests should be borne in mind in making 'genesis' decisions. As Parfit and others have shown, though, it is impossible to say that these future persons will be harmed by an act that brings about their existence, *provided* the lives into which they are born are not so awful (for them) as to be worse than non-existence.

While the Non-Identity Problem/Principle is recognised by most commentators in the field, many seek to get around it by relying instead on some version of a utilitarian Non Person-Affecting principle, which creates duties to 'the class of potential future children who might exist' or, more commonly, to the world at large. I have tried to show, though, that such theories are themselves problematic, giving rise as they do to duties more onerous, and more impersonal, than their proponents would be likely to accept.

In the next chapter, I turn to some of the other candidates who might claim to be harmed, either by the very existence of a genetic supermarket, or by the specific decisions made by those who avail themselves of it. For the moment, though, it would appear that the overwhelming majority of choices that prospective parents would or could make about the genetic composition of their future children are harmful neither to the children themselves, nor, in any meaningful sense, to 'the world'. This conclusion may feel, at some level, less than satisfying for anyone whose concern is with the quality of lives of existing and future persons; Glover has written that 'it is hard to accept that society should set no limits to the genetic choices parents can make for their children',[88] while Parfit himself seems far from satisfied by this conclusion.[89] It is significant, though, that neither those two eminent philosophers, nor any other contributors to this debate, have offered an intelligible model which can account for the intuition that the pro-choice approach to GCTs violates the principle of non-maleficence.

I therefore propose a reading of s 13(5) that is consistent with the Non-Identity Principle, that is, a narrow reading that would prevent the implantation only of those embryos likely to develop into children with WTN lives. Any embryos affected by lesser conditions should not be excluded from implantation; while the children they may become will be exposed to certain harms from which 'normal' children will be spared, their creation will not, predictably, constitute harms on balance, or at least not harms to *them*.

The children of the genetic supermarket – both those who owe their existence to their parents' choices, and those insubstantial entities whose potential lives were prevented by GCTs – look, at first glance, to be the most obvious candidates to be harmed by it. In fact, closer inspection suggests that this will very rarely be so. In the former case, this is because they are likely to come out ahead, on balance, from decisions that gave them life, to have few valid complaints against their parents that don't boil down to a genuine wish never to have been born. In the latter case, all talk of harm is philosophically muddled; we cannot sensibly attribute interests to beings who never possessed even the most rudimentary consciousness, and to worry about the possible people who might have been born but for the use of PGD is morally akin to worrying about all the children the Pope might have had but for his vow of celibacy.

This conclusion, though, cannot exhaust our search for the genetic supermarket's possible victims. For there are parties less immediately affected by germinal choice decisions who might claim that their interests are adversely affected.

88 Jonathan Glover, *What Sort Of People Should There Be?*, London: Penguin, 1984, p 48.
89 Parfit, *Reasons and Persons*, op. cit., fn 1, p 443.

Chapter 5

Disability, gender and the threat to the already disadvantaged

Over the past couple of chapters, I have tried to show that the pro-choice approach to germinal choice technologies poses no credible risk of harm – or at least, no harm that was not outweighed by benefit – to the potential children who are born as a result of those choices. The only credible exception would be those rare cases where prospective parents used GCTs to ensure the birth of a child afflicted with some genetic disorder so dreadful that the subjective quality of life of the child was worse than non-existence.

In this chapter, I want to look at the possibilities of harm to other parties, less directly affected by the choices made by prospective parents, but who may nonetheless have interests that will be adversely affected by those choices. Typically, the 'negative externalities' considered here will arise (if at all) not from one or two isolated uses of reproductive choice, but from the cumulative effect of many such choices. The risk of such harms, it seems, derives from the prospect of GCTs becoming commonplace, and from those who use them making predictable, and similar, choices. Hans Reinders has expressed this concern in the following terms:

> side effects of individual decisions made by people using their repro-ductive freedom, though unintended, can collectively have very dam-aging effects in society. The question then is whether the proliferation of genetic tests should be restricted and whether such restriction is suf-ficiently justified on the grounds of the unintended but harmful side effects of large-scale use of such tests.[1]

Who, then, are these third parties who might be at risk of harm from the genetic supermarket?

---

1 Hans S Reinders, *The Future of the Disabled in Liberal Society: An Ethical Analysis*, Notre Dame, Indiana: University of Notre Dame Press, 2000, p 86.

People with disabilities

In August 2005, the United Kingdom's Human Fertilisation and Embryology Authority launched a public consultation, seeking views on the use of preimplantation genetic diagnosis for the detection of cancer genes.[2] The issue was considered by the Authority to be a possible source of particular controversy because it involved extending the range of conditions for which PGD can be licensed in a potentially important way: as well as testing for genes that would *definitely* cause disease traits, such as cystic fibrosis and muscular dystrophy, this would involve genes that would only *possibly* manifest themselves phenotypically. In other words, there is a very real chance that such an application of PGD would result in the destruction of perfectly healthy embryos.

Aside from the possible danger of 'false positive' results, this further extension of PGD seems likely to provoke a range of familiar responses to the technology. On the day that the consultation was launched, Josephine Quintavalle, Director of Comment on Reproductive Ethics (CORE), argued on CORE's website: 'We are looking at issues which go to the heart of our attitudes to disability, and the offensive message that is sent in this instance is that the disabled or sick are better off not being born.'[3]

While CORE's underlying agenda might have more to do with protecting embryos than with possible harm or offence to disabled or sick people,[4] Quintavalle's comment is resonant of a particular species of objection to GCTs, a species of objection concerned about what some see as a judgment inherent in such techniques about the value of certain lives. Sometimes described as 'expressivist' objections,[5] these have proved some of the most genuinely troubling for proponents of a pro-choice approach towards PGD.

While some objections to GCTs rely on religious or conservative views about the 'naturalness' of reproductive technologies[6] or the status of the

---

2   'Should embryo screening help parents prevent passing on a wider range of inheritable diseases?', 11 August 2005, at http://www.hfea.gov.uk/PressOffice/Archive/1123751318.

3   'Kill the carrier? New HFEA consultation', 11 August 2005, at http://www.corethics.org/document.asp?id=cpr110805.txt&se=2&st=4.

4   Colin Gavaghan, ' "Pro-life" tactics on tissue typing', *BioNews Commentaries*, 15 April 2003, at http://www.bionews.org.uk/commentary.lasso?storyid=1642.

5   See, for example, S D Edwards, 'Disability, identity and the "expressivist objection" ', *Journal of Medical Ethics* (2004); 30: 418–20; Rosamund Scott, 'Prenatal testing, reproductive autonomy, and disability interests', *Cambridge Quarterly Healthcare Ethics* (2005); 14(1): 65–82.

6   Conservative commentator Francis Fukuyama, who has recently turned his attention to biotechnology, has written of 'a desperate need for philosophy to return to the pre-Kantian tradition that grounds rights and morality in nature'. *Our Posthuman Future: Consequences of the Biotechnology Revolution*, New York: Faber, Strauss and Giroux, 2002, p 112. Another eminent 'biocon', Leon Kass, has regularly argued along the lines that '[s]eeking to escape entirely from nature (in order to satisfy a natural desire or a natural right to reproduce!) is self-contradictory in theory and self-alienating in practice'. 'The wisdom of repugnance: Why we should ban the cloning of human beings', *New Republic* (1997); 216 (22): 17–26.

embryo,[7] and others – as I have argued – rest on philosophically questionable fears of harm to the resulting children, the expressivist objection raises a concern that transcends political or religious views. What is more, the threat of which it warns is posed not to hypothetical future people, or non-sentient embryos, but to living people with actual rights and interests.

If I am to succeed in showing that a future genetic supermarket does not violate the principle of non-maleficence, then I must consider the possible harms done to people with disabilities, either those who are in existence now, or those who will come into existence despite the presence of GCTs.

Disability-oriented objections to PGD

Not all concerns about the effect of widespread use of GCTs on disabled or ill people are properly regarded as expressivist in character. In fact, it may be the more substantial body of disability-oriented arguments are of a substantially different sort. Before scrutinising the differences, though, it is perhaps informative to consider the common factors shared by all such arguments.

Although they differ in other respects, all the objections considered here proceed on the basis that, however widespread the use of PGD eventually becomes, there will continue to be *some* disabled people in our society. Otherwise, these objections would be meaningless; what would it mean to harm disabled people in a society in which there are no disabled people? Predicting the future is a perilous task, but it is almost impossible to imagine a future society without disability of any sort. For one thing, PGD will not eliminate the possibility of disability through accident (including injuries sustained at birth). Second, it is probably safe to assume that, even as PGD becomes more accurate, it will remain imperfect, meaning that some genetic disabilities will 'slip through the net'.

Perhaps most significantly, it seems highly unlikely that every prospective parent will rush to use PGD, or such other GCTs as become available. A public consultation carried out jointly by the HFEA and the Human Genetics Commission, the results of which were published in November 2001, revealed that 30% of individual respondents were opposed to PGD in general,[8] while eight of the 20 respondents 'who indicated some experience of disability, including carers, families as well as disabled individuals themselves'[9] voiced general opposition. Even in the dystopia of *Gattaca*, where PGD is all but compulsory, some non-conformist parents elect to entrust their children's genes to chance, having what are regarded as 'faith babies'.

---

7   Fukuyama, *Our Posthuman Future*, op. cit., fn 6, p 91.
8   Joint Working Group of the HFEA and Human Genetics Commission, *Outcome of the Public Consultation on Preimplantation Genetic Diagnosis*, November 2001, p 12.
9   Ibid, p 11.

For those who believe human life acquires full moral status at conception, the use of IVF deliberately to create more embryos than will ever become children is itself ethically troubling, irrespective of how the decision is made about which of them to implant. Such people, we can surely presume, will never use PGD technology. Furthermore, some of the very people whose concerns this chapter explores – those disabled people who object to the use of PGD to 'screen out people like them' – may prefer in most cases to entrust the genetic endowment of their own children to chance, or occasionally to make more surprising choices about how to use PGD.

Another common factor among the (otherwise varied) disability-oriented arguments is the belief that a pro-choice approach to PGD will cause harm or offence to those disabled people already alive, or who will be born in the future. This 'harm' may be relative to (a) their present status, (b) the 'able-bodied' population, or (c) some notion of what their status *should* be in a future society; how we respond to such claims may depend very much on which of these adverse comparisons is being postulated.

In other respects, though, the various disability-oriented arguments differ substantially. I have attempted a fairly simplistic division into what I call 'objective' and 'subjective' concerns. It is only the subjective concerns that I refer to as 'expressivist',[10] and it is predominantly with those that I am concerned here. The objective harms, though somewhat more tangible, are – for reasons I will explain – harder to evaluate; all the same, they certainly merit some response, and it is to them that I will first turn.

Objective harms

Probably the most concrete of this class of possible harms relates to the actual impact of widespread GCTs on the status and prospects of the disabled within society. This involves an objective determination – whatever they might think, their position actually *is* made worse. The most straightforward suggestion is that a reduction in the numbers (either absolutely, or as a proportion of the population) of people affected by particular conditions will reduce the perceived importance of finding cures, treatments or ways to improve the lives of those remaining affected people. As regular commentator on disability issues Tom Shakespeare says:

> as a condition becomes rarer, the impetus to discover a cure or treatment diminishes. This reinforces my wider feeling, that genetic screening will never be total, which means that the proportion of congenital impairment may be reduced, but not eliminated, which means that disabled

---

10 Rosamund Scott draws a similar division between disability-oriented arguments; see 'Prenatal Testing, Reproductive Autonomy, and Disability Interests', fn 5.

people will be further isolated, face increasing prejudice, and the pressure to make society accessible to all will be reduced.[11]

This is what Allen Buchanan has deemed the 'loss of support' objection.[12]

Shakespeare offers no empirical evidence in support of this contention, but it seems to me that his thesis is not implausible. Is it, we might reasonably wonder, likely that millions of pounds of research funding would be given over to the investigation of potential treatments for conditions that affect only a handful of people? Is it likely that buildings and buses would have been rendered 'wheelchair accessible' if there were but a few dozen wheelchair users?

It is also possible, though, that in certain practical respects, the position of some existing disabled people (or those who will nonetheless come to exist) may be *improved* by a reduction in the number of similarly affected people. A condition (such as cystic fibrosis) which may require access to kidney dialysis or to organ transplantation will often see affected parties forced to 'compete' with other candidates for scarce resources. Their chances of receiving treatment, we might reasonably expect, will improve in inverse proportion to the number of similarly affected individuals who are also vying for those resources.[13]

Even were we to accept, though, that existing affected people will, on balance, come out worse as a result of the use of GCTs, it isn't entirely obvious how we should respond to this concern. We might consider that the fear of a loss of support to existing disabled people could, and should, be met by guarantees of support, not necessarily by requiring reluctant parents to add to their numbers. Furthermore, as several writers have noted, if the 'loss of support' concern is deemed to outweigh all other concerns or interests, it seems to have implications beyond the issue of genetic testing. After all, reductions in the numbers of disabled persons might be brought about just as

11 Tom Shakespeare, 'Back to the future? New genetics and disabled people', *Critical Social Policy* (1995); 15 (2/3): 22–35, p 31. Susan Wendell has expressed a similar concern in *The Rejected Body: Feminist Philosophical Reflections on Disability*, London: Routledge, 1996, p 54.

12 Allen Buchanan, 'Choosing who will be disabled: genetic intervention and the morality of inclusion', *Social Philosophy & Policy* (1996); 13(1): 18–46, p 21. Laura M Purdy also writes of the notion that 'acting so as to avoid such births will lead us to reduce the social resources now allocated to the disabled'. 'Loving Future People', in Joan C Callahan, (ed), *Reproduction, Ethics and the Law: Feminist Perspectives*, Indiana University Press, 1995, p 312. See also Phillip Kitcher, *The Lives To Come*, London: Allen Lane: The Penguin Press, 1996, p 200.

13 Philip Kitcher offers just such an example, of beta thalassaemia in Cyprus: 'As the incidence of thalassaemia has diminished, help for the afflicted has increased: Because there is now less demand for blood transfusions and other treatments, the lives of thalassaemia sufferers are now better than they were.' *The Lives To Come*, op. cit., p 85.

surely by workplace safety laws[14] and treatments that cure, rather than 'screen out', those affected by disabling conditions.[15] Does the 'loss of support' argument require that we abandon such initiatives and treatments?

In pointing to such extreme (and perhaps absurd) consequences, I don't mean to ridicule or trivialise the concerns that underpin the 'loss of support' position. It is entirely plausible that people affected by uncommon disabilities face all manner of obstacles that would be made easier were there more similarly affected people.[16] But it is surely obligatory to consider whether there are other, less restrictive, ways in which the lot of such people might be improved, before taking the extreme step of abolishing health and safety laws, or requiring reluctant parents to give birth to severely handicapped babies.

Creating a class of 'undeserving disabled'

A slightly different version of the same concern has been expressed by Hans S Reinders, in his book *The Future of the Disabled in Liberal Society*. For Reinders, it is not a question of the decreased size of the disabled population that will constitute a problem for remaining disabled people, but the perception that their existence was a matter of parental choice rather than biological chance:

> Assuming that disabled people will always be among us, that the proliferation of genetic testing will strengthen the perception that the prevention of disability is a matter of responsible reproductive behavior [*sic*], and that society is therefore entitled to hold people personally responsible for having a disabled child, it is not unlikely that political support for the provision of their special needs will erode. If this development takes place, their access to social services, welfare, education, and the labor market will be in danger . . . At any rate, it will be much more in danger than when the general conviction is that disabled people should enjoy these social goods because of the special needs that they have without any fault of their own.[17]

Specifically, Reinders talks of the danger that 'the general attitude will be

14 James Hughes, *Citizen Cyborg: Why Democratic Societies Must Respond to the Redesigned Human of the Future*, Westview Press, 2004, p 144.
15 Buchanan, Brock, Daniels, Wikler, *From Chance to Choice: Genetics and Justice*, New York: Cambridge University Press, 2000, pp 266–9.
16 Buchanan et al point to the example of so-called 'orphan' drugs, ie treatments for conditions so rare that it is not economically viable for pharmaceutical companies to develop or manufacture them. Ibid, p 268.
17 Hans S Reinders, *The Future of the Disabled in Liberal Society: An Ethical Analysis*, Notre Dame, Indiana: University of Notre Dame Press, 2000, pp 14–15.

that people with special needs should be legitimately entitled to social benefits but that it is fair to withdraw such benefits as soon as these special needs are no longer a matter of misfortune but can be attributed to personal responsibility'.[18]

Is it in fact likely that such an attitude will be brought about by the presence of the genetic supermarket? Although I can claim no expertise in social sciences, a couple of reasons occur to me that cause me to doubt Reinders' hypothesis. The first derives from the reasons why we do, or should, provide benefits or assistance for disabled people in the first place, while the second relates to what precisely it is possible for prospective parents to avoid.

The answer to why we think it morally important to devote some resources to those affected by disabilities derives, at least in part, from a notion of justice. As Allen Buchanan says:

> there is an obligation to devote some social resources to preventing or correcting undeserved differences in initial social or natural assets that result in some persons' [sic] suffering significant limitations on their opportunities – limitations so serious as to interfere with their having reasonable prospects for a decent life.[19]

This notion of justice, then, regards it as unfair that anyone should be abandoned to a poorer or more restricted life because of factors that were not the product of their choice or control, be they social, environmental, or genetic. Is this obligation weakened when the disabilities or disadvantages are the product of their own choice? Some commentators certainly think so,[20] though the preponderance of academic bioethical opinion seems to favour the view that, at least regarding the provision of medical treatment, such value judgments are inappropriate.[21]

18 See fn 17, p 79.
19 Allen Buchanan, 'Choosing who will be disabled: genetic intervention and the morality of inclusion', *Social Philosophy & Policy* (1996); 13(1): 18–46, p 25. See also Jonathan Wolff: 'one is responsible for those results of one's freely chosen actions or decisions, but should receive compensation (or pay tax) for the results of bad (good) luck.' 'Tin genes and compensation', in Justine Burley, (ed), *The Genetic Revolution and Human Rights*, Oxford: Oxford University Press, 1999, p 133.
20 See, for example, Moss and Siegler, 'Should alcoholics compete equally for liver transplantation?' *Journal of the American Medical Association* (1991); 265(10): 1295–8; 'Should smokers be offered coronary bypass surgery?', debate in (1993) 306 *BMJ* 1047.
21 Raanan Gillon's position, for example, is 'that patients should be given treatment in relation to their medical need, and that scarce resources should not be prioritised on the basis of a patient's blameworthiness'. 'On giving preference to prior volunteers when allocating organs for transplantation', *Journal of Medical Ethics* (1995); 21: 195–6, p 196. See also Cohen and Benjamin, 'Alcoholics and liver transplantation', *Journal of the American Medical Association* (1991); 265(10): 1299–301. One possible response to the view that individuals should

Perhaps more damaging to the 'argument from responsibility' is the fact that, even were we to adopt a 'tough' stance on self-induced disadvantage or disability, the parties whose choices have 'caused' the disability (or more accurately, allowed it to come into existence) are different people entirely from those who will be affected by it, and who may require assistance in the form of state benefits, medical assistance or whatever else. Even if society came to view the decision to have a 'faith baby' as reckless and irresponsible, it would be unfair and irrational to visit the adverse consequences of such recklessness upon the entirely innocent children themselves. Is it possible that public opinion will follow this unfair and irrational path, will come to resent this 'tax for other people's bad genes',[22] and exert pressure upon their political representatives to withhold or reduce the benefits payable to such children? Perhaps. But the blame for any such attitudes would surely lie with a societal mindset that habitually blamed children for their parents' bad choices, rather than the fact that such choices existed.[23]

The second reason why the 'argument from responsibility' might not constitute a compelling argument in this context derives from the fact that, insofar as it is intelligible to hold individuals responsible for the consequences of their own actions or inactions, it is only logical to do so when there were other alternatives available to them. Hence, it would be intelligible to hold parents responsible for the birth of their 'faith babies' only if the option of screening embryos had been open to them, and they had declined it.

How likely is it that PGD will ever be a practically accessible option for all? On Nozick's approach, certainly, prospective parents will be free from state interference or restriction with such choices, and in that sense PGD will indeed be an option. But, as has been often noted, freedom *from* interference with a choice is not synonymous with freedom *to* act upon that choice. The other side of Nozick's laissez faire approach would, presumably,

---

be left with the consequences of their own choices would ask whether, and to what extent, those 'choices' were themselves the product of factors outwith their control, such as a genetic predisposition to addiction or poor education during childhood.

22 Reinders, *The Future of the Disabled in Liberal Society*, op. cit., fn 17, p 90.

23 Libertarian commentator Hillel Steiner has argued that the genetic revolution 'shifts responsibility from nature to particular persons', specifically to the parents of genetically disadvantaged children insofar as they had it within their power to prevent such disadvantages; thus, in such cases, compensation to the child should be from the negligent parents and not the state. However, even leaving aside the question of whether the parents may possess the means adequately to redress this disadvantage, Steiner concedes that – in view of the Non-Identity Principle – this transfer of responsibility would be appropriate only in cases where gene therapy (which he supposes to be non identity-altering) was available, but not where PGD was declined. 'Silver spoons and golden genes: Talent differentials and distributive justice', in Justine Burley, (ed), *The Genetic Revolution and Human Rights*, Oxford: Oxford University Press, 1999, pp 146–8.

deny that it is the responsibility of the state, or of other people, to provide the means to act upon that choice – what I refer to later as the 'hard' version of the genetic supermarket hypothesis. While the prospect of a pro-choice model in which only 'the rich' have choice presents its own problems (see Chapter 7), it does perhaps provide one possible response to the argument from responsibility: it is illogical and unfair to hold a parent responsible for not utilising PGD when, for reasons of inadequate resources, they could not afford to do so. And, given that this objection is directed at those who will, or whose disabled children will, be reliant upon state benefits, it is perhaps not implausible to imagine that they will not constitute the wealthiest section of society.[24]

Again, it is not my contention that the general public *would* subscribe to such a view; it is always possible that those for whom PGD lies beyond their means would be subjected to a sort of 'double jeopardy', blamed both for their poverty and for the consequences of that poverty. However, we should at least bear in mind that, at least according to the common conception of justice considered later, the attribution of responsibility *should* take note of what was, in reality, possible for the parents of disabled children. If it is reasonable to penalise children for the bad choices of their parents – and I maintain that it is not – then it is at least surely unreasonable to penalise them when any such choices were, in fact, illusory.

Subjective harms: causing disabled people to *feel* devalued

If our concern is instead about how existing disabled persons will feel in the face of this technology, then the measurable impact, in terms of reduction in political strength or public sympathy, may be less relevant than the personal, subjective testimony of actual disabled people. And there exists ample evidence of distress and offence in the face of the perceived message that, as one commentator put it, 'some of us are "too flawed" in our very DNA to exist; we are unworthy of being born'.[25] To evaluate this concern, we must consider who, precisely, it is that is thought to be sending this message. For these purposes, I have considered separately the suggestions that (a) it emanates from parents, and (b) it emanates from 'society'.

---

24 Of course, I recognise that more severely disabled children may require full-time care or assistance, or specialist treatment, which may lie beyond the means of even moderately wealthy families, families for whom PGD would have been affordable. Nonetheless, insofar as this objection derives its emotional force from its seeming concern with the least wealthy, it is worthy of note that they should, by rights, be excluded from any such attribution of 'blame'.

25 Marsha Saxton, 'Disability rights and selective abortion', in Solinger, (ed), *Abortion Wars: A Half Century of Struggle*, Berkeley: University of California Press, 1998, pp 374–93, p 391.

a. By their parents

Marsha Saxton has contributed some obviously deeply personal contributions to several collections on reproductive technologies. In one chapter, she recalls her own first exposure to the choices posed by the existence of prenatal testing:

> I remembered the spina bifida newsletter when I first read about the AFP [alpha-feto protein] test available to detect spina bifida and other neural tube defects. I remember having mixed feelings. Could I choose to abort a baby with my own disability, end the life of someone somehow an even closer kin to me than my own child? . . . Another thought emerged: if this test had been available to my mother I might never have been born.[26]

The last sentence seems to describe psychological anguish arising from a sort of counterfactual parental rejection. If my mother had had the option of this test, Saxton seems to be saying, she would have rejected me.

A similar sense of hurt has been expressed by Deborah Kent, who has written of her disappointment in the face of the reactions from her parents and husband at the prospect of giving birth to a child that shared her genetic blindness:

> I feel that I have failed when I run into jarring reminders that I have not changed their perspective. In those crushing moments I fear that I am not truly accepted after all.[27]

It is not difficult to understand how such a belief – that their very existence was a result only of their parents' lack of choice, and that given that choice they would have been rejected – could be painful to anyone who values their relationship with, and the esteem in which they are held by, their parents. Does this, then, provide a concrete example of harm caused by PGD (or, as in Saxton's scenario, to prenatal tests)?

There are at least three possible responses to the 'rejection' concern that, while not necessarily allaying all of the concern felt by people like Saxton and Kent, at least give pause with regard to the coherence of those concerns, or their direct relevance to a pro-choice approach to PGD. First, it might be pointed out that, in one way or another, most of us owe our existence to the lack of choice open to our ancestors; had sex education, effective

---

26 Marsha Saxton, 'Born and unborn: the implications of reproductive technologies for people with disabilities', in Arditti et al, (eds), *Test-Tube Women: What Future for Motherhood?*, Pandora Press, 1984, p 301.

27 Deborah Kent, 'Somewhere a mockingbird', in Parens and Asch, (eds), *Prenatal Testing and Disability Rights*, Washington, DC: Georgetown University Press, 2000, p 62.

contraception and perhaps the notion of female reproductive autonomy been available to the generations that preceded us, it is more than likely that, somewhere in our genetic lineage, an ancestor would have elected not to have as many children, not to have children at precisely that time, or indeed not to have children at all, with the result that *we* would never have come to exist. Presumably, few of us would consider that this provides a reason for denying those choices to women today.[28]

Should this realisation prove comforting to those who, like Saxton, are concerned about what her mother might have done had prenatal testing been available to her? Perhaps she might retort that, while my ancestors may indeed have elected not to have a child, or another child, or a child at that precise time, they would not have been rejecting *this particular child*, and certainly not on the grounds of certain characteristics that this child possessed. This is the position adopted by Theresa Degener –

> Of course, the non-selective abortion of a pregnancy that was undesired from the start also views the fetus as a burden, but this evaluation is not based on an individual characteristic of the potential child, but on aspects that are unrelated to the fetus, such as the woman's living conditions and the way she wants to lead her life. The special character of selective abortion lies in wanting to opt for a so-called norm(al) child and reject a disabled child.[29]

– and is what Erik Parens and Adrienne Asch have deemed the 'any-particular distinction': while 'most abortions reflect a decision not to bring any fetus to term at this time . . . selective abortions involve a decision not to bring this particular fetus to term because of its traits'.[30]

Are these writers correct to assume, though, that a decision to 'screen out' a disabled embryo is unique in its implicit negative connotations about certain existing children? Are decisions to avoid the birth of a fifth or sixth child, a child born into conditions of poverty, or, as in Parfit's famous example, a child born to a girl too young to look after it properly, devoid of any such connotations? In exactly the same way as, for Saxton, the decision to

---

28 Even more troubling examples exist of choice-denying or even coercive circumstances that gave rise to great lives. The parents of the great abolitionist, Frederick Douglass, were a slave mother and a slave-owning father who may very possibly have raped her. It is surely possible to celebrate Douglass's life while at the same time celebrating that the circumstances that led to his birth will never be repeated.

29 Theresa Degener, 'Female self-determination between feminist claims and "voluntary" eugenics, between "rights" and ethics', *Issues in Reproductive and Genetic Engineering* (1990), 3(2), 87–99, pp 92–3.

30 Erik Parens and Adrienne Asch, 'The disability rights critique of prenatal testing: reflections and recommendations', in Parens and Asch, (eds), *Prenatal Testing and Disability Rights*, Washington, DC: Georgetown University Press, 2000, p 15.

avoid the birth of disabled children constitutes a rejection of, and affront to, existing disabled people, do not these other decisions tacitly imply negative evaluations of children born into large families, into poverty or to young teenaged mothers? Precisely this point is made by James Lindemann Nelson:

> even granting, for sake of argument, that abortion to prevent disability sends a disrespectful message to disabled people, why would abortion on the basis of family size, or poverty, or for any other reason, not send similarly disparaging messages to children of large families, or the poor, or to those who share with the fetus whatever properties that were the basis of the abortion decision?[31]

Those who agree with Saxton, then, must demonstrate why a decision to avoid the birth of a disabled child sends an emotionally harmful message to existing disabled people, while a decision to avoid the birth of a child into difficult social or economic – as opposed to genetic – circumstances does not send an analogous message to poor families, large families or families with very young mothers, all groups who are already, to some extent, the subjects of social stigma.[32]

The second objection takes issue with the assumption that, in opting not to give birth to a disabled child, prospective parents are devaluing life with disability. Hans Reinders has suggested that it is possible for prospective parents to screen out (or abort) an embryo (or fetus) with a particular

---

31 James Lindemann Nelson, 'Prenatal diagnosis, personal identity, and disability', *Kennedy Institute of Ethics Journal* 10.3 (2000) 213–28, p 216.

32 Perhaps the danger of conveying such a negative message to disabled people is more acute in view of the extent to which disabled people have already been devalued, discriminated against and excluded from many aspects of society. It has also been argued (by, among others, an anonymous reviewer of an article I wrote on this subject) that these hardships have led to a shared sense of identity among disabled people, and that it is this identification with other disabled people that renders the expressivist message so hurtful. It would be unsurprising if the history of disabled people has given rise to certain distinct fears and concerns, but nonetheless, Nelson's analogy may not be entirely inaccurate. That poor people have, historically and currently, been excluded from many aspects of society – work places, social clubs, academia, legislature and judiciary – can be demonstrated by reference to any number of sources (see, for example, Gordon Marshall, Adam Swift and Stephen Roberts, *Against the Odds? Social Class and Social Justice in Industrial Societies*, Oxford: Clarendon Press, 1997). Furthermore, that a sense of shared identity has grown up among poor people is, arguably, at least as true as the analogous claim regarding disabled people. That is, such a shared identity does exist, up to a point, and political movements have been built on the basis of the common obstacles they face (including the UK Labour Party), but it is by no means true that all people from economically deprived backgrounds, or with disabilities, regard those factors as being integral to their identities, nor that they feel a sense of community or identity with other poor/disabled people.

condition without making a discriminatory judgment about people with that condition:

> If a couple after having had a prenatal test decides to abort the fetus because it is affected by Down [sic] syndrome, they can justify this decision by referring to what they think they are capable of in raising a family.[33]

As Allen Buchanan notes, there may be a number of reasons why parents wish their children to possess certain traits that do not necessarily presuppose a discriminatory attitude against those who lack them: 'One may wish to avoid serious strains on one's marriage, on one's ability to fulfil responsibilities to one's other children, or on scarce social resources.'[34] Furthermore, prospective parents may simply wish their children to share certain of their own characteristics, perhaps in pursuit of some kind of 'genetic immortality', perhaps because they simply feel that they will be more easily and happily assimilated within the existing familial environment if they do.[35]

I have already mentioned one interesting, though controversial, example of such a desire for similarity, in the well-publicised attempts by Candy McCullough and Sharon Duchesneau to ensure their child was 'deaf like them'.[36] Such attempts did not presuppose a belief that the life of the hearing was in any sense inferior to that of the deaf, merely that their lives are sufficiently different to constitute a barrier to sharing certain of the same experiences as their parents.

Whatever the precise reason, there may be a number of possible explanations for parents preferring a child with certain qualities, none of which involve a generalised assumption of inferiority of those without those qualities. In the case of those traits conventionally regarded as 'disabilities', the reason may simply be a recognition, or belief, that they themselves lack the financial, physical, social or emotional resources necessary to raise such a

---

33 Hans Reinders, *The Future of the Disabled in Liberal Society: An Ethical Analysis*, Notre Dame, Indiana: University of Notre Dame Press, 2000, p 93.

34 Allen Buchanan,. 'Choosing who will be disabled: genetic intervention and the morality of inclusion', *Social Philosophy & Policy* (1996); 13(1): 18–46, p 32. A similar point is made by Bonnie Steinbock in her chapter 'Disability, prenatal testing, and selective abortion', in Parens and Asch, (eds), *Prenatal Testing and Disability Rights*, op. cit., fn 30, p 119.

35 A point of view expressed by Mary Ann Baily, who candidly admits her own unease at the prospect of any future child she bore being co-opted into a 'disability culture' from which she herself was excluded; 'Why I had amniocentesis', in Parens and Asch, (eds), *Prenatal Testing and Disability Rights*, op. cit., fn 30, pp 68–9.

36 M Spriggs, 'Lesbian couple creates a child who is deaf like them', *Journal of Medical Ethics*, Online eCurrent Controversies, 2 May 2002.

child; they may be recognising their own limitations, rather than deeming the child as 'sub-standard' or 'unfit to live'.[37] As Degener notes,

> there is as little harm in wanting to have a nondisabled child as there is in wanting to have a disabled child. . . . It is only when this wish for a nondisabled child is declared universal and it becomes mandatory to resort to supposedly infallible technological means to ensure that it is fulfilled that it becomes a danger and a duty.[38]

The third possible response to Saxton's objection is that, whether or not the choice of PGD is made available to today's potential parents, she will none-theless have to confront the evidently uncomfortable possibility that, had she had a choice, her mother might have opted for an abortion. At most, denying the option of PGD to another generation of potential parents will simply give rise to another generation like Saxton who will wonder, with varying degrees of emotional discomfort, what their parents might have done had they had the choice. After all, we might think, the only way to be *sure* how people really feel is to give them the choice, and see how they act.

b. By 'society'

The view that 'society' is sending a negative message to disabled people is well summarised by Susan Wendell. In *The Rejected Body*, she addresses the issue of prenatal testing, followed by abortion of any fetuses found to be disabled:

> the widespread use of selective abortion to reduce the number of people born with disabilities . . . sends a message to children and adults with disabilities, especially people who have genetic or prenatal disabilities, that 'we do not want any more like you'.[39]

In a similar vein, Reinders observes that:

> it appears as though our society is simultaneously sending two messages to the disabled and their families. The first message says, 'Since you're here, we're going to care for you as best we can,' but the second says, 'But everyone would be better off if you were not here at all'.[40]

---

37 See Nelson, 'Prenatal diagnosis, personal identity, and disability', op. cit., fn 31, pp 215–16. See also Parens and Asch, 'The disability rights critique of prenatal testing', op. cit., fn 30, p 15.
38 See Degener, 'Female self-determination between feminist claims and "voluntary" eugenics, between "rights" and ethics', fn 29, p 95.
39 Susan Wendell, *The Rejected Body: Feminist Philosophical Reflections on Disability*, London: Routledge, 1996, p 153.
40 Reinders, *The Future of the Disabled in Liberal Society*, op. cit., fn 1, p 4.

while Bill Albert of Disabled Peoples' International has argued that 'No one should have to live . . . in a society which values them so little it makes a social and medical virtue out of eliminating people who might be like them'.[41] In this sort of objection, then, the offence arises not so much from the choices parents make, but from the choices society allows, or assists, them to make.

Is it necessarily true, though, that 'screening out' of certain genetic conditions implies a devaluing of *people* with those conditions? Attempts to eliminate smallpox, leprosy, or rickets were not taken to imply that those affected by such conditions were devalued, and it is unlikely that they regarded attempts to eliminate such diseases as offensive. As Reinders says,

> If research to eliminate cancer does not imply an attitude that supports discrimination against persons who suffer from this disease, why should clinical genetics be different?[42]

Reinders calls this the Distinction between the Person and the Condition (DPC) argument, according to which 'The charge of negative evaluation is completely unjustified, therefore. It is based on the false identification of persons with their conditions'.[43]

As he goes on to acknowledge, though, whereas it is possible to destroy cancer cells while leaving alive those persons who were affected by them, the same cannot be said of screening out genetic disorders, where the only means by which the disorder can be avoided necessarily involves 'avoiding' the person as well.[44] In other words, it is not simply the disorder that is being rejected, but the whole package of person-plus-disorder. As Edwards has written,

> That there could be an 'identity constituting' relationship between disability and identity is something which those who dismiss the expressivist objection rarely consider.[45]

---

41 Bill Albert, 'The new genetics and disability rights', Presentation to EU Conference 'Human genetic testing, what implications', Brussels, 6 May 2004, available at http://www.dpi.org/en/resources/topics/bioethics/05–10–04_balbert.htm. See also 'Disabled people speak on the new genetics', DPI Europe Position Statement on Bioethics and Human Rights, available at http://www.dpieurope.org/htm/bioethics/dpsngfullreport.htm; Laura M Purdy, 'Loving future people', in Callahan, (ed), *Reproduction, Ethics and the law: Feminist perspectives*, Indiana University Press, 1995, p 312; Meg Stacey, 'The new genetics: a feminist view', in Marteau and Richards, (eds), *The Troubled Helix*, Cambridge: Cambridge University Press, 1996, p 343.

42 Reinders, *The Future of the Disabled in Liberal Society*, op. cit., fn 1, p 55.

43 Id.

44 Ibid, p 56.

45 S D Edwards, 'Disability, identity and the "expressivist" objection', *Journal of Medical Ethics* (2004); 30: 418–20.

This, perhaps, is distinct from attempts to eliminate somatic (or even treatable genetic) disorders.

Even were we to agree with Edwards about the 'identity constituting relationship between disability and identity', it does not obviously follow that this should be restricted to disability that is genetic in origin. Rather, there is a school of thought that views other conditions, particularly those which act upon the brain, as potentially 'identity defining'. This possibility has at least been seriously considered by a number of bioethicists in relation to conditions such as Alzheimer's disease.[46] Indeed, at least one author would argue that this expressivist objection could be applied to practically any attempt to 'cure' a disabling condition, genetic or otherwise:

> If abortion on the basis of prenatal diagnosis sends a 'we don't want your kind here' message, why would therapeutic interventions not do so as well – and the more successful the therapies are, the more effective the message? ... If testing and abortion militate against social acceptance of disabilities as examples of human variation, why would testing and treating not do so as well?[47]

This is another of the counter-intuitive claims about which I warned at the outset. Anyone who has ever watched someone they cared about succumb to the ravages of dementia would, I am sure, welcome a cure without reservation, and certainly without the sort of existentialist speculation in which I am indulging here.

Yet certain issues in medical law and bioethics have made it impossible to ignore such questions. Suppose I write a document – a 'living will' – setting out my wishes about how I should be treated in the event of my becoming seriously demented. Those wishes include a firm conviction that, in the latter stages of any such disease, my life should not be prolonged by medical intervention. What should happen if the events I have anticipated do indeed come to pass, but it appears that I am quite content in my demented state, blissfully untouched by concerns with autonomy, independence and

---

46 An intriguing discussion of Alzheimer's disease and continuity of identity has centred on the issue of advance directives. See, in particular, Rebecca Dresser, 'Advance directives, self-determination, and personal identity', in Hacker, Moseley and Vawter, (eds), *Advance Directives in Medicine*, New York: Praeger Publishers, 1989, and 'The incompetent patient on the slippery slope', *Hastings Center Report* July–August 1994, 6–12 (with P J Whitehouse). See also Mark Kuczewski, 'Whose will is it, anyway? A discussion of advance directives, personal identity, and consensus in medical ethics', *Bioethics* (1994) 8(1): 27–48; Helga Kuhse, 'Some reflections on the problem of advance directives, personhood and personal identity', *Kennedy Institute of Ethics Journal* (1999) 9(4): 347–64.

47 Nelson, 'Prenatal diagnosis, personal identity, and disability', op. cit., fn 31, p 219. See also Walter Glannon's example of potentially identity-affecting gene therapy, *Genes and Future People: Philosophical Issues in Human Genetics*, Oxford: Westview Press, 2001, pp 81–2.

dignity? Should the living will nonetheless provide a reason not to prolong my life?

For some commentators, the answer to how I should be treated depends on whether the person who wrote the living will, and the contentedly oblivious demented person, is in fact the same person. If so, then we could see the living will as a projection of his competent, considered wishes into a situation of incompetence. But if we think otherwise, if we regard the onset or progression of senility as constituting a radical break in identity, then the living will is better seen as an attempt by one person to make decisions for another.

Perhaps an answer to this question requires us to consider what it is that constitutes identity. In the previous chapter, I looked at the Zygotic Principle, which held that an embryo made up of different gametes would turn into a different person. But it does not follow that who we are is *only* determined by our genes (a view that would, after all, cause all sorts of problems for identical twins!). Instead, we might also regard a number of mental properties as relevant: memories, values, religious or political beliefs, likes and dislikes, ambitions and fears, relationships with other people. I can forget something, or change my mind about someone, or discover a preference for real ale rather than red wine, without feeling that I have become a completely different person. But if *all* of those elements were to change over a short period of time, if the entirety of my personality were to be replaced by something quite different, I should not be surprised if my friends (or the people I *previously* thought of as my friends, as I suppose this would have to change too) began seriously to wonder if they were looking at the same person at all.

On this view, then, a condition that radically altered my personality might be thought to be 'identity defining' just as surely as a different complement of genes. Even without determining precisely *which* disabling conditions might be 'identity defining' in this way, we can at least take seriously the possibility that some – those which impact most severely upon cognitive functioning, awareness of self, memories and aspirations – can be said to come within the ambit of the expressivist objection. A treatment for Alzheimer's disease would result in a society where 'different' people existed than one where Alzheimer's is not cured. If this is true, then attempts to eliminate Alzheimer's may well carry an implicit statement devaluing or rejecting those affected by the disease. Can we therefore conclude that society devalues or disrespects or rejects those with late-stage Alzheimer's?[48]

---

48 Following the logic of the Non-Identity Principle, and assuming that Dresser et al are correct about the discontinuity of identity between those with, and those without, Alzheimer's, a somewhat more alarming prospect arises: that, in attempting to cure Alzheimer's, at least for those in the latter stages of the disease, we would in truth be seeking to replace one – existing – individual with a different, presently merely hypothetical one. If the discontinuity thesis is taken to its logical conclusion, would this amount to 'killing' one human being in order that another might come into existence?

The analogy between genetic screening and attempts to reverse the effects of plausibly identity-defining conditions such as Alzheimer's disease is, it seems, stronger than some exponents of the expressivist objection seem to recognise. If this is so, then if we conclude that genetic screening sends a negative message to existing disabled people, then this must be equally true of existing mentally impaired individuals when we pursue 'cures' for their conditions; 'cures' which, we might well think, would replace them with different persons just as surely as PGD. If, on the other hand, we do not regard these efforts as implicitly devaluing existing mentally impaired individuals, then neither should we regard PGD as implicitly devaluing those affected by genetic disorders.

On this view, then, 'screening out' certain conditions does not, or need not, send out a negative statement to anyone, by anyone, or in any event at least no more so than an attempt to cure a disease such as Alzheimer's. Even if this view is rejected, though, there exist a number of other reasons to doubt that a pro-choice approach to PGD would communicate a negative value judgment to the disabled.

Whether or not the use of PGD/GCTs sends out a negative societal message about disability depends very much on what we understand by 'society'. There are probably many different senses in which we use this term, but two in particular seem relevant to this discussion. First, we might think of 'society' as applying to those people and bodies entrusted, elected or appointed to make decisions in the interests of the populace as a whole, while at the same time presumably safeguarding the rights and interests of minority groups or individuals within that populace; in the United Kingdom, for instance, we might see 'society' as embodied in the decisions of Parliament, of the courts and of the HFEA.

The second sense of 'societal' offence might take an even more direct form, as when individual women or couples made the same sorts of decisions in sufficient numbers to communicate a single message to a particular section of the population – in this case, disabled people. If the majority of women or couples faced with a choice elected to screen for and reject embryos affected with cystic fibrosis, this might be thought to convey a negative message to those living with CF as to how they are viewed by, and the extent to which they are valued or accepted within, the society in which they live.

This latter concern is similar to an objection I looked at earlier. Disability activists like Marsha Saxton already appear (not implausibly) convinced that unrestricted and widespread access to PGD would result in negative judgments about certain traits becoming the norm in practice. Yet if it is this judgment – not by any state or executive agency, court or regulatory body, but by individual potential parents – that is offensive or devaluing to existing disabled persons, then we must ask whether we offer much solace by denying access to the means of implementing or demonstrating that judgment. Presumably some disabled persons will still be aware, or at least highly suspicious, that such attitudes exist, and that the only reason they are not routinely implemented is that 'society' in its other conception – the legislature, the courts and the regulatory bodies – prohibit them from being so.

It is even likely that those denied access to what they now recognise to be a technologically possible option may demonstrate their value judgments in other forms; by lobbying the legislature, for example, or appealing to the courts, writing to newspapers or – as in the case of the Whitaker[49] and Masterton[50] families – travelling to less restrictive jurisdictions to give effect to their choices. Perhaps most straightforwardly, it might be assumed that opinion polls and public consultations will continue to demonstrate wide public sympathy for abortion on the grounds of serious fetal abnormality, and PGD for 'serious inherited conditions'[51] a response that presumably conveys quite unambiguously the sort of value judgment some disabled persons find offensive.

The notion, then, that we could prevent 'society' in the sense of the aggregate of potential parents from communicating negative value judgments by restricting their access to GCTs is conceptually flawed, since it is likely that those values will continue to be expressed in other forms and through other media, and since it is likely that the more sensitive of observers will continue to *suspect* that such values exist in any event. The only way in which 'society' in this sense could avoid the infliction of the offence that lies in the mass rejection of disabled embryos would be by exercising that choice in a manner that does not devalue such embryos. Depriving them of that choice, at best, does no more than mask the offensive judgment, or more accurately – and perhaps more significantly – one of many possible manifestations of that offensive judgment.

What, then, of the role of 'society' in that other sense, as embodied in the decisions, permissions and proscriptions of its decision-making bodies? Here, the response offered to the first sense of 'societal' criticism seems less valid. I have suggested that a ban on certain uses of PGD may do little to reassure disabled persons that they are not being devalued by the 'community of potential parents', since the only thing preventing them from acting according to those judgments is a system of legal restriction. Presumably, though, the same thing cannot be said of the authors of these very restrictions. If

49 R Dobson, ' "Saviour sibling" is born after embryo selection in the United States', *British Medical Journal* (2003); 326: 1416 (28 June).

50 'Because sex selection is banned in Britain, the couple paid an Italian clinic £30,000 for three attempts to conceive a girl but none was successful.' 'Couple abandon battle for baby of their choice', *The Sunday Times*, 23 January 2005.

51 Approximately 69% of respondents to the HGC/HFEA Public Consultation on PGD agreed that PGD should be available only where there is a known family history of serious genetic disorder or to cases of aneuploidy. 'Analysis of the Responses to the Joint HFEA/ACGT Consultation Paper on PGD', para 16.

lawmakers elect to draw a line, permitting PGD for certain genetic traits or conditions but not for others, it is easy to see how this could be seen as a value judgment as between those traits or conditions. As Parens and Asch have said:

> Enlisting medical professionals to list the conditions approved for tests and exclude others as 'not serious enough or burdensome enough' turns individual, private, parental decisions into socially supported ones. Also, it increases the likelihood that an explicitly devaluing message will be sent about people whose conditions are listed as 'serious enough to avoid'.[52]

At present, the HFEA allows PGD for the purpose of avoiding cystic fibrosis, but refuses to allow it for, say, avoiding a child with brown rather than blue eyes. Assuming that the debit side of the equation – the reasons *against* allowing PGD, such as the intrinsic value attributed to the embryo, or the dangers inherent in the procedure – remain constant in both decisions, the justification for the differing response to these two uses of PGD must reflect a particular judgment as to the desirability of avoiding, respectively, children with CF and children with blue eyes. This judgment may rely on beliefs about the burdens such children may themselves experience, the burdens their births will impose on their parents, or the contribution they will be able to make to their 'society', but it seems that some such belief is implicit in this act of line-drawing; and it is precisely in such beliefs that commentators like Saxton and Wendell discern an offensive message.

Suppose, though, that the role of 'society' (as embodied in the legislature or the HFEA) in the decision of which traits to 'screen out' was wholly value neutral; that is, if the choice were entirely that of the prospective parents. In such a circumstance, we could reasonably say that 'society' sends no message to anyone, beyond the message that it is willing to respect the individual choice of individual potential parents in such matters. (The question of the extent to which it should adopt a facilitative or enabling role, providing the means for prospective parents to make such decisions, is an important one, and I will consider it in Chapter 7.)

Is the role of society in such decisions really as passive as this contention seems to require? Well, at present, this is certainly not the case in the UK, where the availability of PGD is strictly curtailed by the terms of the Human Fertilisation and Embryology Act, and by the requirement of licensing by the Human Fertilisation and Embryology Authority. PGD is available only for those traits the Authority permits, and so far it has sought to restrict this to those likely to pose 'a significant risk of a serious genetic condition being

---

52 Parens and Asch, 'The disability rights critique of prenatal testing: reflections and recommendations', op. cit., fn 30, pp 30–1.

present in the embryo'.[53] Furthermore, it has explicitly excluded screening on the grounds of embryonic sex and – initially – for HLA compatibility alone.

What message does the Authority send out when it restricts the use of PGD in such a manner? All other considerations aside, it assuredly sends the signal that choices about PGD are not wholly private matters, to be arrived at by the prospective parents alone. As Reinders has said:

> Society does not allow us absolute freedom in any area of social life. . . . Free choice, therefore, is always restricted to publicly acceptable uses of freedom. . . . Consequently, if society accepts the prevention of disability as justified, it is because and only because it is regarded as a legitimate use of personal freedom. . . .[54]

PGD, then, will be permitted only where there is a sufficiently compelling justification. But it is important to consider the possible implication of restricting PGD to 'serious genetic condition[s]'. If there is merit in the objection that 'society' sends out negative signals to disabled persons when it allows prospective parents to screen them out of existence, then how much reinforced is that message when 'society' expressly prohibits every other kind of screening?

I will take a closer look at the HFEA's approach to tissue typing in the next chapter. For now, though, it is worth noting that the HFEA clearly regarded the use of PGD in the Hashmi case as being for the benefit of the future child; were this not so, then the fact that its use by the Whitakers would *not* benefit their future child would not amount to a significant distinction. Given that there was no prospect of curing beta thalassaemia, this could only be taken to mean that the potential future Hashmi child possessed some kind of interest in avoiding being born with the burden of this disease. Yet what message does this decision send to Zain Hashmi, or to others who live every day with that same illness? A clearer example of PGD sending a societal message that 'it would have been better had you not been born' would be hard to find.

If, in contrast, Parliament and/or the Authority were to permit any prospective parents to screen for *any* trait, whether or not it is associated with what is conventionally seen as a 'disability', then it would be possible to argue that the value 'society' is upholding is that of reproductive choice, whatever that choice may be. With regard to the specific traits that prospective parents might desire or reject, they could with some plausibility argue that they are entirely neutral; it would, after all, be difficult to argue that 'society' was

---

53 Joint Working Group of the HFEA and Human Genetics Commission, *Outcome of the Public Consultation on Preimplantation Genetic Diagnosis*, November 2001, Recommendation 11.
54 See Reinders, *The Future of the Disabled in Liberal Society*, op. cit., fn 1, p 64.

implicitly devaluing the 'disabled' if it allowed couples like Duchesneau and McCullough to select genetically deaf embryos for implantation.

Clinical geneticist Angus Clarke espoused what is probably the orthodox line with regard to PGD when he wrote that 'society must determine what types of disorder are sufficiently severe to warrant prenatal-screening programmes with the termination of "affected" pregnancies'.[55] However, in allowing screening only to eliminate conditions deemed 'sufficiently severe', it may be that some validity is accorded to the arguments of those who, like Marsha Saxton, feel that their society is making a statement that they are unwanted. The state's acceptance of PGD to screen out CF, Duchenne muscular dystrophy or beta thalassaemia embryos would, perhaps, seem less value-laden, less offensive, perhaps even less sinister to those living with such conditions were it also to accept the use of PGD to screen out embryos who had blue eyes, who were boys, or who had normal hearing, however much media hysteria was generated by such choices.[56]

The media response generated by the HFEA's 2005 consultation on genetic testing for cancer genes was predictable in its hyperbole, and it was not long before allusions were being made to 'eugenics'. But while it might be thought that an analogy between an optional test such as this, and the coercive measures that accompanied the worst excesses of the eugenics movement, is somewhat strained, there is a sense in which the UK's present approach to PGD might be thought eugenic in character. When law and policy restrict the use of PGD to the avoidance of children with genetic defects, denying it to those with other values and priorities, it becomes at least arguable that our approach to this technology, far from being driven by an agenda of promoting individual choice and respecting diversity, is underpinned by judgments about the value of those lives that are avoided. It is scarcely surprising if those affected by genetic illnesses or disabilities, or those who care about or for such people, look with some offence and suspicion at those laws and policies.

I think we should seriously consider, though, that their concerns could better be addressed by loosening the regulations applicable to PGD, thereby

---

55 Angus Clarke, 'Response to: "What counts as success in genetic counselling?" ', *Journal of Medical Ethics* (1993); 19: 47–9, p 48. See also Jeffrey R Botkin: 'As the range of conditions for which we can test prenatally expands, society and the medical profession need to develop guidelines about which tests ought to be offered and which ought not to be.' 'Fetal privacy and confidentiality', *Hastings Center Report* (1995); 25(5): 32–9, p 32.

56 It could be suggested that any ostensibly value-free approach would in reality be undermined by the fact that the overwhelming majority of PGD-users would in fact use it to screen out 'disabilities' and not more 'frivolous' traits, still less to use it to screen *for* disability. My suggestion is that this need not undermine a genuine claim of state neutrality, any more than the constitutional commitments of the USA to neutrality on the question of religion are undermined by the fact that, in practice, a substantial majority of their citizens use, and have always used, that freedom to practise as Christians.

allowing those like Sharon Duchesneau and Candy McCullough, Alan and Louise Masterton, Michelle and Jayson Whitaker or any other prospective parents to utilise this technology to implement their own values and preferences. In so doing, we might avoid the imposition by the state of a single, simplistic view of what constitutes 'normality' and 'disability', a view that is clearly not universally shared. The appropriate response – from the state, from the public, and from the Authority itself – to the HFEA's question about the desirability of testing for cancer genes should be: 'We hold no view on this, other than that prospective parents should be permitted to make informed choices for themselves, free from coercion, and safe in the knowledge that whatever choice they make will be respected and supported.' Nothing, I submit, could be further removed from the pernicious taint of eugenics.

The need for line-drawing?

A value-neutral approach to GCTs, then, could circumvent at least some expressivist objections. Does such an approach, though, require that all potential parents have access to all possible preimplantation tests? And if not, how might a line be drawn between those which are available and those which are not?

Jeffrey Botkin is one of the few authors to have not only attempted to make the case for line-drawing in preimplantation and (particularly) prenatal testing, but to demonstrate where, or at least on what basis, such lines might be drawn. In a series of articles,[57] he has set out the case for setting limits on the range of genetic traits for which testing should be available, according to both practical and ethical considerations. The practical aspect of his argument relies on the prediction that, as information about genetics expands, so to will the range of possible tests which might be carried out on an embryo's genome, expanding perhaps to encompass thousands of traits of varying degrees of rarity, and thousands of tests with varying degrees of accuracy. How, Botkin asks, is it 'remotely feasible' for a doctor or genetic counsellor to have a 'meaningful conversation' with a pregnant, or prospectively pregnant, woman about 'thousands of rare conditions'?[58]

On Botkin's model, the line between those tests which would be 'available', and those which would not should be drawn according to two criteria: 'risk' and 'value'. Risk would reflect the likelihood of the trait which the test is intended to detect actually existing; for Botkin, the cut-off point might be

---

57 'Fetal privacy and confidentiality', *Hastings Center Report* (1995); 25(5): 32–9; 'Line drawing: Developing professional standards for prenatal diagnostic services', in Parens and Asch, (eds), *Prenatal Testing and Disability Rights*, op. cit., fn 30, pp 288–307; 'Prenatal diagnosis and the selection of children', *Florida State University Law Review* (2003); 30: 265–93.
58 'Line drawing: Developing professional standards for prenatal diagnostic services', loc. cit., p 295.

where there is 'a prevalence of less than one in a thousand or one in ten thousand births . . . below which physicians need not offer prenatal testing for the condition as standard care'.[59]

The second criterion employed by Botkin in his line-drawing exercise is 'value', that is, the impact a given condition will have on 'family life'.[60] Impact, he suggests, can be measured in terms of four characteristics: 'the likely severity of the condition with respect to health', 'the age of onset of the condition', 'the probability that the child's genotype will manifest as a significant clinical disease' and 'the probability that the condition will occur in those without specific risk factors'.[61]

It is in this attempt at value-based line-drawing that Botkin, as he acknowledges, runs into difficulties; first with relevance to the lack of consensus on the relative 'severity' of various traits. Although he is doubtless correct in his observation that certain conditions, such as Tay-Sachs, would be regarded as very severe by almost anyone familiar with their symptoms, identifying one extreme does not provide much assistance with drawing lines.

In attempting this line-drawing, Botkin attempts to draw analogies between the burdens imposed by unwanted children and by disabled children. If, he argues, we allow abortion on 'social' grounds where women are too young, or too poor, or simply too reluctant to bear these children, then the cut-off point for allowing genetic testing should be where the disability in question would impose 'problems for the parents of a similar magnitude to the birth of an unwanted child'.[62] Which genetic conditions, he enquires, would be approximately as burdensome on a family as an unplanned and unwanted child?

Specifically, he identifies 'conditions that are often fatal in childhood', 'conditions that result in a child who is chronically ill or who has recurrent illnesses of sufficient gravity to require repeated hospitalization', 'conditions that will not permit the child to achieve independence in his or her adult years' and 'disabilities of such severity that there are constant demands on the parents for time, effort, and financial resources'.[63] He would exclude,

---

59 See fn 58, p 297.
60 Note that Botkin's approach is concerned primarily with prenatal testing, and hence, his approach is premised substantially upon an analogy with abortion for 'social' reasons. Thus, he asks not just how the condition will impact upon the child – as he points out, conditions such as anencephaly or Down's syndrome may not be 'bad' for the child – but whether and to what extent it will harm the family.
61 Botkin, 'Fetal privacy and confidentiality', fn 57, p 37.
62 Id.
63 Id. Botkin then goes on to enumerate specific genetic conditions that he believes meet his criteria, including 'hemophilia, Down [sic] syndrome, sickle cell anemia, Menkes syndrome, Fanconi's syndrome, fragile X syndrome, muscular dystrophy, osteogenesis imperfecta, Hurler's syndrome, cystic fibrosis, Tay Sachs disease, many cases of spina bifida, and many inborn errors of metabolism. The burdens of these conditions for the parents are roughly

however, 'any condition affecting children that can be cured or effectively treated so that the affected individual does not experience significant mental or physical impairments and in which the cure or treatment does not cause a serious financial burden to the family';[64] 'those conditions affecting children that may not be amenable to cure or effective treatment, but for which some treatments may be available or the conditions usually have a limited impact on the life of the child and family in terms of effort, time, and financial resources';[65] and 'those conditions that do not affect children'.[66]

Assuming that Botkin's prediction turns out to be accurate, and it does become possible to test for thousands of traits, what implications might this have for the genetic supermarket hypothesis? Would it in fact necessitate an exercise in line-drawing? At different points in his argument, Botkin seems to offer at least two different, and potentially mutually irreconcilable, answers to the question of why there is a need for line-drawing at all. On the one hand, he appears to argue that prenatal testing is inherently ethically problematic and therefore in need of justification. At one point, he contends that 'the knowledge that our parents fashioned us to their liking' is potentially harmful, offending against 'a personal sense of independence and individuality'.[67] He goes on to argue that 'other values, such as respect for prenatal life' must be weighed in the balance against 'the welfare of prospective parents'.[68]

In Chapters 3 and 4, I looked at these sorts of objections to the genetic supermarket hypothesis, and suggested that they might not be especially compelling. But if these do constitute genuine (or plausibly likely) harms, then it would be entirely right to argue that a weighty case must be made out for permitting genetic testing, and it may well be correct to argue that some tests would outweigh this harm while others might not. At other points in this chapter, though, Botkin himself seems to take the view that these are not sufficiently weighty harms to require a prohibition of those tests which do not meet his criteria, but merely that tests for these 'below the line' conditions should not be *required*. In the final paragraph of his conclusions, he says the following:

similar, if not much greater, than the burdens of an unwanted child in terms of the effort, time, and financial resources necessary to care for these children, not to mention the tragic early deaths caused by some of these diseases' (p 38).

64 'Examples would include PKU, galactosemia, polydactaly, hypothyroidism, most cases of asthma, and cleft lip and palate' (p 38).

65 'Examples include G6PD deficiency, many of the thalassemias, Tourette [*sic*] syndrome, spherocytosis, Marfan syndrome, and icthyosis vulgaris.' Id.

66 '. . . including Huntington disease, polycystic kidney disease, and many of the hereditary predispositions to cancer, such as those secondary to the BRCA1 gene.'

67 'Line drawing: Developing professional standards for prenatal diagnostic services', fn 57, p 302.

68 Id.

My conception of a line corresponds to a professional standard of care, not legal prohibitions on the provision of services. . . . Practitioners could choose not to conform to the standard, by offering either more or less testing than the standard (although they could be held legally liable through wrongful birth suits for failure to provide sufficient information).[69]

Yet if Botkin's argument is that line-drawing is required because the harms inherent on below-the-line tests require to be outweighed by competing harms, it is difficult to see why the provision of such tests should be at the discretion of practitioners.

Considerably more plausible, I think, is his claim that it is impractical to provide all possible tests, or even information about all possible tests, to all prospective parents. If his prediction is accurate, and it does in future become possible to test for thousands of conditions, is it necessary to allow access to every possible test to every prospective parent?

The answer to this question depends very much on what, precisely, it is asking. If the question is whether the state (in the form of the criminal law and licensing bodies like the HFEA) should *restrict* access to PGD, then I have already suggested that no such restrictions (subject to a very few rare exceptions) are justified. If, on the other hand, it is asking whether the state (for example, via the auspices of the NHS) should be subject to a *positive* obligation to provide access to PGD, even for incredibly rare conditions (where there is no reason to suspect heightened susceptibility) or 'flippant' choices, then two distinct options arise. The first is what we might refer to as a 'hard' conception of the genetic supermarket. This would propose that, while potential parents could avail themselves of whatever tests they wished, free from state interference, access to such tests would not be provided for them by the state. If the state will not pay for *any* PGD, then we need not concern ourselves with the task of specifying *which* tests it will provide.

On an alternative, 'soft' conception of the genetic supermarket hypothesis, the state's obligation would not only be negative – to refrain from interference – but positive – to provide the means to act on those choices. Assuming that neither the public will nor the practical means would provide access by *anyone* to *any* possible test, such a model would necessitate an exercise in line-drawing akin to that attempted by Botkin. As such, it would leave itself open to two charges. First, we might think that any such lines would, in the absence of any consensus as to 'severity', be arbitrary. While the other three of his criteria rely on objective judgments (though we might question the accuracy with which they can presently be made), 'severity' denotes a subjective value judgment, about a matter on which there is no underlying agreement within

69 See fn 57, p 306.

the medical profession or among those affected by those conditions or their families or carers.

Botkin seeks to circumvent this absence of consensus by relying on what most parents might be assumed to deem intolerably burdensome; his line will reflect 'prudent standards of care', and not the 'idiosyncratic or highly subjective expectations'[70] of a few parents. Yet there is reason to doubt any generalisation as to the extent of the familial burden imposed by a particular condition. Philip M Ferguson, Alan Gartner and Dorothy K Lipsky, writing in the same collection as Botkin, refer to research that casts serious doubt on widespread assumptions about how disabled children impact upon pre-existing families, while several authors – including Deborah Kent, Alison Davies and Hans Reinders – have pointed to the disjunction between the perception of life with a given disability shared by those with direct experience of it, and the perception held by the public at large. For such writers, it seems likely that Botkin's line would be set at too low a level, designating some conditions 'sufficiently severe' which, they would argue, are entirely compatible with a good standard of life, both for the affected child and the family into which it is born.

On the other hand, as we saw in Chapter 3, bioethicists like John Harris and Julian Savulescu argue for an ethical obligation to avoid, as far as is possible, any condition which would 'harm' a future child. For such influential academics, it would seem that Botkin's line would be set too high, excluding a great many harmful conditions.

And then there are those potential parents who actively seek children who would, on Botkin's analysis, fall on that side of the line for which testing should be available. What of the couple of very restricted height who wish to avoid the birth of a child who will soon grow big enough to present practical problems for their domestic arrangements?

A 'soft' conception of the genetic supermarket, then, where the choices of prospective parents would not only be permitted but would be funded by the state, would necessitate an exercise that would certainly not please all interested parties, and would inevitably be open to the charge of arbitrariness. Furthermore, such an exercise would expose the line-drawers (presumably the HFEA or some similar body) to exactly the expressivist critique that I have been trying to find a way around.

There is one more sense in which the question of whether lines are needed might be interpreted. This would see it as asking which tests should be routinely offered by practitioners, in the sense of informing prospective parents as to their availability. The question is really asking: do the dictates of good clinical practice require that practitioners alert their patients to options which may be available privately, but which will not be provided by

70 'Fetal privacy and confidentiality', op. cit., fn 57, p 37.

the NHS? Is it even possible that a practitioner who fails to inform a prospective parent of her options in terms of self-funded PGD may leave himself exposed to a delictual claim, either in negligence or for 'wrongful birth'?

Sex selection

Disabled people are not the only third parties who might be harmed by private use of GCTs. Among the most widely publicised – and widely feared – potential applications of such technologies is the opportunity to select children's sex. This possibility has formed the basis for numerous ethical evaluations, some of which are considered here, but has recently been given a more immediate concern by the attempt by Alan and Louise Masterton to secure access to this technology.[71]

In Chapter 2, I explained that the Mastertons, having lost their only daughter, sought to use PGD to ensure that their next child was a girl (they also had four sons). In that chapter, I also argued that the Mastertons had a strong (reproductive) liberty interest in being allowed to deal with their loss, and to plan their reproductive future, as they best saw fit; the challenge for those who would prevent them is to demonstrate some harm that would result, or some other important ethical principle that would be violated, by their choice.

However, the Mastertons' attempts to choose the sex of their next (and last) child faced an immediate problem. Since 1993, the HFEA had instructed licensed providers of infertility treatment that they 'should not select the sex of embryos for social reasons',[72] a position it has recently reiterated in its response to a consultation process on sex selection.[73] Why, though, did the Authority reach this decision?

In this section, I will consider some such arguments against a pro-choice approach to sex selection. Although many such arguments have been put forward, it is questionable whether they are in fact of sufficient weight and sufficient intellectual rigour to tip the scales against reproductive autonomy. Yet the flawed case against choice has been accepted whole-heartedly – and largely unanimously – by the regulatory community in the UK.

---

71 'Baby sex choice couple speak out', BBC Online, Monday, 13 March 2000, 18:03 GMT http://news.bbc.co.uk/1/hi/scotland/675652.stm. See Chapter 2.

72 Open letter to Parliamentary Under-secretary of State, 15 July 1993. See also HFEA Code of Practice, fifth edn, March 2001, para 9.9.

73 'Sex selection for non-medical reasons should not be permitted', in *Sex Selection: Report Summary*, key HFEA recommendations, available at http://www.hfea.gov.uk/AboutHFEA/Consultations/Final%20sex%20selection%20summary.pdf

Sex discrimination

The danger of sex discrimination was outlined in the Consultation Document in the following terms:

> To permit sex selection for non-medical reasons is implicitly to condone sex discrimination – for example, the kind of discrimination whereby male children are favoured heirs when questions of inheritance are considered.[74]

Assuming for the moment that the designation of such choices as sexist is reasonable, does this render them harmful? While sexist choices might be thought to be inherently objectionable, can they be said to harm anyone? Mary Anne Warren certainly regarded the inherent sexism in the choice as giving rise to nonconsequentialist, rather than harm-based objections.[75] Other writers, though, have argued that sex selection, at least for sexist reasons, can be harmful either to the child born or to women in general. Their arguments, it seems, are rather similar to some of those concerned about harms to disabled people. Helen Bequaert Holmes has claimed that such actions can result in '[s]tereotypes about the sexes becom[ing] more firmly ingrained',[76] while Michael Bayles has argued that the practice of sex selection for sexist reasons 'would probably reinforce sexist attitudes both in those who practice it and in others'.[77]

It is easy to understand the view that such choices reflect sexist attitudes. Why would parents go so far as to reject otherwise healthy embryos on the grounds of sex if they did not hold a marked preference for children of one sex or the other? And is such a belief not, by definition, sexist? On closer inspection, though, it is not so clear that sex selection for family balancing – that is, its use by a family who already have a child, or children, of one sex, and who now want a child of the other sex – invariably denotes such a preference. The Mastertons, after all, have four sons whom they profess to love dearly; their desire for a daughter *as well* surely does not imply a preference for girls over boys. Hence, Savulescu and Dahl have argued:

> Since their choice is simply based on the gender of already existing children, and not on the absurd assumption that one sex is 'superior' to

74 Consultation paper, para 81.

75 Mary Anne Warren, *Gendercide: The Implications of Sex Selection*, New Jersey: Rowman and Allanheld, 1985, pp 83–6.

76 Holmes, 'Choosing children's sex', see fn 88, p 167.

77 Michael Bayles, *Reproductive Ethics*, New Jersey: Prentice-Hall, Inc, 1984, p 36. See also Buchanan, Brock, Daniels and Wikler, *From Chance to Choice*, op. cit., fn 15, p 184: 'The practice depends on and reinforces a systematic bias against women. That bias is indefensible on grounds of justice and works in various ways to produce injustice against women.'

another, the claim that these couples are making a sexist choice is an unjustified accusation.[78]

Nonetheless, it may be thought that the use of sex selection for family balancing still reflects sexist attitudes. As the HFEA Consultation Paper put it, 'it is liable to involve the imposition of stereotypical gender roles on a child of the "right" sex who has been born by this technique'.[79] A similar argument has been advanced by Wertz and Fletcher:

> Even in the US where most couples desire to have one child of each sex, there are preferences for boys. Even if the selection were in favor of girls, however, the fact remains that sex selection is inherently sexist because it is premised upon a belief in sexual inequality.[80]

We might, then, recognise that the Mastertons do not prefer girls to boys, but still want to know what they mean when they speak of restoring 'the female element' to their family. Does this statement not reflect an inherently sexist view that a girl child, whatever her individual characteristics, will bear similarities to Nicole that set her apart from her brothers?[81]

There could, in fact, be two objectionable aspects of a choice underpinned by such beliefs. First, there is the danger that preconceptions about 'how girls are' will impact badly on the new child, perhaps by constraining her life choices according to her parents' preconceived notions about how a girl should behave.[82] It might also be thought that the child may sustain psychological or emotional harm when it learns that it was selected for sex.[83]

Such a suggestion may be far from implausible. For decades, it has been known that, from infancy, how children – 'normal', non-sex selected children – are treated depends substantially on their gender, or on which gender they are perceived to be. One of the most famous demonstrations of the latter was in the oft-cited Jack-in-the-box experiment.[84] This gauged the responses of a selection of adult observers to the perceived emotional responses of young

78 Julian Savulescu and Edgar Dahl, 'Sex selection and preimplantation diagnosis: A response to the Ethics Committee of the American Society of Reproductive Medicine', *Human Reproduction* (2000); 15(9): 1879–80, p 1880.
79 Consultation paper, para 97.
80 Dorothy C Wertz and John C Fletcher. 'Fatal knowledge? Prenatal diagnosis and sex selection', *Hastings Center Report*, May/June 1989, 21–7, p 22.
81 A similar point is made by Bayles, *Reproductive Ethics*, op. cit., fn 77, p 35. See also Buchanan, Brock, Daniels and Wikler, *From Chance to Choice*, op. cit., fn 15, p 184.
82 John A Robertson, 'Preconception gender selection', *The American Journal of Bioethics Online*, Winter 2001, 1(1): 2–9, p 4.
83 Consultation paper, para 89.
84 J Condry and S Condry, 'Sex differences: A study of the eye of the beholder', *Child Development* (1976); 47: 812–19.

children to a startling stimulus (a Jack-in-the box). The study famously revealed that the same response was typically deemed to be 'fear' when the child in question was believed to be female, and 'anger' when it was believed to be male.[85]

Such preconceived attitudes, whether conscious or subconscious, are often thought to characterise parents' relations with their children. Furthermore, in those cases where prospective parents have gone to such lengths as to seek out, and perhaps pay for, sex selection, we might perhaps expect that such attitudes already exist. If this is so, then *whatever* child that is born to such parents will be subject to these attitudes, and whatever harms may be thought to accompany them; the harms, then, will eventuate irrespective of whether they are permitted or prohibited from using sex selection technologies.

To a large extent, these potential harms might be analogous with those arising from heightened parental expectations more generally. In Chapters 3 and 4, I argued that any harm arising from such unfair expectations or con-straints would be unlikely to be *harms on balance*, that is, harms so severe that a proportionate step would be to prevent the child's birth altogether. To deny access to these technologies to parents like the Mastertons would be impli-citly to proclaim that, for such children, the benefits of existence would not outweigh the disadvantages of a sexist environment. I suggested earlier that this was an unpersuasive conclusion, and I think the same can be said here.

If sex selection is not bad for particular children, then, what of the notion that they are potentially harmful to women in general, that – as Holmes, Bayles, and others have argued – they do not only passively reflect but *actively reinforce* sexist attitudes within society? The precise mechanism by which such reinforcement might take place is not examined by any of its proponents cited above, but we might think that a societal context in which sexist choices were common, well publicised and permitted would encourage sexist attitudes in others.

Such a concern might be thought to bear similarities to the expressivist concerns I considered earlier, the difference being that in this case the pre-conceived prejudicial attitudes are against women (or less commonly, men) rather than those characterised as 'disabled'. They are also subject to some similar responses. In much the same way as it is possible to wish to avoid the birth of a disabled baby without harbouring negative opinions about disabled people per se, so too can it be argued that sex selection of one's offspring need not be a manifestation of negative attitudes towards one or other sex. Just as deaf parents may wish to have a child that will share in their experience of a deaf life, Mary Anne Warren has observed that women may have a rational reason for preferring daughters:

---

85 The children were dressed either in pink or blue, but this did not, contrary to the expectations of the observers, correspond to their actual gender.

A son might be able to share most of their particular interests and activities, but he could not share the basic experience of being female in a
society which still values males more highly. However much he may sym-
pathize with the plight of women, he will still be a member of the more
privileged sex.[86]

Such a choice, then, will not be inherently sexist, but will rather be a rational
response to an already heavily gendered society. In other societies, Warren
notes, the pre-existing sexism could lead women in the other direction: in a
society that favours boys and men, a woman who wishes the best for her child
may well try to ensure that child is male. Whatever difficulty we would find in
reconciling such an attempt with the Non-Identity Principle, it would, Warren maintains, be unfair to blame women for contributing to the sexism that
characterises that society when they are in reality merely trying to make the
best they can of life within its confines:

> So long as these many forms of oppression persist, it is absurd to suggest
> that women are guilty of sexism if they wish to have male children in order
> that the latter may enjoy the freedoms which women are still denied.[87]

The apportionment of blame, however, does not necessarily answer the consequentialist question of whether such a choice is potentially harmful. We
may understand and sympathise with the motivations of women who make
such decisions within a context that was not of their making, while still
recognising that '[e]ach act of son-preference . . . further devalues women as a
class'.[88] However, it is as well to keep in mind that, in such contexts, prohibition of sex selection may be inflicting non-trivial harms on the women who
seek to avail themselves of this technology.

Ruth Macklin's interviews with Indian women led her to conclude that,
whatever the ethical problems with sex selection as practised there, 'to prohibit it by law is probably causing more harm than good to the very people
it seeks to protect – members of the female sex'.[89] In the absence of any
prospect of instantly reversing centuries of entrenched sexism, Macklin
maintains, the choice is between, on the one hand, allowing the use of sex
selection, and on the other, further limiting the already narrow range of
choices open to such women, and in so doing forcing them to accept the

---

86 Warren, *Gendercide*, op. cit., fn 75, p 87.
87 Id.
88 Helen Bequaert Holmes, 'Choosing children's sex: Challenges to feminist ethics', from Joan
    C Callahan, (ed), *Reproduction, Ethics and the Law: Feminist Perspectives*, Indiana University
    Press, 1995, p 167.
89 Ruth Macklin, *Against Relativism: Cultural Diversity and the Search for Ethical Universals in
    Medicine*, Oxford: Oxford University Press, 1999, p 154.

inevitable social stigma (and sometimes ostracisation and even violence) attendant on the failure to produce a son. In such circumstances, she concluded, the greater of the two evils lies in martyring actual, existing women on the altar of western egalitarian values.[90]

Furthermore, the potential harm to 'women as a class' seems to rely on the assumption that sex selection will be used predominantly to choose boy rather than girl children; without this assumption, it is impossible to see how the technique could be regarded as devaluing women. If such a belief transpired to be well founded, then it may be that other, more concrete harms could result from the inevitable distortion of demographic trends. It is to this possibility that I now turn.

Demographic distortions

Is it likely that preimplantation sex selection would result in a skewing of the balance between males and females? And if it did, would this be harmful? The former assumption certainly seems to underpin many feminist critiques of sex selection.[91] In fact, the available evidence, inconclusive though it is, suggests that such a fear may be exaggerated. First, though, to the question of whether, and why, a society with more males than females would be something to be concerned about.

Perhaps the most controversial claim has been that a society with significantly more males than females is likely to be more aggressive and violent. This belief may derive either from a perception that males are inherently more violent than females, or a perception that the relative absence of women would lead to tensions among (particularly) young men who would become rivals for the attentions of the relatively scarce available women.

Whether societies with majority male populations are indeed more violent is a complex sociological question, and any answer to it must take account of myriad variables over and above gender ratios. Furthermore, as Warren has pointed out, we must be wary of overly rash assumptions about the causal relationship between the trends:

> Where there is an association between the two phenomena, it is at least as likely that the violence of the society contributes to son-preference and the consequent high sex ratios than the reverse. The American and

---

90 See also Warren, *Gendercide*, op. cit., fn 75, pp 196–7.
91 'Few doubt that if sex selection were cheap and effective, many more males than females would be born.' Helen Bequaert Holmes, 'Choosing children's sex', fn 88, p 152. More emotive is Robyn Rowland's claim that sex selection technology 'could mean the death of the female'. 'Motherhood, patriarchal power, alienation and the issue of "choice" in sex preselection', from Gena Corea et al, (eds), *Man-Made Women*, Bloomington: Indiana University Press, 1987, p 75.

Australian frontiers were probably not violent because of the scarcity of women. Rather, women were scarce because life on the frontier was difficult and unsafe.[92]

The second concern about societies that are male-dominated in population terms relates to the position of women within them; the fear is that they will become male-dominated, or more male-dominated than they already are, in the other, patriarchal rather than demographic, sense. One version of this claim bears a marked resemblance to the claim from Tom Shakespeare that the political strength of disabled people would decline in proportion to their numbers. Thus, Rowland has argued that:

> Women are the most exploited, manipulated, oppressed and brutalized group in the world, yet we have the numbers. What would our status be as a vastly outnumbered group? And how many women would be prepared to accept a world where their value as breeders or sexual objects only would be recognized?[93]

In response to the suggestion that the status of those women who are born into such a society might rise as a result – 'Because of her scarcity woman will be "highly-valued" ' – Rowland maintains that 'she will be valued for sexual and breeding purposes rather than for her intrinsic worth as a person'.[94] She then proceeds to catalogue a range of specific problems that a reduction in the percentage of women would pose, including the empirically unsubstantiated assertion that 'I would suggest that female suicide rates would escalate'.[95]

Warren has examined the various claims relating to the likely status of women within male-dominated societies, and has found the evidence and arguments to be unpersuasive in either direction. Insofar as any specific prediction can be discerned as to the likely effect, Warren claims that the effect for 'women' is likely to depend on the pre-existing nature of the gender relations in that society. Thus, she suggests:

> Where polygyny is not practiced and single women have few means of earning an adequate living, a shortage of men is bound to result in more women living in poverty. In contrast, women who have adequate means of survival outside of marriage may benefit from low sex ratios.[96]

---

92 Warren, *Gendercide*, op. cit., fn 75, p 127.
93 Rowland, 'Motherhood, patriarchal power, alienation and the issue of "choice" in sex preselection', fn 91, p 83.
94 Ibid, pp 81–2.
95 Ibid, p 83.
96 Warren, *Gendercide*, op. cit., fn 75, p 135.

Furthermore, the effect on 'women' will depend on precisely which women we are discussing:

> The potential benefits to women of increased sex ratios include greater opportunities to form stable relationships with men, and a greater subjective sense of power within the traditional female roles. The potential liabilities include a loss of freedom to deviate from these traditional roles, exclusion from most high-status positions, and the absence of a strong feminist movement to combat such injustices.[97]

Whether a particular woman stands to benefit in such a society, then, will depend in part on whether she, personally, has interests bound up with a stable traditional role as a wife and mother, or with opportunities to pursue other, less traditional avenues, such as a career.

Such predictions, as Warren concedes, are necessarily highly speculative. There is simply insufficient empirical data to allow for a confident prediction of how a greater gender imbalance would affect the position of women. Fortunately, for present purposes, such data may not be required in order to respond to this particular suggested harm. For the available data relating to attitudes to sex selection suggest that the possibility of a predominantly male society is highly remote.

The literature review that formed part of the HFEA's report following the consultation process found that 'There were surprisingly few general population surveys regarding attitudes to sex selection published since 1990',[98] and that 'The majority of specific sex selection surveys appear to have been carried out in the US during the 1970s and 1980s'.[99] These were the studies that formed the basis of Mary Anne Warren's research, and which led her to conclude that there was, at that time, no empirical basis for the fear that (1) there would, in the USA, be substantial demand for sex selection, and (2) among those who did make use of it there would be a pronounced preference for boys rather than girls. What the research to which Warren referred *did* suggest, however, was a slight statistical preference for first children to be boys. This led her to speculate as to the effects of a society of 'big brothers and little sisters'.[100]

---

97 See fn 96, pp 135–6.
98 Dr Catherine Waldby, 'Literature review and annotated bibliography: Social and ethical aspects of sex selection', p 2. Interestingly, the opinion poll conducted by MORI on behalf of the HFEA, and the results of which form part of the report, did not attempt to fill this lacuna by enquiring whether respondents would wish to utilise these techniques, had they the option. Instead, the poll asked only about attitudes to regulation of other people's choices. See Michele Corrado and Konrad Collao, 'Sex selection – public consultation: Research study conducted for Human Fertilisation and Embryology Authority', January 2003.
99 Ibid, p 3.
100 Warren, *Gendercide*, op. cit., fn 75, pp 138–42.

The most recent research pertaining to UK attitudes referred to in the HFEA report was reported in a letter to *The Lancet* in 1993, and recorded the attitudes of already pregnant women.[101] The results revealed that, of the 1,824 women recruited into the survey, '58% of responders said they had no preference for a child of a particular sex; 6% said they would prefer a boy and 6% a girl; 12% would quite like a boy and 19% a girl'. The authors conceded that '[t]hese data tell us nothing of what women would do if they could select the sex of their baby', but nonetheless noted that 'most pregnant women have no particular preference', while 'of those who expressed a sex preference for their unborn child, that preference was as likely to be for a girl as for a boy'.[102] This led them to conclude that 'fears of unbalancing the sex ratio are not supported by our data'.[103]

The HFEA review also referred to research published in 1995 which examined the ethnic composition and specific gender preferences of over 800 couples seeking sex selection at the London Gender Clinic.[104] Although this is informative from another point of view (see below) the self-selecting nature of the couples in question sheds no light on the likely rates of uptake of such services were they widely available.

Since the publication of the HFEA report, a further study[105] has suggested that a significant minority – 21% – of the UK population would be willing to pay £1,250 to avail themselves of sex selection were the option available, with 7% claiming to be undecided as to whether or not they would use it.[106] (This was contrasted with only 6% of Germans responding that they would exercise the choice.[107]) Does the prospect of as many as 30% of the population potentially availing themselves of sex selection techniques lend substance to the fears of demographic skewing?

The authors of this particular article certainly did not interpret their data as a cause for alarm. Rather, they noted that while 3% of respondents would prefer only boys in their family, this was largely counteracted by the 2% who wanted only girls, while 68% favoured an equal number of boys and girls, and

---

101 Helen Statham, Josephine Green, Claire Snowdon, Merry France-Dawson, 'Choice of baby's sex', *The Lancet* (1993); 341(8844): 564–5.

102 Ibid, p 565.

103 Id.

104 P Liu and G A Rose, 'Social aspects of > 800 couples coming forward for gender selection of their children', *Human Reproduction* (1995); 10(4): 968–71.

105 Dahl, Hinsch, Beutel and Brosig, 'Preconception sex selection for non-medical reasons: a representative survey from the UK', *Human Reproduction* (2003); 18(10): 2238–9.

106 The fact that 71% of respondents had no interest in choosing their babies' sex did not prevent the BBC from reporting the study under the headline 'Britons "would choose baby's sex"'. BBC Online, 25 September 2003.

107 Dahl, Beutel, Brosig and Hinsch, 'Preconception sex selection for non-medical reasons: a representative survey from Germany', *Human Reproduction* (2003); 18(10): 2231–4.

16% 'simply do not care about the sex of their children'.[108] While a slightly higher number of respondents indicated that they would prefer a boy (16%) rather than a girl to be their first-born child, a large majority (73%) expressed no preference, and 10% preferred a first-born girl. If such data accurately reflect the views of the UK population as a whole, then it seems unlikely that the suggested advantages enjoyed by first-born children[109] need significantly reinforce the existing advantages enjoyed by males.

While it would be foolhardy to infer too much from a single study, it is perhaps equally rash to assume that the preference for boys would be both present and substantial enough to cause demographic problems. To date, none of the published studies have provided evidence of a significant parental preference for boys over girls; insofar as any common preference is discernible, it is for an equal number of children of each sex, or for at least one of either sex within a bigger family. Whether or not such preferences derive from sexist assumptions about the likely characters and attributes of, respectively, boys and girls, they certainly do not provide a reason to believe that a pro-choice approach to preimplantation sex selection will give rise to significant demographic distortions.

Of course, if such trends did begin to appear, and if they looked like becoming a problem, a case could be made for adopting measures to constrain choice. But for the time being, when what little evidence is available suggests that most prospective parents would either have no interest in making this choice, or would actively strive to promote gender balance, worries about skewing gender ratios seems prematurely pessimistic.

Furthermore, the widely held beliefs that sex selection in other societies (India and China are oft-cited examples[110]) would be used overwhelmingly to avoid the birth of girls, Macklin and Warren have both provided reasons to doubt whether prohibitions in those communities would actually benefit women there. In any event, the fact that a particular technology would present problems in another part of the world hardly constitutes a reason to prohibit its use in the United Kingdom, any more than the practice of footbinding in China would have been ended by banning the sale of bandages from London pharmacists.[111]

---

108 Dahl et al, 'a representative survey from the UK', fn 105, p 2238.
109 See Warren, *Gendercide*, op. cit., fn 75, pp 138–42.
110 See, for example, Buchanan, Brock, Daniels and Wikler, *From Chance to Choice*, op. cit., fn 15, p 183.
111 Over the past decade, the HFEA's position on sex selection appears to have been influenced to some extent by the belief that, while there may be little demand for sex selection among the general population, it is likely to be used in a more problematic way by 'certain ethnic communities'; see Open letter to Parliamentary Under-secretary of State, 15 July 1993. Such concerns may have been lent some credence by the research of Liu and Rose, which revealed that, of the 800 or so couples in the survey, all of whom were attending a London clinic offering sex selection, 57.8% were of 'Indian' ethnic origin, while 'Asian and Middle Eastern

Conclusion

Unlike some of the arguments I considered in earlier chapters, the 'third party concerns' I have looked at in this chapter cannot be discounted out of hand. Unlike the 'children of the genetic supermarket', these parties do not owe their existence to the choices in question. As such, it is difficult to argue that they have gained more than they have lost; rather, any harmful effects of this technology are likely to come unmitigated by corresponding benefits.

What is less clear is that the risks to these parties are better addressed by restrictions on reproductive choice. 'Loss of support' concerns are serious, but the suggestion that they are best met by increasing the numbers of disabled people in society is deeply problematic. As Tom Shakespeare acknowledged in his evidence to the Science and Technology Select Committee,[112] such a position would mean that we should prevent women from taking folic acid during the early stages of pregnancy to reduce the chances of spina bifida; after all, in reducing the incidence of spina bifida, we would be weakening the numbers, and the political influence, of those already born with that condition.

With regard to less tangible 'expressivist' concerns, I have suggested that these could be best addressed by more, rather than less reproductive choice. An approach that limits the use of PGD to the elimination of embryos affected by 'serious disorders' inevitably makes a very definite, very negative statement about people with such disorders: that we, as a society, would rather that they were not born. But an approach that allows prospective parents to use this technology to select whatever traits they choose (from the narrow range likely to be available to them) sends a different message, a message that the value being upheld is one of reproductive autonomy rather than any sort of eugenic ideas.

couples overwhelmingly wanted boys, whereas European couples showed a slight preference for girls.' The notion that sex selection is likely to give rise to demographic problems among UK ethnic minorities was, however, called seriously into question by the Qualitative Research Study commissioned by the HFEA, which found 'the views expressed amongst Asian groups very similar to other groups. That is, from a personal, moral perspective, they felt serious medical conditions [the] only justifiable reason for sex selection.' In marked contrast to the apparent expectations of some commentators, most respondents from the Asian groups (there were separate groups for Hindu/Sikh and Muslim respondents) felt that 'it was discriminatory to argue that girls were less desired or valued than boys', and that 'girls were as likely, if not more likely, to become economically successful and want to look after elderly parents.' *Sex Selection – Policy and Regulatory Review. A Report on the Key Findings from a Qualitative Research Study*, October 2002. Of course, responses in a 'focus group' might be thought a less reliable guide than what people actually do in practice. But since preimplantation sex selection has been unavailable in the UK since 1993, such surveys of professed opinion are the most reliable indicator we have, and certainly more accurate than unsubstantiated generalisations about ethnic minorities.

112 Select Committee on Science and Technology, Examination of Witnesses, 10 November 2004, Q1038.

With regard to sex selection, I have sought to show first that a preference for a child of one sex rather than another does not, invariably, demonstrate a preference for one sex over another. For a variety of reasons, parents with a child, or children, of one sex may have preferences regarding the sex of their next child. Most practically, restricted living space may mean room-sharing, which for many people would be easier with a family of all boys or all girls, especially as the children grew older. For others, the concern is with 'family balancing', having the different experiences of raising both boys and girls. Occasionally, tragic cases like the Mastertons might arise, where parents seek to restore a lost element to their family dynamic.

None of these motives is entirely uncontroversial. In particular, all are likely to strike some people as involving, to a greater or lesser degree, sexist attitudes. What does it mean to want the distinct experience of raising a boy if I do not attribute some particular traits to boys that girls lack? How will I feel if the son onto whom I have projected these ideas prefers to shop for clothes with his mother, rather than to watch football with me? What if the Mastertons' were able to have the girl child they so badly wanted, and she transpired to be a scruffy tomboy rather than the 'wee princess' of which they dreamed?

Having children is like that. Our own tastes and characters are rarely a perfect fit with parental aspirations and expectations. In most cases, it seems, this does not prevent a fairly good relationship between parents and child. In some, though, it can be the cause of serious emotional and psychological distress. The House of Commons Select Committee on Science and Technology heard evidence about a couple whose marital problems apparently derived from the fact that, at the age of five, the husband 'became very aware of his parents' desire to have a girl and that affected him very severely for all the rest of his life'.[113]

Even assuming that the causal relationship between the parents' attitudes and the later emotional distress was as straightforward as the witness assumed, though, we might well ask what this tells us about the use of PGD for sex selection. As the Select Committee's Report pointed out, 'if this takes place in the normal course of events, what justification is there for citing psychological problems when technology has been involved?'[114] If this example shows us anything, it is that children can be damaged by their parents' sexist expectations *with or without PGD*.

The notion that widespread social sex selection will result in damaging demographic distortion is, I have suggested, highly questionable on empirical grounds. Such evidence as is available suggests that few people would have much interest in choosing their children's sex, while that minority that would do so seem more interested in ensuring 'family balancing' than in skewing

113 Oral evidence from Ms Philippa Taylor, see fn 112, Q141–3.
114 Select Committee Report, para 139.

the ratio one way or the other. If the opinion polls are to be believed, demographic distortion is a phantom menace.

Yet that, we might argue, is a very substantial 'if'. What people tell pollsters about theoretical choices may differ substantially from what they actually do when that choice becomes real. What if a large proportion of people *do* choose to have more sons than daughters? Or what if, despite my arguments, widespread use of PGD *does* turn out to be harmful to the interests of disabled people? Is it not foolhardy to assume the least worst outcome, especially when the stakes are so high?

We might, however, question quite how high the stakes are. PGD is not, after all, what we might call a 'stable door' issue. Unlike, for example, genetically modified organisms or xenotransplantation, the danger is not that a new pathogen will be released that cannot be recaptured or returned to its previous non-harmful state. Unlike certain environmental issues, such as nuclear power or nuclear weapons, the danger is not of a sudden, cataclysmic event that will unfold too quickly to avoid the resultant (terrible) harms.

Rather, the demographic dangers posed by PGD are, by their very nature, gradual dangers, appearing over the course of generations. While it does not follow that they are trivial dangers, their slow-release nature affords us the opportunity to monitor them, to determine whether any of the troubling trends discussed here are actually manifesting themselves in the real world. If they do, if it transpires that more people are choosing all-boy or all-girl families than the surveys predicted, then we would at least have some concrete evidence of harm on which to proceed.

Chapter 6

Saviour siblings and the 'means-ends' imperative

Thus far, I have considered two important ethical principles (or three, if beneficence is regarded as a distinct principle from non-maleficence, as opposed to the other half of a utilitarian yin and yang). This has led me to the following conclusions: first, that the principle of respect for autonomy provides a pro tanto reason for allowing prospective parents to choose as they see fit; and second, that the principles of non-maleficence and beneficence provide no compelling reason to curtail that choice, the presumably very rare occurrence of 'worse then nothing' lives notwithstanding.

Over the next two chapters, I will examine my pro-choice approach in the light of two other widely recognised ethical principles. In Chapter 7, I will consider the claim that a genetic supermarket would be contrary to ideas of justice. In this chapter, though, my concern is with the notion of instrumentality, the ethical principle that warns us against using other people as means rather than as ends in themselves. The principle is widely recognised, both by professional ethicists and the public at large. What is less certain is how it applies to the sort of choices that GCTs make available. Is it, we might wonder, even possible to treat a 'potential future child' as an end in itself?

In recent years, this sort of question has become more than an abstract thought experiment for academic philosophers. Rather, concern about means and ends seems to have been central to the decisions the HFEA have made in relation to a particular use of PGD. The Authority's handling of the so-called 'tissue typing' cases have become the subject of much scrutiny, and no little criticism. Indeed, even within the HFEA, there appears to have been significant uncertainty about how to approach such cases, as is evidenced by its policy change in August 2004.

Much of the controversy related to doubts as to the precise meaning of certain clauses within the 1990 Act. But the ethical deliberations surrounding these cases also provide us with a context within which to assess the 'ends and means' objections.

The Hashmis: background

Zain Hashmi suffers from beta thalassaemia major. This is an autosomal recessive genetic disorder, which causes an abnormally high rate of breakdown of red blood cells, and leads in turn to severe anaemia. Sufferers require frequent blood transfusions, but such a regimen can cause iron overload and consequent organ deterioration. Indeed, the only long-term solution, and certainly the only *cure* for Zain's condition, lay in a transfusion of stem cells.

Until recently, the only source of such cells was bone marrow.[1] The extraction of bone marrow can be a painful procedure, rendering it ethically (and potentially legally) questionable whether pre-competent children should be used as 'donors'. However, developments in the field of stem cell technology may well have made it unnecessary in cases like Zain's. This is due to a discovery that '[c]ord blood from neonates contains substantial numbers of haemopoietic stem cells, which can be harvested at delivery, frozen, and then transplanted to patients who would not otherwise have a donor'.[2] Rather than subjecting the donor to the painful process of bone marrow retrieval in the future, then, all that would be required was a quantity of blood from his or her umbilical cord.

Since neither Zain's parents, nor any of his three elder siblings, were compatible to act as bone marrow donors, this option was particularly important for the Hashmis. They were still faced, though, with the problem of finding a supply of Human Leukocyte Antigen (HLA) compatible umbilical cells. Desperate to save Zain, the Hashmis undertook to have another child that could act as a donor for him.

Their first attempt ended in unfortunate circumstances; prenatal testing revealed that the child Shahana Hashmi was carrying would be afflicted with the same condition as Zain, and she elected to have an abortion. A second pregnancy was more successful, in that the child was unaffected, but it became quickly apparent that this child was not a suitable tissue match and could therefore not provide the required transplant. This outcome was not entirely surprising; as the HFEA Ethics Committee was to explain, even among siblings, the odds were not especially favourable:

> The chances of the technique being successful (i.e. resulting in the birth of a healthy, unaffected, tissue-compatible donor) will need to be calculated separately in each case. With an autosomal recessive condition, for example, on average three-quarters of embryos created would be unaffected, although one half would be carriers. As one quarter would be

1   G Lucarelli, M Andreani, E Angelucci, 'The cure of thalassemia with bone marrow transplantation', *Bone Marrow Transplantation* (2001); 28: S11–3.
2   A L Lennard, G H Jackson, 'Stem cell transplantation', *British Medical Journal* (2000); 321: 433–7.

HLA compatible, this gives . . . a 1/16 chance of a normal HLA compatible embryo or a 3/16 chance of an unaffected HLA compatible embryo.[3]

Around this time, Mrs Hashmi discussed her problem with Dr Simon Fishel, the Director of Centres for Assisted Reproduction Limited (CARE), the 'largest single provider of in vitro fertilisation . . . services in the United Kingdom'.[4] Fishel was aware of a groundbreaking procedure being piloted at the Reproductive Genetics Institute (RGI) in Chicago, and he brought this to Mrs Hashmi's attention. The procedure Fishel described comprised five steps:

1. the creation by in vitro fertilisation of several embryos, using gametes from Mr and Mrs Hashmi;
2. the biopsy of a single cell from the embryos thus created;
3. the use of PGD to screen those embryos for the presence of beta thalassaemia (henceforth referred to as Phase 1 screening);
4. simultaneous screening of the embryos to ensure HLA compatibility with Zain (referred to by the court as 'tissue typing', but henceforth referred to as Phase 2 screening);
5. jettison of those embryos found either to be affected by the disease or to be HLA-incompatible with Zain.

Although PGD had already been used for the screening out of embryos that carried genetic diseases, Phase 2 screening had not been carried out in the UK before. Fishel therefore enquired of the HFEA whether a licence would be granted for such a procedure.

The HFEA appears to have found this question somewhat troubling. In 1999, a Joint Working Party (JWP) of the HFEA and the Human Genetics Commission had been established to consider the extent to which, and circumstances in which, PGD should be available. When it reported in 2001, the Working Party recommended that PGD 'should only be available where there is a significant risk of a serious genetic condition being present in the embryo'.[5]

The use of PGD to ensure the birth of a suitable tissue donor had not been specifically considered in the consultation process preceding the Report, but

3   Ethics Committee of the Human Fertilisation and Embryology Authority (2001), *Ethical Issues in the Creation and Selection of Preimplantation Embryos to Produce Tissue Donors*, 22 November 2001.

4   *R (on the application of Quintavalle) v Human Fertilisation and Embryology Authority* [2003] 3 All ER 257, per Lord Phillips of Worth Matravers MR, p 259.

5   Joint Working Group of the HFEA and Human Genetics Commission, *Outcome of the Public Consultation on Preimplantation Genetic Diagnosis*, November 2001, Recommendation 11.

it is clear that it was tacitly precluded by the terms of this Recommendation. The first phase of screening, to ensure the new child would itself be free from genetic illness, certainly seems to fall within the terms of Recommendation 11. But the second phase, to ensure compatibility with the existing child, clearly would not. Indeed, the Report went on to make this rejection of HLA typing explicit, at least until further discussion of the perceived ethical difficulties took place.[6]

This further discussion was carried out by the HFEA's Ethics Committee, a body set up by the HFEA and comprising the Authority members 'with the most relevant experience'.[7] In December 2001, the Ethics Committee published a document entitled 'Ethical issues in the creation and selection of preimplantation embryos to produce tissue donors'.[8] These new guidelines allowed for the possibility of the use of PGD for this purpose, but such use was tightly restricted by the conditions which it attached.

The Ethics Committee's recommendation seems to have satisfied the HFEA that Dr Fishel's clinic should be granted the licence, and that the Hashmis should therefore be permitted to make use of the two-phase screening technique.[9] (As I will discuss in due course, though, not all of the Ethics Committee's recommendations were taken on board by the Authority.)

In contrast to many accounts of developments at the 'cutting edge' of reproductive and genetic technology,[10] the HFEA's decision in the case of Raj and Shahana Hashmi was widely welcomed, by the popular press as well as the medical profession.[11] The HFEA, it was thought, had adroitly picked a path through an ethical minefield, balancing the life of Zain Hashmi, and the reproductive freedom of his parents, against the possible ethical perils of 'designer' and 'spare-part babies'. The latter concerns were, it was widely thought, reflected in the strict guidelines on tissue typing which the Authority

6 See fn 5, para 29.
7 Sally Sheldon and Stephen Wilkinson, 'Hashmi and Whitaker: An Unjustifiable and Misguided Distinction?' *Medical Law Review* (2004); 12: 137–63, p 162.
8 Opinion of the Ethics Committee of the Human Fertilisation and Embryology Authority, 'Ethical Issues in the Creation and Selection of Preimplantation Embryos to Produce Tissue Donors', 22 November 2001, available at http://www.hfea.gov.uk/PressOffice/PressReleases-bysubject/PGDandtissuetyping/Ethics%20Cttee%20PGD%20November%202001.pdf.
9 Human Fertilisation and Embryology Authority Press Release, 13 December 2001, 'HFEA to allow tissue typing in conjunction with preimplantation genetic diagnosis'.
10 For one example among literally hundreds, consider the front page story in the *Metro* on 3 July 2003, in response to the revelation that Chicago scientist Dr Norbert Gleicher had injected male cells into female embryos in an attempt to find treatments for genetic disorders. Under the headline 'Now scientists create a he-she', the story went on to describe the breakthrough as 'the latest in a chilling series of genetic announcements', and pointed to alleged parallels with 'the work of concentration camp doctor Josef Mengele' who 'experimented on Jewish prisoners in an effort to create a master race'.
11 'Why Mr and Mrs Hashmi were right to choose life', *Independent on Sunday*, 24 February 2002; 'The virtue of IVF', *The Observer*, 24 February 2002.

had published a few months prior to the decision.[12] As then-chairwoman Ruth Deech reassured the press, '[t]he authority will only approve the treatment in very rare circumstances and under strict controls'.[13]

The Select Committee on Science and Technology

Not everyone was as approving of the Authority's conduct. In July 2002, the HFEA's decision in relation to tissue typing, together with Chairwoman Ruth Deech's defence of that decision, were the subjects of scathing criticism from the House of Commons Select Committee on Science and Technology.[14] Noting that the public consultation process had not addressed the scenario that arose in the Hashmi application, and that the only consideration of this particular practice had been before the HFEA's Ethics Committee, the Select Committee took the view that:

> The HFEA's decision to allow tissue typing in conjunction with pre-implantation genetic diagnosis went beyond the scope of its own public consultation. It is vital that the public are taken along with decisions of such ethical importance.[15]

In response to Ruth Deech's submission that the fact that the HFEA took the decision on PGD 'protects Members of Parliament from direct involvement in that sort of thing',[16] the Select Committee retorted that 'Parliament does not need protecting and democracy is not served by unelected quangos taking decisions on behalf of Parliament'.[17] The Select Committee concluded on this issue by drawing attention to the fact that '[a] pressure group, Comment on Reproductive Ethics, is seeking judicial review in the High Court on PGD on the grounds that the 1990 Act only permits distinguishing between embryos on the basis of whether they are healthy or not or for providing treatment services to the mother', warning that '[s]hould this ultimately be successful, Parliament's intervention may be inevitable'.[18]

---

12 Human Fertilisation and Embryology Authority, 'A Summary of the One Hundred and Thirteenth Meeting of the Human Fertilisation and Embryology Authority' on 29th November 2001, at http://www.hfea.gov.uk/aboutHFEA/archived_minutes/00028.htm.

13 Clare Dyer, 'Watchdog approves embryo selection to treat 3 year old child', *British Medical Journal* (2002); 324: 503.

14 House of Commons Select Committee on Science and Technology, Fourth Report, 18 July 2002, at http://www.parliament.the-stationery-office.co.uk/pa/cm200102/cmselect/cmsctech/791/79103.htm.

15 Ibid, para 17.

16 Ibid, para 18.

17 Id.

18 Id.

The case

The licence in question was granted on 22 February 2002, but the HFEA's policy decision to permit HLA tissue typing was by this time already the subject of a legal challenge. Josephine Quintavalle, backed by the pressure group Comment on Reproductive Ethics (CORE), sought judicial review of the HFEA's decision, on the grounds that it had acted ultra vires of the powers vested in it by the Human Fertilisation and Embryology Act 1990.

(The Quintavalle family was by this point no stranger to the English civil courts, Mrs Quintavalle's son, Bruno, having already attained prominence by challenging – initially successfully, although he ultimately lost on appeal to the House of Lords – the efficacy of the 1990 Act in prohibiting human cloning.[19] It is interesting to speculate on the extent to which the courts are likely to replace the legislature as the primary forum within which bioethical disputes will be played out.)

Although Mrs Quintavalle's opposition to tissue typing was one of principle, her legal challenge to the HFEA's decision was highly technical. It was based on the precise wording of the 1990 Act, and comprised four elements:

1. Section 3 of the Act prohibits the creation or use of any embryo 'except in pursuance of a licence'.[20]
2. Section 11 of the Act limits the circumstances within which the Authority may issue a licence to those set out in Schedule 2.[21]
3. Schedule 2 provides, inter alia, that a licence may only be issued if 'it appears to the Authority to be necessary or desirable for the purpose of providing treatment services'.[22]
4. The definition of 'treatment services' is in turn spelt out in section 2(1), which provides the following definition: ' "treatment services" means

---

19 *R (on the application of Quintavalle) v Secretary of State for Health* (2002) 63 BMLR 167, (2003) 71 BMLR 209.

20 3. **Prohibitions in connection with embryos**

    (1)   No person shall
        (a)   bring about the creation of an embryo, or
        (b)   keep or use an embryo,
        except in pursuance of a licence.

21 11. **Licences for treatment, storage and research**

    (1)   The Authority may grant the following and no other licences –
        (a)   licences under paragraph 1 of Schedule 2 to this Act authorising activities in the course of providing treatment services,
        (b)   licences under that Schedule authorising the storage of gametes and embryos, and
        (c)   licences under paragraph 3 of that Schedule authorising activities for the purposes of a project of research.

22 Schedule 2, para 1(3).

medical, surgical or obstetric services provided to the public or a section of the public for the purposes of assisting women to carry children.'

Quintavalle's contention was that the Hashmis' intention to use IVF/PGD for tissue typing did not fall within the definition of 'providing treatment services', and therefore fell outwith that range of purposes for which the Authority could legitimately issue a licence.

The Authority's response was that it was indeed within its power to grant a licence for this purpose, since tissue typing was 'at least desirable for the overall purpose of providing fertility treatment'.[23] Quintavalle, though, maintained that the purpose of tissue typing was not to 'assist women to carry children', but rather, 'to ensure that a child born to a particular woman would have tissue that was compatible with the tissue of a sibling'.[24]

On 20 December 2002, at the High Court, Justice Maurice Kay decided in favour of Mrs Quintavalle.[25] Contrary to the Authority's submission, he held that the procedure *could not* be licensed, since – as Mrs Quintavalle had contended – tissue typing could not be said to be 'necessary or desirable for the purpose of assisting a woman to carry a child'.

The Authority appealed against this decision, and was supported in that appeal by the Secretary of State for Health, who was concerned that the decision, were it to stand, could impede the use of PGD more generally, and specifically for the purpose of eliminating genetic disease.[26] The trial judge's interpretation of the relevant section as being restricted to allowing a woman to become pregnant and carry a child to term was arguably not wide enough to permit screening for genetic disorders that would not manifest themselves phenotypically until after birth.[27] Certainly, it is clear from CORE's website that their objection was not solely to tissue typing, but to PGD more generally.[28]

The basis of the Authority's appeal was that:

the entire treatment, comprehending creation of the embryo, biopsy for PGD and tissue typing, the analysis of the cell removed by the biopsy

---

23 See fn 22, para 17.
24 Ibid, para 18.
25 [2003] 2 All ER 105.
26 A concern shared by the Authority itself; see [2003] 3 All ER 257, p 281, para 116.
27 Ibid, pp 281–2, para 116.
28 'PGD is purely and simply another example of modern eugenics, practised ever earlier on developing human life. . . . With PGD the purpose of diagnosis is simply to identify who should be killed. Neither for the disabled baby in the womb, nor for the disabled embryo do you offer any choice but the final solution – death.' From CORE's Response to Human Fertilisation and Embryology Authority/ Advisory Committee on Genetic Testing Consultation Document on Preimplantation Genetic Diagnosis, available at http://www.corethics.org/document.asp?id=fresponse.htm&se=3&st=5.

and the implantation of the embryo, if it proved to be free of disease and a tissue match for Zain[29]

amounted to treatment 'for the purpose of assisting a woman to carry a child'. Counsel for the Authority disputed Justice Kay's narrow interpretation of that phrase, which seemed to see 'treatment services' as 'hav[ing] as their sole object the assistance of the physical process of producing a child'.[30] Rather, a broader reading of the phrase – one which, it was contended, was closer to legislative intention – took account of the fact that, in some circumstances, allowing a woman to eliminate the possibility of genetic disease could be regarded as assisting her to carry a child, since '[w]ithout such knowledge some women who carried genetic diseases would not be prepared to have children'.[31]

Were it to be accepted that PGD for the 'screening out' of genetic disease fell within the definition, counsel for the Authority went on, it followed that the purpose for which Mrs Hashmi wished to use PGD should also be so regarded, since:

> In the same way tissue typing would assist Mrs Hashmi to carry a child, for her wish to do so was conditional upon knowing that the birth of that child would be capable of saving the life and health of Zain.[32]

When challenged as to whether such a wide reading of the Act could allow PGD for the selection of *any* traits to be regarded as 'assisting', and thence the subject of a possible licence, counsel for the Authority conceded this possibility, but regarded the policing of the use of this technology to be the proper responsibility of the Authority, and not a reason to read the governing legislation restrictively.

While Justice Kay had agreed with Quintavalle's restrictive reading of the legislation, the judges in both the Court of Appeal and, ultimately, the House of Lords favoured the Authority's interpretation. For the Law Lords, the question of tissue typing was inextricably bound up with the question of whether PGD could be licensed at all. As Lord Brown of Eaton-Under-Heywood said, using this technology to ensure the birth of a genetically healthy child 'assists a woman to carry a child only in the sense that it helps her decide whether the embryo is "suitable" and whether she will bear the child'.[33] It is not a treatment for infertility – the woman would be able to have children without it – and would therefore be precluded by a very narrow reading of 'assist[ing] women to carry children'. Alternatively, if PGD is to be

29 See fn 26, p 264, para 20.
30 Ibid, para 21.
31 Ibid, p 264, para 21.
32 Id.
33 [2005] 2 AC 561, p 579.

allowed for the avoidance of genetic disease, then the line cannot be drawn at the point favoured by CORE. In the words of Lord Hoffmann:

> if the concept of suitability . . . is broad enough to include suitability for the purposes of the particular mother, it seems to me clear enough that the activity of determining the genetic characteristics of the embryo by way of PGD or HLA typing would be 'in the course of' providing the mother with IVF services and that the authority would be entitled to take the view that it was necessary or desirable for the purpose of providing such services.[34]

The Law Lords, then, favoured an interpretation that regarded both uses of PGD – for disease avoidance and for tissue typing – as potentially licensable.

To the concern that such a ruling could open the proverbial floodgates to any choices prospective parents might want to make about their children's genetic constitution, Lord Brown had this to say:

> In the unlikely event that the authority were to propose licensing genetic selection for purely social reasons, Parliament would surely act at once to remove that possibility, doubtless using for the purpose the regulation making power under section 3(3)(c). Failing that, in an extreme case the court's supervisory jurisdiction could be invoked.[35]

Between them, then, the Authority, Parliament and the courts offered sufficient reassurance against a 'genetic supermarket'; allowing tissue typing did not set society on any sort of slippery slope.

It may seem, then, that the response of both the Authority and the Court of Appeal to tissue typing might be seen as a first victory for supporters of a pro-choice approach to GCTs. On the first occasion that an attempt was made to curtail parental choice in use of PGD, both regulatory authority and judiciary have supported that choice. However, a closer examination of the Authority's reasoning, the conditions and caveats with which it sought to delimit this decision, and perhaps most tellingly, the contrasting approach it adopted when a similar case appeared before it a short time later, paint a somewhat different picture.

First, the Ethics Committee recommended, and the HFEA subsequently accepted, that 'all other possibilities of treatment and sources of tissue for the affected child should have been explored'[36] and that the use of HLA typing

---

34 See fn 33, p 570.
35 Ibid, p 579.
36 'Ethical issues in the creation and selection of preimplantation embryos to produce tissue donors', 22 November 2001, para 3.12.

should be limited to 'severe or life-threatening' cases.[37] And this view was reiterated in even starker terms when the Authority released its revised PGD guidelines in July 2004, in which it clearly stated that 'The HFEA regards preimplantation tissue typing as a last resort'.[38]

In taking this line, the HFEA might be thought to be making a statement about the pro tanto wrongness of the technology. If there was nothing inherently wrong in the practice, there would be no need to find such compelling justification for its use; and it certainly would seem an odd thing to require that existing children be subjected to the discomfort of bone marrow harvesting rather than sanction this use of PGD, unless it was felt that the former course of action is less ethically troublesome.

What, then, might the Authority regard as being ethically problematic about using PGD for tissue-typing? And is it reasonable to conclude that these concerns were more adequately addressed when the conditions listed are met? At the outset of its consideration, the Committee identified three questions which it hoped would guide it in framing its recommendations:

- Is PGD with HLA typing compatible with the 'welfare of the unborn child'?
- Is licensing PGD with HLA typing compatible with the public good?
- Can morally significant criteria be found to demarcate 'acceptable' and 'unacceptable' reasons for the conception and selection of embryos?

The last of these three questions might be thought to presuppose the answers to the first two, in that no such demarcation would be necessary unless there actually exist unacceptable reasons. It seems, therefore, that the question of the pro tanto wrongness of PGD/HLA rests in the first instance on its likely impact on this question of welfare, and in the second on the likely impact on the public good.

To a significant extent, the first of these questions is inextricably tied to my conclusions about non-maleficence more generally; any harms resulting from the child's unorthodox origins must be viewed as the unavoidable costs of the child's coming to exist at all. That being so, and assuming that existence can be predicted to bring many more positives than negatives for the child (an especially likely state of affairs given the lengths that parents such as the Hashmis and Whitakers are likely to go for the benefit of their existing children), it follows that for the 'welfare' concern to count against allowing PGD/HLA, there must be some very substantial risk of very significant harm to the resulting child.

37 See fn 36, para 3.13.
38 HFEA Report: Preimplantation Tissue Typing, para 23.

Welfare of the unborn child

In considering the welfare of the future child, the Ethics Committee considered a fairly traditional formulation of the 'welfare principle', asking 'whether the outcome of the technique adversely shifts the balance of benefit and harm', (para 2.14) together with a more unusual formulation considered in the next section. The first, and more straightforward, of these conceptions of welfare asks whether the donor child will experience a balance of benefit over harm as a result of the technique in question. Such concern may seem entirely valid in this context. Is the use of a child as a 'walking medicine chest'[39] not a clear example of harm to that child?

It is certainly the case that, while UK law allows parents to consent to medical treatment on behalf of their precompetent children, it does not allow them carte blanche in volunteering them for non-beneficial surgery. Rather, the overriding principle with regard to consent exercised for a child is the best interests of the child him- or herself. Can the decision of the Hashmis credibly be thought to satisfy this criterion?

In attempting to answer this question, it is essential to clarify which of the Hashmis' decisions we are scrutinising: the decision to create *a* child, the decision to screen the embryos, the decision to implant *a particular* embryo or the later decision to consent to retrieval of umbilical blood. With regard to the first decision, it may validly be asked whether it is legally necessary, or indeed even *possible*, for the decision to be based on the best interests of the child. Given that, at the time of the decision, the child in question has only a hypothetical existence, it cannot possess any sort of interests, far less best interests. How, then, can its 'best interests' inform the decisions?

It might be thought that this requirement relates to the likely foreseeable interests that the child will possess if it is brought into existence. Should not such interests be taken into account in deciding whether to create the child? Two responses might be thought to cast doubt on this requirement. First, we might ask why it should be incumbent on the prospective parents to give priority to the hypothetical interests of a future child, over the actual interests of their existing children. The decision to have another child might have a profound effect, positive (as in Zain Hashmi's case) or negative (as in the case where the parents already barely possess enough resources to provide for the children they have), on the existing children. Is it not appropriate that any future reproductive decisions take account of such impacts? Indeed, as we have seen, section 13(5) of the 1990 Act specifically requires that any decision to provide access to reproductive technologies take account of precisely this.

Furthermore, as Sheldon and Wilkinson point out, the 1990 Act apparently does not require the best interests of the future child to be the

---

39 A term employed by an anonymous reviewer of an article I submitted on this topic.

paramount consideration but merely that account be taken of the welfare of such a child;[40] the juxtaposition of this requirement with the reference to 'any other child who may be affected by the birth' may be thought to suggest that the welfare of the created child is but one of, potentially, several parties whose interests should be of relevance to the decision.

Could the best interests requirement be satisfied by the decision to use PGD for the purposes of ensuring (or maximising the likelihood of) an HLA-compatible child? Again, this requirement would find itself embroiled in some complex metaphysical speculation. Given that the effect of PGD is to inform a decision as to which of several 'candidate embryos' to implant, for the 'rejected' embryos, the effect will be (as discussed in Chapter 3) to ensure that they never develop interests at all. To apply the best interests test to the latter group is all but meaningless.

While the selected embryo or embryos possess no interests, the children they will (hopefully) become will be interest-bearers. Does it therefore make sense to require that PGD satisfies a test of their (prospective) best interests? The difficulty here is that if we make it a prerequisite of any procedure carried out on an embryo that it benefit that embryo, or the child it will become, then that must apply equally to the act of *implanting* that embryo. How can implantation be said to be in the future child's best interests? The only interest that can conceivably be furthered thereby is some notional 'interest in becoming the sort of being that possesses interests', a metaphysically awkward construction, but one necessary to circumvent the requirement that implantation satisfies the best interests test.

Assuming, for the present, that we can say that their best interests have been furthered by a choice that led to them possessing any interests at all, then this must apply not only to implantation, but also to the use of PGD to ensure that they, and not one of the other candidate embryos, was selected for implantation. (Indeed, we may need to take this a step back and note that the real precondition of their existence was the use of IVF rather than natural conception, a course of events that only unfolded – in the case of fertile couples like the Hashmis – because of the availability of PGD.)

If implantation satisfies the best interests test, then so too, I suggest, does PGD. Alternatively, we may prefer the view that sees neither satisfying that test (since it cannot, we might think, be in a being's best interests merely to allow it to develop interests), but which sees the best interests test as being inappropriate for and inapplicable to preimplantation decisions. This, I think, is the more plausible view. After all, the 1990 Act allows for the possibility of non-beneficial – indeed, destructive – research on embryos up to 14 days,[41] a practice that would clearly fail any conception of a best interests test.

---

40 Sheldon and Wilkinson, 'Hashmi and Whitaker', fn 7, p 158.
41 Human Fertilisation and Embryology Act 1990, s 3.

What, then, of the last of the parents' decisions, the decision to consent to the child acting as a tissue donor? Should that, at least, not be required to be a decision positively in the interests of the child herself? In the Hashmi case, however, there was no prospect of intrusive surgical intervention to harvest the required tissue, but rather, as explained previously, to retrieve it from the discarded umbilicus.[42] Hence, the necessity to satisfy the best interests test may, we might think, be irrelevant.[43]

The same could not, of course, be said of an attempt to harvest bone marrow from the child, still less an attempt to transplant a non-regenerative organ such as a kidney. Such donation could only be justified if it could be shown to be in the child's own best interests. *Re Y (Mental Incapacity: Bone Marrow Transplant)*[44] demonstrated how this requirement can be met in the case of incompetent adults, but no analogous case law exists with regard to precompetent children.[45]

However, assuming similar logic were applied, it seems that tissue donation from a child that was required to save a family member could conceivably be justified where the child enjoyed a close relationship with that relative,[46] at least where the tissue required was regenerable (blood or bone marrow). Indeed, Sheldon and Wilkinson have suggested that a more prospective approach could be adopted to best interests, according to which 'it could surely be argued that A [the selected sibling] would benefit from B's [the existing child] company and may well derive pleasure from knowing that she has saved B's life',[47] while the authors of another article on tissue typing have gone so far as to suggest that 'parents who want to have another child anyway, have an obligation to try this last possibility of saving their sick child'.[48]

---

42 This has been disputed by CORE, whose website proclaims that 'Dr Fishel reiterated at a recent public debate against CORE that it is indeed blood [sic] marrow which they intend to harvest, rather than the placental and cord blood which is usually referred to'. Press release, 'Tissue-typing hearing tomorrow', available at http://www.corethics.org/document.asp?id=CPR310303.htm&se=2&st=4.

43 The question of whether the child might have some sort of property interest in its own tissue or cells is, of course, a separate question, and one that has never, to my knowledge, been definitively answered in UK law. See, however, *Moore v Regents of the University of California* (1988) 249 Cal Rptr 494 (Cal CA) for an example of how such a claim has failed in another jurisdiction.

44 [1997] Fam 110, (1996) 35 BMLR 111.

45 Though Sheldon and Wilkinson seem convinced that a UK court would apply the same principles were the potential donor a precompetent child rather than an incompetent adult; see 'Hashmi and Whitaker', fn 7, pp 160–1.

46 Or even, as in the *Re Y* case, with another person who would be adversely affected by their failure to donate.

47 Sheldon and Wilkinson, 'Hashmi and Whitaker', fn 7, p 151.

48 G Pennings, R Schots and I Liebaers, 'Ethical considerations on preimplantation genetic diagnosis for HLA typing to match a future child as a donor of haematopoietic stem cells to a sibling', *Human Reproduction* (2002); 17(3): 534–8, p 536.

In any event, the decision as to whether the retrieval of tissue and subsequent transplant should take place would be determined at a later time, by weighing up the harms and risks and benefits attendant to the donation, and would be likely to require judicial approval. There is no question that the procedure would go ahead merely on the parents' say-so. We might think, then, that the interests of the child, once born, will adequately be protected by the courts, a fact that the HFEA seemed to acknowledge.[49] Certainly, the prospect of a court deciding whether the bone marrow harvest could be in the child's interests seems a more plausible and proportionate mechanism for safeguarding the child's interests than the intervention of the HFEA to prevent it ever being born.

What, then, of the possible emotional and psychological burdens that may be experienced by a child who grows up knowing that it was created for such a purpose? That their relationship with the parents who conceived them for that reason, or with the sibling they saved, will be adversely affected? Certainly, concerns have been expressed about the possibility of 'damage to his [the new child's] self worth',[50] while Paul Tully of the Society for the Protection of the Unborn Child has rhetorically asked 'How will this child feel knowing that he or she was selected from a group of embryos just to serve as a tissue donor to a sibling?'[51]

Such possible objections begin to look less compelling, of course, when we recall the nature of the alternative for the child in question. Because, as I explained in Chapter 3, for this particular child, the alternative to being born as a tissue donor is not to be born into a more conventional family setting, but rather, *not to be born at all*. Once this is accepted, then it becomes difficult to conclude that the child created as a tissue donor is harmed by those decisions upon which its very existence is dependent. Unless we foresee that its life is likely to be so unremittingly awful that existence itself will be a burden, we must conclude that it is better off (or at least no worse off) being born into these unusual circumstances than never being born at all. There may well, as I have conceded, be conditions and circumstances so subjectively unpleasant for those affected as to be worse than non-existence. It is difficult, though, to imagine that being born in the hope that your life will help save the life of a sibling would constitute such a circumstance.

Furthermore, if our concern is with the possibility of psychological harm to the future child, we must consider the possibility that a family deprived of the use of tissue-typing might attempt a normal pregnancy in the hope that the resulting child will be HLA compatible with the existing child. Given the

49 Human Fertilisation and Embryology Authority, press release, 13 December 2001, 'HFEA to allow tissue typing in conjunction with preimplantation genetic diagnosis'.
50 Richard Nicholson, 'We are some way down a slippery slope', The Guardian, 20 June 2003.
51 'The painful dilemma over babies by design', The Daily Telegraph, 3 August 2002.

low probability that any resulting child will be both unaffected and a tissue match, we should consider what unique psychological burdens will be placed on such a child. If it is harmful to begin life knowing that one was conceived as a saviour, how much harder might it be to know that one was conceived as a saviour and 'failed' in this role, however illogical the attribution of blame for such an unchosen quality as HLA compatibility?

While there is no legal mechanism available to scrutinise the motives nor to control the actions of parents who choose to entrust the creation of a 'saviour sibling' to the reproductive lottery in this way, the possibility that desperation would drive them to attempt this should, it might be thought, be borne in mind before the tissue typing route is blocked by those who profess concern for the welfare of 'the child'.

Treating the child as an end in itself

It seems, then, that there are no harms likely to be associated with tissue typing that require me to abandon my pro-choice stance, or indeed, that justify the 'cautious' approach adopted by the HFEA to this practice. The HFEA's position, though, did not rely entirely on harm-based arguments. Although its reasoning is sometimes rather obliquely explained, it seems as though its caution in this area was also substantially informed by the sort of concerns about 'instrumentalisation' to which I alluded at the outset of this chapter. Having identified a fairly traditional conception of the welfare of the resultant child as one of its primary concerns, the HFEA's Ethics Committee went on to elaborate that 'positive consideration of the welfare of the child requires respect for beings as ends and that the putative child be treated not simply as a means to a further end but also as an "end in itself" '.[52]

The principle that all humans should be treated as ends in themselves is often thought to originate in the writings of the great philosopher Immanuel Kant, and in particular his imperative to 'Act in such a way that you always treat humanity, whether in your own person or in the person of any other, never simply as a means, but always at the same time as an end'.[53] For all its antiquity, though, it remains a principle that commands contemporary adherence.[54] Certainly, it is a theme that has been revisited in subsequent discussions of the tissue typing decisions. One of the clearest statements of the objection came from Professor Alasdair Campbell, in his evidence before the Select Committee on Science and Technology:

The 'saviour sibling' scenario is one of double jeopardy in that not only

---

52 Para 2.9.
53 *Groundwork of the Metaphysics of Morals* (1785) 4.429.
54 See, most notably, Alan Donagan's *The Theory of Morality*, Chicago: University of Chicago Press, 1977.

are you going to be doing that to this child once born, if that is what you do, but in fact the whole reason for conceiving that child is for the sake of someone else. I do not believe our society should go down that path of creating children in order to serve the ends of others.[55]

It is therefore quite understandable that the Authority, and its Ethics Committee, would wish to keep this concern in mind during its deliberations. What, though, does it mean to treat someone as a means and not as an end? As Beauchamp and Childress point out, this ethical rule is often misinterpreted as meaning simply that it is objectionable to use someone as a means to furthering one's own objectives.[56] As they explain, this could not be so without casting ethical opprobrium on every transaction between customer and vendor, employer and employee, client and service provider; when I hire a plumber to unblock my sink, or when I buy a newspaper from my local newsagent, I am treating them as means to my desired ends, i.e., having a sink that drains properly and reading the day's newspaper. If other means were available to attain that same objective – if non-sentient robots and vending machines were able to carry out the same tasks – I would be equally satisfied.

Since, as Beauchamp and Childress write, even Kant would not have regarded such transactions as intrinsically unethical,[57] there must be more to the Kantian imperative than treating other people as a means to my own ends. This extra element is encapsulated in the 'merely' element of the imperative, i.e., the proscription of treating them 'merely or exclusively as a means'[58] and not also as an end in themselves. That is to say, there is nothing objectionable per se in using someone as a means, provided I do not lose sight of the fact that s/he is also an end in him/herself.

On this reading, it would be untenable to allow the Hashmis to use the new child as a means to furthering their own, or Zain's, interests without taking into account any interests of its own which might be affected as a consequence. As I have already suggested, any such interests as may be attributed to the embryonic Hashmi child would relate to the sort of life it might reasonably be expected to enjoy (or endure) once it attained even rudimentary sentience. Those deselected embryos which will never attain sentience will simply never develop interests of any kind, never attain the capacity to be harmed; to speak of their being used as means and not ends is meaningless in a context where taking account of their interests is impossible.

The same, of course, cannot be said of the child who will be born as a result of tissue typing. It is not inconsistent or illogical to be concerned with

55 13 October 2004, Q761.

56 Beauchamp and Childress, *Principles of Biomedical Ethics* fifth edn, Oxford: Oxford University Press, 2001, p 351.

57 Id.

58 Id.

the possibility that such a child will be viewed or treated as a means rather than an end in itself. Certainly, on the analysis I have offered, we might expect such a child to gain more than it loses from the steps which brought it into existence. We should remember, though, that this ethical principle is not merely a rephrasing of the principle of non-maleficence, but something quite distinct from it. Thus, even – as seems likely – if all parties involved are net beneficiaries in terms of harms and benefits, we may have done something ethically wrong if, in the process, we treated some of them as mere instruments.

What is less clear is whether this is a valid objection to levy at the Hashmis. To answer this, it is necessary to look a little closer at what the 'means–ends' principle actually involves. Alan Donagan is a leading contemporary adherent to and interpreter of Kantian ethics. For him,

> Kant's formula of the fundamental principle may be restated in a form more like that of the spiritual commandment that is its original: *Act always so that you respect every human being, yourself or another, as being a rational creature.*[59]

Before examining what Donagan understands this to involve, it is perhaps worth clarifying that the imperative to respect a being as a rational creature is, for him, in no way dependent upon its being capable of rational thought. Rather, any genetically human organism is, by virtue of its species membership, entitled to respect as a rational creature, regardless of its state of cerebral development.[60] This being so, then, following a Donaganian interpretation of Kant's imperative, the Ethics Committee would have been conceptually correct to regard the embryonic Hashmi child as the sort of being that must be shown 'respect . . . as a rational creature'.

What sort of duties, then, are owed to a being by virtue of its status as a rational creature? Much of Donagan's book is given over to a discussion of this question, and he identifies various 'precepts' that derive from the core imperative. He maintains, for example, that 'it is impermissible for anybody at will to use force upon another',[61] a precept that itself gives rise to derivative precepts prohibiting killing, inflicting bodily injury or holding another in slavery;[62] that '[i]t is impermissible not to promote the well-being of others by actions in themselves permissible';[63] that it is impermissible to lie;[64] and that

---

59 Donagan, *The Theory of Morality*, op. cit., fn 54, p 65.

60 Ibid, p 83.

61 Ibid, p 82.

62 Ibid, p 83.

63 Id.

64 'It is impermissible for anybody, in conditions of free communication between responsible persons, to express an opinion he does not hold'; ibid, p 88.

there exists a duty (subject, as are almost all of these 'first-order precepts', to certain exceptions) to obey the law.[65]

One striking aspect of these precepts is that they seem to give rise to a more obvious case *in favour of* tissue typing in cases like those of the Hashmis and Whitakers than they support the contrary position. For while Donagan has nothing to say about the sort of scenario about which the Committee was asked to deliberate, the precept that imposes a positive duty of beneficence – '[i]t is impermissible not to promote the well-being of others by actions in themselves permissible' – gives arise to an ostensible obligation to rescue Zain and Charlie. Of course, the caveat 'by actions in themselves permissible' prevents us from leaping too readily to this conclusion. But nonetheless, a first reading of Donagan's precepts seems to see the scales tilt in favour not only of allowing HLA-typing in life-or-death cases such as those under consideration, but perhaps in cases of less serious illness too; the precept, after all, does not stop at imposing a duty to save life, but rather speaks of 'promot-[ing] the well-being of others'.

The question that remains is whether the actions in question are 'in themselves permissible'. This is the sort of issue on which scholars of Kantian philosophy might be likely to diverge. What we can say, though, is that it is not at all obvious that HLA-typing would contravene the duty to respect the new child as an end in itself in any of the ways specifically identified by Donagan. The new child would certainly not be killed, exposed to bodily harm or enslaved. As discussed above, the positive duty to promote its interests is problematic in a context where the future child does not presently possess any interests, and there is certainly no obvious sense in which such a possibility exists but is being neglected. And duties in relation to truthfulness, honouring contracts, and obeying the law are irrelevant in this context.

What the Kantian imperative seems to require, then – at least as Donagan interprets it – is that the well-being of Zain and Charlie should be promoted unless it can be demonstrated that some other aspect of the duty – presumably as owed to the new child – is being violated. It is for scholars of Kant, of Donagan and of such duty-based ethics more generally to ascertain whether any such competing obligation exists and, if so, whether it can outweigh what Donagan clearly recognises as a duty to Zain and Charlie. But it is by no means uncontroversial or obvious that this ethical obligation to which the Ethics Committee attached such weight, namely to respect all humans as ends in themselves and as rational beings, weighs *against* HLA-typing, either in life-or-death cases or in cases where it is only well-being rather than life itself that is at stake. Indeed, it may even be that this obligation – contrary to the Ethics Committee's apparent assumption – pulls in the opposite direction.

A similar approach to the Kantian imperative has been advanced by Walter

---

65 See fn 54, p 109.

Glannon, this time in relation to the possibility of reproductive human cloning. Glannon invites us to imagine a (far from implausible[66]) scenario wherein:

> the parents of a recently deceased or dying child want to clone an individual who is genetically identical to that child and thus 'replace' it to compensate for their loss or else carry on the family line.[67]

Glannon acknowledges that, if 'the sole intent of the parents is replacement or compensation, then the cloned individual would be treated solely as a means', and that this 'would deny the intrinsic dignity and worth one possesses in virtue of the fact that one is a human agent with the capacity for reason.'[68] However, for Glannon, the motives with which the clone was created would be less important than the manner in which it is treated throughout its life:

> if the clone were loved and treated with the dignity and respect commanded by its intrinsic worth, then cloning might be morally justifiable on Kantian grounds. Although the intention to clone the child suggests that he or she would be treated instrumentally, the fact that the child is treated as a unique individual once she exists is enough to dispel any moral qualms about the parent's behavior [sic].[69]

In short, 'how one is treated by others over the course of one's life is more morally significant than the reasons for causing one to exist'.[70]

Yet even if this is an erroneous interpretation of the duty, and HLA-typing presents greater difficulties for the duty to respect the new child as an end in itself than has been recognised here, it is by no means clear that the recommendations at which the Committee arrived would follow from this. For if it is felt that 'being born to be a donor' is incompatible with being treated as an end in oneself, then it is difficult to see how this is so only when the anticipated recipient is a parent, but not a sibling.

In neither case is the prospective child able to consent to the donation, nor of course to its creation. In both cases the decision involves consideration for a party other than the putative child itself. In both scenarios, in other words,

---

66 Ian Wilmut, one of the scientists responsible for the creation of Dolly the sheep, has told of the demand for such treatment: 'I fielded many of the telephone calls that flooded into Roslin Institute in the days after we went public with Dolly, and quickly came to dread the pleas from bereaved families, asking if we could clone their lost loved ones.' Introduction to Wilmut, Campbell and Tudge, *The Second Creation*, London: Headline Book Publishing, 2000, p 16.

67 Walter Glannon, *Genes and Future People: Philosophical Issues in Human Genetics*, Oxford: Westview Press, 2001, p 118.

68 Id. See also Pennings, Schots and Liebaers, 'Ethical considerations . . .', fn 48.

69 Id.

70 Ibid, p 120.

the donor child is being created at least partly as a means to some other end. The next section will consider this most perplexing of restrictions.

The parental exception

The fact that the Committee had wandered into areas of ethical confusion, and perhaps departed from its original remit, became clearest when it came to consider the possibility of utilising this technology to provide a tissue donation to a parent. Among its final recommendations, it proposed that 'because it [the Committee] favours a principle of qualified parental decision-making with respect to the use of the technique *the technique should not be available where the intended tissue recipient is a parent*'.[71] No further justification is offered for such a condition in this paragraph, and it is necessary to search the remainder of the document in some depth to locate some indication of the Committee's reasoning.

Paragraph 2.21 concluded with the claim that 'it appears *prima facie* to be morally less acceptable than selecting an embryo to provide tissue to treat a sibling, as it seems to replace concern with another with concern for oneself'. There are several observations we could make about this assertion. First, it may be seen to conflate that which is morally *acceptable* with that which is morally *commendable*. Undertaking a physically, emotionally and perhaps financially demanding process such as IVF and pregnancy in order to save the life of another may perhaps scale heights of altruism and selflessness greater than undertaking these burdens to save one's own life. But that is not to say that the latter course of action is morally unacceptable. To make out the case for moral unacceptability, the Committee would need to have demonstrated some aspect of the treatment that contravened some ethical principle.

Second, the Committee's assessment perhaps overlooks the contribution and sacrifice of the other parent. If, for example, it had been the father who suffered from a debilitating and life-threatening condition requiring stem cell transfusion, and if the couple had undergone the same procedure in an attempt to find a suitable donor, would the requisite element of sacrifice and altruism not have been displayed in the mother's willingness to go through ova retrieval, embryo implantation, pregnancy and labour to save her husband?

The Committee commenced its enquiry by identifying consequentialism and deontology as the ethical principles that would guide it, but seems at this point to have imported a third ethical principle, one that sees only acts of supreme and selfless sacrifice as being acceptable. Yet even on those somewhat idiosyncratic terms, it is not at all clear that applying this technique to benefit a parent should not be acceptable.

Neither the 1990 Act, nor the common law, require parents to have wholly

---

71 Paragraph 3.15, original emphasis.

or primarily non-selfish motives when they act on behalf of their children. The parent whose selfish decision happens to coincide with his child's interests will not have his motives scrutinised for any hint of self-interest. Why, we might ask, should such an unfeasibly high standard be set for prospective parents seeking to use PGD-HLA?

Indeed, we might also ask whether it is not invariably the case that, by the very fact of its conception and birth, a child is serving as a means to some other end. It is perhaps unlikely that any pregnancies are commenced wholly or predominantly out of beneficence towards the future child. Couples or individuals have children for a wide variety of reasons, ranging from the fulfilment of long-harboured life plans to unwelcome accidents, via myriad psychologically complicated motivations involving self-fulfilment, tradition, peer expectation, strengthening ailing relationships and a – perhaps sub-conscious – quest for some sort of genetic immortality. As Julian Savulescu has said:

> Parents have many desires related to their children: perhaps to have a companion, to have a friend to the first child, or to hold a marriage together. It is unlikely that any parent ever desires a child solely as an end in itself. . . . Provided that parents love their child as an end in itself, there is no problem with the child's life also fulfilling some of the parents' desires for their own lives.[72]

It is also entirely common to hear parents citing a desire for companionship for an existing child as a reason.[73]

Whatever the precise reasoning, however, the fact that couples *want* to be genetic parents is a selfish, or at best a mixed, motive, just as surely as the fact that one of them needs a donation of stem cells. It may be that in other times and in other societies, couples greeted the news of pregnancy with a stoical acceptance that they were fulfilling an unhappy duty, but it would be difficult to see this as a preferable state of affairs to one where the forthcoming birth of a child is seen as a joyous event for all concerned.

For the most part, we want parents to satisfy their own wants and ambitions when bringing a child into the world. Of course, if these wants and ambitions were likely to harm the child once it is in existence – if the child was wanted as a slave or a sacrifice, for example – that may be problematic. But the mere fact that the creation of a life symbiotically benefits the parents is not only accepted, but is for the most part expected and welcomed.

---

72 Julian Savulescu, 'Sex selection: the case for', *Medical Journal of Australia* (1999); 171(7): 373–5, p 373.
73 See, for example, Pennings, Schots and Liebaers, 'Ethical considerations . . .', fn 48, and Sheldon and Wilkinson, 'Hashmi and Whitaker', fn 7, p 147.

Whether the parents are motivated by altruistic concern for other children, or selfish concern for their own health, they are nonetheless viewing the new child as a means to some other end. But provided they do not view it, and more importantly do not treat it, *only* as a means, they have not violated its interest in being treated with the respect due.

The Whitaker case: an arbitrary distinction?

The Quintavalle challenge, then, demonstrated that the Law Lords were content to entrust to the HFEA the responsibility for ensuring that PGD is used only in 'appropriate' circumstances. The manner in which this task is being carried out has, I suggest, been cast into doubt by the apparent ethical confusion underlying the conditions attached to the decision about HLA tissue typing. Even greater reason for dissatisfaction lies in the Authority's handling of the next application for a licence to carry out tissue typing.

Charlie Whitaker suffered from Diamond Blackfan Anaemia (DBA), a rare blood disorder requiring day-long blood transfusions. In that the condition is painful, debilitating and impossible to cure without transfusion, it is analogous to Zain Hashmi's thalassaemia. The distinction, upon which the HFEA placed so much reliance, is that DBA is rarely a hereditary condition; indeed, tests of Michelle and Jayson Whitaker revealed that they were not carriers, and that Charlie's condition was attributable to a spontaneous mutation.

As already noted, the Joint Working Party's Recommendation 11 restricted PGD to cases where the embryo being screened was itself at significant risk of developing a particular genetic condition. While the future Hashmi child satisfied this criterion – both Shahana and Raj Hashmi being asymptomatic carriers – any future child the Whitakers may have would be at no greater than average risk of developing DBA. The terms of the Recommendation, therefore, would not be satisfied in the latter case.

However, the HFEA Ethics Committee, charged specifically with the role of considering the ethics of HLA tissue-typing, reached an entirely different conclusion. Paragraph 3.14 of the Committee's Report addressed precisely the scenario in which the Whitakers found themselves, and recommended that PGD should be available in those circumstances. In announcing in August 2002 that the Whitakers would be denied access to PGD for tissue-typing only,[74] the HFEA acted against the recommendation of its own Ethics Committee in this matter. While it is of course free to do so, it is difficult to discern what ethical or legal basis the HFEA was relying on when it made this decision.

---

74 HFEA, Press Release, 'HFEA confirms that HLA tissue typing may only take place when preimplantation genetic diagnosis is required to avoid a serious genetic disorder', 1 August 2002, available at http://www.hfea.gov.uk/PressOffice/Archive/43573563.

The Minutes of the first HFEA meeting after the Ethics Committee's Report contain only a fairly cursory discussion of the issue:

> Members felt that to allow PGD for tissue typing alone would run contrary to the requirements of the welfare of the child assessment. Therefore, it was agreed that tissue typing using PGD should only be offered where PGD was already necessary to avoid the passing on of a serious genetic disorder.[75]

As discussed earlier, the Ethics Committee had in fact identified the 'putative child's actual moral, psychological, social and physical welfare' as an issue of great significance.[76] Its Report considered both a fairly traditional formulation of the 'welfare principle', asking 'whether the outcome of the technique adversely shifts the balance of benefit and harm',[77] together with a more unusual formulation where the Committee considered the proposition that:

> It could be suggested that positive consideration of the welfare of the child requires respect for beings as ends and that the putative child be treated not merely as a means to a further end but also as an 'end in itself'.[78]

It is unclear which of these concepts of 'welfare' the HFEA felt to be compromised by the Whitakers' application, though not by the Hashmis'. The first version, concerned with the prospect of harm to the future child, seems to be answerable in terms of the Non-Identity Principle in exactly the same manner as in the Hashmi scenario. Unless we can predict with confidence that either child will suffer a net balance of harms over benefits as a result of its existence, it is impossible to conclude that the very fact of its creation constitutes harm to it.

Had the HFEA contended that the Whitakers would be likely to neglect or abuse the new child, regarding it literally as an instrument to save Charlie's life, to be tossed aside when that end was attained, then there may have been a case to answer (although the option of adoption – a very real possibility when the child's plight was inevitably trumpeted by the nation's media – would cast into doubt whether even those circumstances would render the

---

75 Human Fertilisation and Embryology Authority, *A Summary of the One Hundred and Thirteenth Meeting of the Human Fertilisation and Embryology Authority on 29th November 2001*, at http://www.hfea.gov.uk/aboutHFEA/archived_minutes/00028.htm.

76 Ethics Committee of the Human Fertilisation and Embryology Authority, *Ethical Issues in the Creation and Selection of Preimplantation Embryos to Produce Tissue Donors*, 22 November 2001, para 3.2.

77 Ibid, para 2.14.

78 Ibid, para 2.9.

new child's birth contrary to its interests). As far as can be ascertained from the Minutes of the November meeting, though, the HFEA at no point seriously considered the possibility that the new child would be treated in a manner likely to give rise to such concerns.

The only indication of the thinking that led the HFEA to conclude that the future child's welfare would be compromised lies in the Minutes' brief reference to 'the psychological burden that may be placed on a child who was an "engineered" match as opposed to a "natural" match'.[79] The terminology used here might be considered imprecise and unfortunate. The Whitakers did not seek to alter the genetic makeup of their future child, as the term 'engineered' is ordinarily thought to denote. If the distinction the HFEA sought to address was between a 'selected' match as opposed to a 'randomly occurring' match, then it is not apparent how the former child would be at a disadvantage. In both cases, there will be an expectation that the child will act as a donor.

Similarly, the second of the Ethics Committee's conceptions of 'welfare' seems ill-suited to distinguish between the Hashmis' case and that of the Whitakers. The concern that the putative child be considered 'not merely as a means to a further end but also as an "end in itself"' requires that we regard the new child as an end in itself, taking account of its interests and rights, and not merely as an instrument of someone else's welfare. As I showed earlier in this chapter, such a principle may – although by no means uncontroversially – be accommodated within a consideration of the welfare of the future child. However, it is by no means clear that the creation of a child to serve as a donor violates this principle – provided that child is treated with the dignity and respect due to an individual, then it has not been treated solely as a means.

Furthermore, it is far from clear how it serves to distinguish the two cases. Both families sought to have a new child, and to use PGD to select that child, at least partly for the good of an existing child. Even if we were to accept that 'first phase' PGD, for disease screening, was in the interests of that future child (a conclusion that poses certain philosophical difficulties), it is surely the case that in both scenarios, the use of 'second phase' screening, for HLA tissue-typing, was sought exclusively for the benefit of another party. If the HFEA's concern is with preventing embryos being screened wholly for the benefit of someone else, then it is difficult to see how it was any more justified for the Hashmis than for the Whitakers.

The decisions of the Court of Appeal and the House of Lords in the *Quintavalle* case, and in particular their recognition that non-pathological factors could be considered as suitable matters for 'treatment' in terms of the

---

79 *A Summary of the One Hundred and Thirteenth Meeting of the Human Fertilisation and Embryology Authority*, op. cit, fn 75.

1990 Act, could be seen to have lent a wide margin of discretion to the HFEA in terms of granting licences for PGD. The manner in which the Authority has exercised this discretion, however, has afforded little room for optimism in terms of ethical coherence or consistency. While ethical principles like non-maleficence and the Kantian imperative have at least been paid lip-service by the Authority and its Ethics Committee, they have been applied in a manner that suggests only a superficial understanding of their implications. In particular, although the welfare of the child figures prominently in these discussions, at no point is the Non-Identity Principle explicitly considered, nor does it appear to influence the eventual decisions at which they arrived.

The categorical imperative, or more specifically that variation thereof that requires that all individuals be treated not merely as means but also as ends in themselves, was imported into the welfare consideration in a manner that may be deemed questionable. Of more concern, however, was the apparent lack of rigour with which that principle was examined and explained, and the lack of consistency with which it was applied to the various permutations of circumstances that might arise. It is, I have argued, by no means certain that creating a child to serve as a tissue donor violates that imperative; certainly, the interpretation of the principle adopted by Alan Donagan, one of its most influential proponents, seems almost to suggest the very opposite.

However, even if the view is taken that creating a child with the principal motive of having it serve as a tissue donor does in fact amount to a contravention of the Kantian imperative, it is by no means obvious how this provides a valid ground to distinguish between (a) the Hashmi scenario, (b) the Whitaker scenario, and (c) the scenario where the intended recipient is a parent. In all three cases, the child is being created to serve as a donor, and in all three cases Phase 2 screening is being carried out precisely for that end. Either the Kantian imperative is violated by none of these – as I suggest – or it is violated by all three.

That being so, the decisions and rules arrived at by the HFEA certainly seem arbitrary, and it may not even be unduly cynical to suggest that they were motivated more by a desire to maintain an appearance of control – in the face of Select Committee criticism, media concern about 'designer babies', and a court challenge from CORE – than about legitimate concern for the 'welfare' of the resulting child.[80]

---

80 Some credence is given to this view by an eye-opening exchange between Professor Tom Baldwin, Deputy Chair of the HFEA and member of the Ethics Committee, and the Chairman of the House of Commons Select Committee, on the subject of the legal challenge to the Hashmi decision:
   'Chairman: You said you were conscious of these things happening. Were you scared stiff of these things happening?
   Professor Tom Baldwin: By 2002, once CORE started taking us to court, yes' (oral evidence, Q635).

The Authority's *volte face*

While medico-legal academics may have hoped that the Whitakers would contest the HFEA's refusal through the courts, affording us the opportunity to ascertain judicial views on the validity of the distinction upon which the Authority relied, the Whitakers availed themselves of a different option. Instead of investing money and time in a potentially fruitless challenge to the obstacles facing them in the UK, they opted instead to travel to the USA, where no such regulatory difficulties presented themselves. In June 2003, after treatment in the Chicago Reproductive Genetics Institute, Michelle Whitaker gave birth to Jamie, a healthy son whose stem cells could be used to treat his brother Charlie.[81] It is a somewhat ironic facet of the tale that the Hashmis, whose efforts to conceive a donor child were supported by the HFEA and the courts, have as yet been unable to do so.

In the event, though, had the Whitakers been prepared and able to wait another year, they would have been able to have the treatment they sought in the United Kingdom. In July 2004, following a review by its Ethics and Law Committee, the HFEA announced a *volte face* on its policy of not allowing tissue typing in such cases.[82] Since then, at least two couples have been able to use tissue typing in the manner that was denied to the Whitakers.[83]

It is impossible to be anything other than delighted for the Fletcher and Mariethoz families. The rationale offered by the Authority for its change of heart, though, is perplexing. In the press release announcing the change of policy, the Authority claimed that its original refusal to grant a licence in the Whitaker type case was premised upon a 'precautionary approach':

> because the technique is invasive and there was a concern about a potential risk of damaging the embryo, so tissue typing was only allowed on cells which had already been taken from the embryo for genetic diagnosis.[84]

The change of policy was, apparently, justified because:

> The HFEA has now carefully reviewed the medical, psychological and emotional implications for children and their families as well as the

---

81 R Dobson, ' "Saviour sibling" is born after embryo selection in the United States', *British Medical Journal* (2003); 326: 1416 (28 June).

82 HFEA press release, 'HFEA agrees to extend policy on tissue typing', 21 July 2004, available at http://www.hfea.gov.uk/PressOffice/Archive/1090427358. Human Fertilisation and Embryology Authority Report: 'Preimplantation tissue typing', available at http://www.hfea.gov.uk/AboutHFEA/HFEAPolicy/Preimplantationtissuetyping/PreimplantationReport.pdf.

83 See Clare Dyer, 'Couple allowed to select an embryo to save sibling', *British Medical Journal* 2004, 329: 592 (11 September); and 'Couple hope "designer baby" helps others', BBC Online, Thursday, 4 May 2006, at http://news.bbc.co.uk/1/hi/england/leicestershire/4973028.stm.

84 Press release, op. cit.; 'Preimplantation tissue typing', op. cit., p 3.

safety of the technique. There have been three further years during which successful embryo biopsies have been carried out, both in the UK and abroad and we're not aware of any evidence of increased risk.[85]

There are a number of reasons why this explanation is unsatisfactory. In relation to the question of the 'potential risk of damaging the embryos', it is simply implausible that it took until July 2004 for the HFEA to be satisfied that no such risk need concern them. In the Introduction to the consultation paper 'Sex selection: choice and responsibility in human reproduction',[86] considered in more detail below, the Authority noted that:

> Because cells must be removed (biopsy) there is a small risk of damage to the embryo as a result of this procedure. Embryo damage during biopsy usually means that the embryos do not develop and are not therefore transferred, so *there is no reason to believe that there is any increased health risk to a liveborn child following from this technique: embryos not damaged during biopsy should continue to develop normally.*[87]

This document was published in October 2002, a mere two months after the refusal to extend the policy on tissue typing to the Whitaker type case. Given that the research that informed the consultation document was commissioned in January 2002,[88] and that its findings were clearly available by October of that year, why would the HFEA make a decision on tissue typing based on the risk of damage to the embryo without waiting for evidence on that very risk, which it had either received by then, or receipt of which its members knew to be imminent? Such a rushed and ill-informed decision, followed by a delay of almost two years in responding to the evidence received, does not speak well of the decision-making process in the body charged with regulating PGD.

Indeed, it is notable that between the report from the HFEA's Ethics Committee,[89] which recommended that tissue typing be allowed in such circumstances, the Press Release announcing that the Authority had ignored

---

85 See fn 84.
86 Available at http://www.hfea.gov.uk/AboutHFEA/Consultations/Final%20sex%20selection %20main%20report.pdf.
87 Ibid, para 44, emphasis added. While the risk of rendering the embryos non-viable may have concerned the Whitakers themselves, it is simply inconceivable that this was the determining factor in a consideration purporting to be concerned primarily with the 'welfare of the child', from which perspective, damaging the embryo sufficiently to render it non-viable might be supposed to be morally equivalent to deciding not to implant that embryo – the very decision for which PGD is sought.
88 Ibid, para 5.
89 Available at http://www.hfea.gov.uk/PressOffice/PressReleasesbysubject/PGDandtissue typing/Ethics%20Cttee%20PGD%20November%202001.pdf.

that advice,[90] and the Minutes of the meeting at which the decision was made, not one mention was noted of this risk which apparently contributed so much to the decision.

With regard to the 'psychological and emotional implications for children and their families', I have suggested that denying access to PGD on this basis is difficult to reconcile with the Non-Identity Principle. Even were this view not taken, however (and it would be interesting to learn how the HFEA circumvented this argument), it is difficult to imagine how the 'further biopsies' to which the Press Release refer could have allayed any such concerns *specifically in relation to Whitaker-type cases*, since no such uses of PGD have been permitted.

In all, then, while proponents of a pro-choice approach to PGD must surely welcome this change of policy, it is difficult to discern anything in the explanation offered to restore faith in the coherence, consistency or, indeed, transparency of the decision-making process that currently regulates this technology.

Altogether easier to discern is an approach that equates caution with stricter regulation; an approach that attaches greater ethical weight to a theoretical risk to a potential person, than to a very real risk to an actual, living child. The concern that embryo biopsy could damage the resulting child is one that the principle of non-maleficence requires we consider – though of course, it is one that could be somewhat complicated by non-identity issues.[91] That same principle, though, requires that we be at least as concerned with the fate of Charlie Whitaker. While risks from embryo biopsy were no more than speculative, the Authority's decision was, in the words of Charlie's father, tantamount to 'handing my son a death sentence'.[92]

A precautionary approach to PGD involves according weight even to theoretical risks, not yet substantiated by evidence.[93] Much more questionable is the elevation of such speculative risks above demonstrable risks, such as that

90 HFEA confirms that HLA tissue typing may only take place when preimplantation genetic diagnosis is required to avoid a serious genetic disorder, 1 August 2002, available at http://www.hfea.gov.uk/PressOffice/Archive/43573563.

91 Indeed, the only circumstance in which non-identity issues would not be relevant would be where the very same embryo would be implanted even if PGD were prohibited. In that case, it might be meaningful to talk about the same child being born with or without the damage caused by biopsy. Assuming that neither the Hashmis nor the Whitakers would have undergone IVF but for the opportunity it afforded to use PGD, however, the prospect of the very same embryo being implanted without PGD, and hence the very same child being born, did not arise. In those cases, the non-identity principle would be highly relevant, and opponents of tissue typing would need to argue that the damaged child would have been better off never born.

92 Jayson Whitaker, oral evidence, Q607, 8 September 2004.

93 *Human Reproductive Technologies and the Law*, Government Response to the Report from the House of Commons Science and Technology Committee, p 6.

posed to Charlie's life. The HFEA had no positive reason to believe that biopsy would result in damaged children, and by October 2002 at the latest, it had evidence to support the opposite conclusion. Even if evidence of damage did exist, it would have to be very severe indeed to lead us to view PGD as 'harmful on balance' to the resulting child.

Against this, it had a living child, whose suffering could be ended and whose life could be prolonged by the use of this technology, and two desperate parents who faced watching their son die unnecessarily. Looked at in this way, it is almost impossible to see how the approach the Authority adopted could have been seen as 'cautious'.

The Authority's revised policy with regard to tissue typing is a marked improvement on the 2001 guidelines. What would be even more welcome, however, would be some indication that it had adopted a more logical approach to questions of safety and harm, an approach that recognised the dangers inherent in refusing licences as well as in granting them. A restrictive approach is not always a safe approach, and sometimes – as in the tissue typing cases – there is no way to avoid all risks. In such a situation, the sensible course is surely to give more weight to risks that are demonstrable than to those that are merely hypothetical; to risks that are posed to actual existing people than to those whose existence is contingent on the technology in question, and for whom questions of benefit and harm are more philosophically difficult than the Authority has ever acknowledged.

Both the HFEA and the Department of Health seem wedded to the idea of a precautionary approach to PGD. That being so, I think they would do well to incorporate the following precautionary rule of thumb: if you don't know either way about risks to potential future children, then at least save the child in front of you.

Chapter 7

Justice and the genetic supermarket

For anyone concerned with notions of justice or equality, Lee Silver's vision of the future is an alarming one. His *Remaking Eden* begins with a snapshot of 2350, by which time humanity will be divided as never before: 'The people of one class are referred to as *Naturals*, while those in the second class are called the *Gene-enriched* or simply the *GenRich*. . . . The GenRich are a modern-day hereditary class of genetic aristocrats.'[1]

In Silver's future, the division began in 'the twenty-first century, when genetic enhancement was first perfected'.[2] Since then, the gap has grown with each generation, and with each technological advance. By 2350, 'all professional baseball, football, and basketball players are special GenRich subtypes'. 'It would,' he tells us, 'be impossible for any Natural to compete.'[3] Indeed, '[a]ll aspects of the economy, the media, the entertainment industry and the knowledge industry are controlled by members of the GenRich class. . . . In contrast, Naturals work as low-paid service providers or as laborers'.[4]

The notion of a species divided has a rich science fictional pedigree. I have already mentioned *Brave New World*, with its state-imposed caste system of Alphas, Betas, Gammas, Deltas and Epsilons, each bred and conditioned to perform – and, most problematically for Huxley, to enjoy! – particular societal roles.[5] But not all dystopian societies have relied on such totalitarian measures. H G Wells' *The Time Machine* imagines a far future in which the labouring and leisured classes have diverged to the point of becoming separate species, the former – denied the civilising influences of high culture and

---

1 Lee M Silver, *Remaking Eden. Cloning and Beyond in a Brave New World*, London: Weidenfeld and Nicolson, 1998, p 4.
2 Ibid, p 5.
3 Id.
4 Ibid, p 6.
5 Aldous Huxley, *Brave New World*, originally published by Harper & Brothers Publishers, 1932.

education – having evolved into the beast-like Morlocks.[6] Recent science fiction reiterates the theme. Both Kim Stanley Robison's *Mars* trilogy[7] and Nancy Kress's *Beggars in Spain*[8] address the tensions that might arise when only one small group of people have enjoyed the benefits of genetic enhancement. Justina Robson's award-winning *Natural History* is one of the more extreme recent examples of such an imagined divergence, though in contrast to Silver's vision, Robson's genetically 'enhanced' population, the Forged, are a slave class, modified for work in extreme environments, who have long since ceased to be recognisably human.[9]

Such extreme examples of divergence may seem fanciful, but the underlying fear of a species divided, or even a new posthuman species, has been given serious attention by eminent philosophers.[10] More common, however, is the fear that unequal access to technologies of genetic selection or enhancement will cause, or exacerbate pre-existing divisions of a more mundane nature. In Chapter 5, I proposed that one means by which the 'arbitrariness' and 'expressivist' objections could be avoided would be by the state declining to fund any uses of PGD – what I describe as the 'hard' conception of the genetic supermarket hypothesis, and, I surmise, the conception that would come closest to Nozick's ideal.

This laissez faire approach, then, may allow the state to profess neutrality as between different choices, and hence between the qualities of different lives. As such, it may address some of the concerns of disabled persons that their lives are being 'officially devalued'. However, this approach inevitably gives rise to another kind of possible concern: a system in which PGD would be available only to those wealthy enough to afford it seems to sit uneasily with many notions of justice.

As with the other ethical concerns I have considered, there are, I think, several different versions of the 'argument from justice'. Some versions are concerned predominantly with the use of GCTs to eliminate or avoid disease. The fear here is that, when the wealthy are able to ensure that their children are free from certain diseases, empathy with, and concern for, sufferers of those diseases will decrease; they risk becoming what Philip Kitcher has

---

6 H G Wells, *The Time Machine*, London: Pan Books Limited, 1953, originally published in 1895.
7 *Red Mars*, London: HarperCollins Publishers, 1992; *Green Mars*, London: HarperCollins Publishers, 1992; *Blue Mars*, London: Voyager, 1996.
8 Nancy Kress, *Beggars in Spain*, London: Penguin, 1983.
9 Justina Robson, *Natural History*, London: Pan Books, 2003.
10 See Jonathan Glover, *What Sort Of People Should There Be?* London: Penguin, 1984; John Harris, *Clones, Genes, and Immortality: Ethics and the Genetic Revolution*, Oxford: Oxford University Press, 1998, Chapter 9, 'The New Breed'; Ronald A Lindsay, 'Enhancements and justice: Problems in determining the requirements of justice in a genetically transformed society', *Kennedy Institute of Ethics Journal* (2005); 15(1): 3–38.

called 'lower-class' diseases.[11] Other concerns relate to the use of GCTs for purposes of 'enhancement'; that is, for the acquisition of traits likely to be advantageous over and above rectifying or avoiding disease or disability. To a substantial extent, debates about enhancement technologies have been concerned with genetic modification (and non-genetic technologies). For reasons that should now be obvious, PGD offers less dramatic possibilities for enhancing normal species functioning. Nonetheless, it does give rise to concerns about justice and fair competition.

What, then, should we say to someone who fears that they will be locked outside the genetic supermarket's doors, left to gamble their children's futures on a chromosomal lottery while their wealthy and influential contemporaries can buy their way out of such worries? Should we regard them as victims of injustice, or merely of bad luck? And if we regard such unequal access to GCTs as presenting problems for the principle of justice, how should we respond? In particular, are we required to abandon the pro-choice model, or are there other, less restrictive ways to prevent a rich-poor genetic divide?

'Lower-class' diseases

Should we be concerned if PGD, or other GCTs aimed at avoiding genetic disease or disability, were available only to the wealthy? Consider the example of the use of PGD would be to avoid passing on single-gene diseases like cystic fibrosis or muscular dystrophy. Even if the tests needed to avoid such diseases were prohibitively expensive, we might still think that the less wealthy would have little cause for grievance. Since they are presently unable to avoid such conditions, a future in which they cannot access the genetic supermarket will be a future in which they are no worse off. The fact that their affluent contemporaries have a new option that is denied to them might give them a cause for envy, but it does not, we might think, give them a cause for justified complaint.

Of course, we might well reject that glib retort. Perhaps it just *is* worse to have a profoundly disabled child when we know that the technology existed to avoid that birth (and still more so if genetic modification could have allowed the defect to be remedied). Prior to the invention of techniques like PGD and IVF, the birth of a handicapped infant could more easily be attributed to bad luck, but in our post-genetic revolution society, being denied access to such technologies is almost invariably a matter of someone's choice. And when human beings are making decisions about who should have access to what, then considerations of justice necessarily arise.

We might also think that a 'hard' genetic supermarket might make life worse for the less wealthy in another way. In a pre-genetic supermarket

11 Philip Kitcher, *The Lives To Come*, London: Allen Lane: The Penguin Press, 1996, p 198.

society, we might think, the inheritance of genetic disease was a misfortune that could befall anyone, regardless of social station. In such a society, enlightened self-interest would lead the wealthy and powerful to ensure that provision was made for profoundly handicapped children, and their families; after all, such a fate could easily befall them.

This concern was perhaps most vividly expressed by journalist and author George Monbiot:

> Just as the escape hatch of the public school enables the wealthiest and most influential people in the country to ignore the under-funding of state education, future genetic screening or gene therapy could allow them to buy their way out of concern for the social and environmental factors which contribute to poor health. Indeed, it's not hard to imagine a future in which only the rich could – through gene technology – escape from the genetic effects of increasing exposure to such pollutants as pesticide residues and radioactive waste.[12]

As we have seen, Phillip Kitcher has couched his concern in similar – if slightly more mundane – terms:

> If prenatal testing for genetic diseases is often used by members of more privileged strata of society and far more rarely by the underprivileged, then the genetic conditions the affluent are concerned to avoid will become far more common among the poor – they will become 'lower-class' diseases, other people's problems. Interest in finding methods of treatment or for providing supportive environments for those born with the diseases may well wane.[13]

This leads Kitcher to the conclusion that 'societies that introduce prenatal testing have a moral obligation to work toward making it available to all their citizens'.[14]

Where Tom Shakespeare argued that a reduction in the numbers of disabled people would lessen societal concern for those who are nonetheless born with those diseases, Monbiot and Kitcher are more concerned with the distribution of these disabling genes. If they are reserved almost exclusively to the less wealthy – and by implication, probably the less influential – members of society, then it is perhaps unlikely that the resources necessary to treat the

---

12 George Monbiot, 'Rock-a-bye baby with the perfect genes', *The Guardian*, 18 February 1997.
13 Kitcher, *The Lives To Come*, op. cit., fn 11, p 198. See also Gregory Stock: 'If tests to screen for almost all genetic diseases, for example, become available, but primarily to the affluent, such disorders will turn into diseases of the disadvantaged.' *Redesigning Humans: Choosing Our Children's Genes*, London: Profile Books, 2002, p 187.
14 Kitcher, *The Lives To Come*, op. cit., fn 11, p 200.

symptoms of those conditions, or to provide a more accessible environment for those affected by them, will be made available.

We might also wonder whether, in a society where illness is avoidable, we might see a reduction in social provision for the sick. The authors of *From Chance to Choice* have speculated as to whether this might be reflected in attitudes towards workplace absences: if the 'genetic elite' were almost assured to be sick only very rarely, would employers be intolerant of those whose health is what we now consider only ordinarily robust? Intolerant to the point of not employing them?[15]

As with Shakespeare's argument, we might accept that such concerns are valid, while wondering how precisely they might be addressed, at least without employing draconian measures. It may very well be that the best way in which to ensure that society as a whole is concerned about illnesses and disabilities is by ensuring that those illnesses and disabilities are shared throughout society. But how is such an equitable distribution of bad health to be effected? The most obvious solution, we may think, would be by declaring that if PGD cannot be afforded by all, then it should be available to none. This would certainly promise to prevent the economically privileged from ensuring that they are also the 'genetically privileged'.

Yet such an approach contains certain disadvantages, some of which may be insurmountable. First, it involves a necessary and substantial interference with the interest in reproductive choice possessed (by definition) by those who would otherwise have used this technology. Of course, it might be argued that any compulsory redistributive measures, including taxation, involve an interference with liberty interests. For reasons discussed in Chapter 2, though, we might think that interference with the interest in reproductive liberty, in denying someone control over what sort of child for whom they will spend the next 20 (or, in the case of profoundly handicapped children, perhaps many more) years bearing a burden of responsibility, we interfere with their interests in a much more profound way than when we requisition and redistribute some of their earnings.[16]

It has also been suggested that the use of PGD even if only by the wealthiest sections of society could provide incidental but nonetheless substantial benefits to the less wealthy. Ronald Dworkin has argued that 'even a diminished demand for a particular therapy will stimulate research, with possibly unanticipated general benefits, that would not otherwise take place'.[17] Such a technological trickle-down effect might be thought unlikely when the effect

15 Buchanan, Brock, Daniels and Wikler, *From Chance to Choice: Genetics and Justice*, New York: Cambridge University Press, 2000, pp 297–8.
16 A point made by Lindsay, 'Enhancements and justice', fn 10, p 23.
17 Ronald Dworkin, *Sovereign Virtue: The Theory and Practice of Equality*, Cambridge, London: Harvard University Press, 2000, p 437.

for those who can afford it is to avoid the birth of affected children, rather than to develop better or cheaper ways to assist or treat them, but it is perhaps not inconceivable that, with repeated use, PGD and its successor GCTs will become more effective and, hence, more affordable. It is possible, for example, that IVF itself will become more effective, in many cases obviating the need for repeated attempts at conception or successful implantation. This may bring the technology within the reach of those who could not afford repeated cycles of treatment, but who could perhaps afford one or two such attempts.

Any possible loss of support in terms of research into (increasingly rare) genetic conditions, then, might be offset by progress (in terms of efficacy and affordability) with GCTs. If this transpires, then the prospect of a genetic supermarket being available only to a privileged elite should not concern us, because that prospect will not arise. If these optimistic predictions are wrong, though, if there is no technological trickle-down, then we are faced with a situation akin to that of the loss of support for disabled people. Just as there is no natural law that prevents us from continuing to offer support and assistance to disabled people even as their numbers decrease, neither is there any inevitability about our diminishing support for their families. Concern for that minority in the developed world who contract tuberculosis surely does not require us to abandon steps to prevent the spread of that disease.

What, though, of Monbiot's vision of 'a future in which only the rich could – through gene technology – escape from the genetic effects of increasing exposure to such pollutants as pesticide residues and radioactive waste'? Well, the obvious retort is that, whatever 'gene technology' he has in mind, it cannot be PGD. Unless the prospective parents have, somewhere in their gametes, some latent immunity to radiation damage, they will have no prospect of passing this trait onto their offspring, with our without PGD. The possibility that other forms of GCT could bring about such a result, though, is not entirely implausible, and it is a concern that I address in the Afterword.

The pro-choice presumption, then, can be defended against the loss of support argument a number of ways. First, there are reasons to suspect that GCTs will become more affordable, which will invalidate one of the empirical premises upon which the argument depends. Second, even if this does not come to pass, there is no reason why we could not in any case choose to continue to support disabled people and their families. And third, even in the worst case scenario, where the existence of an exclusive genetic supermarket does result in a diminution of support for those who cannot afford to use it, we might think that effectively forcing sick or disabled children onto reluctant parents is a disproportionate step.

If such responses are not entirely reassuring, we should perhaps not be surprised. The first two rely upon suppositions that may seem less than likely. GCTs may well become more affordable at some time in the future – but when? How much comfort should we derive from the knowledge that IVF and PGD will be universally affordable 20, or 50, years hence? And by that time, what new GCTs will be in existence, available only to the privileged? Similarly, the knowledge that society *could* or *should* continue to support the 'genetically disadvantaged' is not to say that such support *would* be forthcoming; whether we think it would or not may depend on how well we think society responds to the needs of its disadvantaged members today. The final response – that reproductive choice is more important – offers no reassurance whatever, only an ethical counterweight to loss of support concerns.

In one sense, of course, unequal access to PGD for the avoidance of diseases does not pose any new problems for the principle of justice. On many occasions throughout the history of medicine, scarcity of resources has meant rationing of state-funded treatments and medicines, with the inevitable consequence that those dependent on state-funded resources had to wait while those possessed of sufficient private means could pass them in the queue. The UK's National Health Service is often described as the greatest in the world, with treatment free at point of delivery, regardless of the patient's means. Yet in 2002, a national newspaper was able to report that:

> Thousands of patients are being denied treatment at Britain's top specialist NHS hospitals because priority is being given to people who can afford to pay huge fees for their treatment.[18]

The story went on to describe how:

> Fee-paying clients are put at the top of operating lists, are less likely to have operations cancelled, and always have access to the top consultants rather than being treated by more junior staff. Private patients – wooed by NHS hospitals with glossy literature and sales teams – are routinely operated on at times of the day reserved for NHS patients, and often bump them down the waiting list.

The issue of wealthy people being able to access expensive treatments, or to circumvent the sort of delays and problems that others simply have to endure is problematic for the principle of justice, but, we might think, it acquires no special significance, and no special ethical complexity, in relation to PGD, or GCTs more generally. Discussion of what distributive justice involves is very common in the context of debates about access to healthcare resources in general, and on one level, access to PGD/GCTs is best approached within that context.[19]

---

18 'Scandal of NHS beds auction', *The Observer*, 6 January 2002.
19 See, for example, Christopher Newdick's *Who Should We Treat? Rights, Rationing and Resources in the NHS*, Oxford: Oxford University Press, 2005; John Harris, *The Value of Life*, London: Routledge & Kegan Paul, 1985, Chapter 5; McKie, Richardson, Singer and Kuhse, *The Allocation of Health Care Resources*, Dartmouth: Ashgate, 1998.

There are, though, several reasons why we might think PGD, and other GCTs, do indeed pose particularly troublesome problems for justice. We might, for instance, pause to wonder who is the subject of any purported injustice. PGD, as we have seen, involves choosing between embryos. It hardly seems reasonable, then, to argue that a disabled child has been treated unjustly because he was not replaced with a different, healthier child.

Could we say instead that questions of justice should be addressed to the parents? I considered in Chapter 6 how the Hashmis might be able to argue that their inability to have a child, safe in the knowledge that it would be free from beta thalassaemia, could be seen as a healthcare need. It might be possible, then, to say that those at higher than average risk of passing on genetic disorders must be considered when attempting a just allocation of healthcare resources.

What, though, of those like the Whitakers, or the Mastertons, whose desire to use PGD did not derive from their carrier status? Neither family, as it happens, sought to make any demands on the taxpayer, but does it follow that such uses of the genetic supermarket pose no concerns for the principle of justice? And if lines are to be drawn between uses of PGD for disorder avoidance, and other uses of PGD, does this not give rise to precisely the sort of expressivist concerns that I sought to avoid in Chapter 5?

The most dramatic problem for justice, though, arises with regard to technologies of enhancement. Allowing a family to avoid the birth of a child with CF or muscular dystrophy might pose no more problems for justice than allowing them treatment for those conditions. Can we say the same, though, when they seek access to GCTs not to avoid disease, but to ensure their children are taller, more athletic, or perhaps even more musical or adept at mathematics? Can the same principles of justice that determine allocation of scarce medical resources be applied to choices of such non-medical traits?

'Silver spoons' and 'golden genes'

George Monbiot has drawn an analogy between 'choosing your children's genes' and 'choosing to educate them privately', both choices that he regards as pernicious.[20] While in certain respects this analogy may be inexact,[21] one aspect that both choices may be thought to possess in common might be

---

20 Monbiot, 'Rock-a-bye baby with the perfect genes', fn 12.
21 It is, for one thing, easier to argue that prospective mothers have a strong personal interest in determining which of their ova should be implanted in their uterus than to argue for a strong personal interest in controlling the education of someone who is, by that stage, a separate individual, with his or her own interests. Even Mill did not argue that individual liberty should extend to making controlling decisions over one's children.

troubling for those concerned with 'justice'.[22] By sending their children to fee-paying schools, parents generally attempt to bestow upon them a competitive advantage over their peers. Since, by definition, fee-paying schools are only open to those who can afford them, and the more renowned of them only affordable by an affluent minority, it might be thought that these schools seek to exacerbate or reinforce the already privileged position of those who attend them, shoring up their inborn economic advantage with a high-quality education and a potentially lucrative network of contacts for later life. Thus, economic and class divisions are reinforced intergenerationally.

In a similar manner, a genetic supermarket affordable only by the already wealthy would complement the economic advantages with which certain children would be born with a series of genetic advantages; they would, in the words of one commentator, be born not only with 'silver spoons' in their mouths, but with 'golden genes' in their chromosomes.[23] Such an objection might become more pronounced were knowledge about genes to extend beyond the identification of the genetic cause for certain diseases, and begin to identify – as many writers have predicted – genetic predispositions to other non-disease attributes such as above-average mental functioning or sporting prowess. Were refinements in PGD to advance in parallel, allowing such traits to be identified in vitro, what would stop a wealthy couple electing to choose a daughter with above-average aptitude in music, or a son with a gift for mathematics?

As we saw in Chapter 2, one limiting factor would of course be whether such abilities were already latent in the gametes of the wealthy couple. The use of PGD, after all, is not an example of what is sometimes deemed 'genetic enhancement'; unlike genetic modification, it cannot add anything to or remove anything from the genes possessed by the couple's embryos. Thus, the selection of traits that will be open to them will be limited by what their own genes already contain. Unless wealthy people generally have a higher genetic aptitude for maths or music than those less economically advantaged, as opposed to advantages resulting from relatively privileged upbringing and education, it is unlikely that they will routinely be able to guarantee their children 'golden genes', or even 'silver genes'.

This response will not, of course, carry much weight if genetic enhancement

---

22 Such criticism of fee-paying schools has a lengthy tradition among socialists and those concerned generally with issues of justice. For example, in 1943, R H Tawney wrote that 'Given the existing economic order, sharp class divisions exist independently of educational organization and policy. . . . It is difficult to deny that the tendency of those schools is to deepen and perpetuate them.' 'The problem of the public schools', first published in *Political Quarterly* April/June 1943, more recently in Rita Hinden, (ed), *RH Tawney: The Radical Tradition*, Middlesex: Penguin Books, 1964, p 63.

23 Hillel Steiner, 'Silver spoons and golden genes', in Justine Burley, (ed), *The Genetic Revolution and Human Rights*, Oxford: Oxford University Press, 1999, pp 133–51.

technologies eventually become available, but it might not even be all that persuasive a reply to concerns about PGD. For while wealthy prospective parents may not be able to guarantee such attributes, the ability to choose between numerous 'candidate embryos' will, perhaps, enable them to make it more likely that any potential for genetic abilities latent in their gametes will be actualised.

If it transpired that there was a genetic trait predisposing affected children to higher-than-average musical ability,[24] but that the genetic trait in question was recessive rather than dominant, then only one in every four embryos would be expected to possess that trait; PGD would allow two musician parents to avoid 'squandering their potential' by inadvertently implanting one of the other three embryos. And since it is likely that, in reality, any such genetic predisposition will be of a far more complex nature, involving the interaction of various different genes, the likelihood of stumbling across the right combination by chance would very probably be considerably longer than one in four.

Wealthy couples, then, may not be able to guarantee their children golden genes, but – to stretch the metaphor – they may be able to identify hidden seams of genetic gold that would be invisible to those excluded from the genetic supermarket. Should this be a cause of concern?

What does justice require?

'Justice' has many different meanings. Retributive justice, for instance, is concerned with punishment,[25] while restitutional justice expresses (very roughly) the idea that people should be compensated for losses that were caused by other people. The notion of justice that is typically thought relevant to discussions about genetic supermarkets is a form of distributive justice; that is, it is about distributing resources 'under conditions of scarcity and competition'.[26]

There are many models of distributive justice, and at least as many approaches to how they relate to GCTs. In this chapter, I want to consider the genetic supermarket notion from four influential perspectives. These I refer to as (1) the 'so what?' approach; (2) the 'lottery ticket' model; (3) the 'species

24 It has been suggested that perfect pitch may have a strong genetic basis; see R Ashcroft, 'Bach to the future: response to: Extending preimplantation genetic diagnosis: medical and non-medical uses', *Journal of Medical Ethics* (2003); 29(4): 213–16.
25 For further discussion of theories of why the law punishes criminals, see Part II of Gorr and Harwood, (eds), *Crime and Punishment: Philosophic Explorations*, London: Ted Honderich, *Punishment: The Supposed Justifications Revisited*, Pluto Press, 2005. For an interesting discussion of notions of punishment as applied to a specific, infamous case, see Simon Lee's chapter entitled 'Child killers: Uneasy mercy', in his *Uneasy Ethics*, London: Pimlico, 2003.
26 Beauchamp and Childress, *Principles of Biomedical Ethics*, op. cit., chapter 2, fn 2, p 226.

normal' approach; and (4) the 'brute luck' model. Although they ostensibly dictate very different approaches to the genetic supermarket, I will hope to show that none of them necessarily requires abandoning the pro-choice approach altogether.

The 'so what?' model

We should not, perhaps, be surprised to learn that the most robust defence of the genetic supermarket in the face of concerns about justice came from Robert Nozick himself. For him, inheritance was predominantly a question of the right of the property owner (the parent) to do with their property as they saw fit: 'Any person may give to anyone else any holding he is entitled to, independently of whether the recipient morally deserves to be the recipient.'[27] Provided the parents did not acquire their assets by unfair means (by which Nozick principally means force or fraud), then they should be entitled to dispose of them as they see fit. If they choose to spend their money ensuring that their children have a better start in life, or indeed a 'better' life, then that is not the proper concern of the state, any more than if they choose to give it to charity, invest it in stocks and bonds, or gamble the lot on the Grand National.

By the same token, the notion that their children would be born with certain competitive advantages over other children should not concern us unduly. Nozick acknowledges that such advantages would not be deserved, but does not conclude from this that they are unjustly held, or that the state is entitled to interfere with them: 'Whether or not people's natural assets are arbitrary from a moral point of view, they are entitled to them, and to what flows from them.'[28] If we have not exactly earned our innate abilities, neither should we have to apologise for them. And anyway, as Nozick points out, natural assets will only confer advantage if coupled with the time and effort to develop them; a naturally gifted athlete will win few medals without intensive training, a naturally gifted scholar will gain few qualifications without at least some study.

For those who find this view appealing, there is no threat posed by the genetic supermarket to the principle of justice. Parents do no wrong when they spend their money to secure genetic advantage for their children, the children do no wrong when they use those genetic advantages, and they in turn would do no wrong if they go on to pass further advantages onto their own offspring.

27 Robert Nozick, *Anarchy, State and Utopia*, Oxford: Basil Blackwell, 1974, 1986 edn, p 217.
28 Ibid, p 226.

The 'lottery ticket' model

The notion that we have some inherent entitlement to use the talents with which we were born probably has some popular appeal – at least if my experience in raising such questions among students is any indication.[29] It may be possible, though, to keep hold of this intuition while stopping short of Nozick's 'so what?' model. A perspective more in accord with our intuitions might be one that proclaimed that we should be allowed to enjoy the fruits of our talents, provided only that everyone had (roughly) the same chance of inheriting these talents. We would not, we might think, begrudge a millionaire lottery winner, even though her victory was attributable wholly to luck rather than effort, talent or sacrifice – provided that we all had an equal chance of winning the lottery.

We might, however, expect a somewhat different reaction if it transpired that the winner was already particularly wealthy, and had spent tens of thousands of pounds on tickets that very week. In Roald Dahl's classic children's novel, *Charlie and the Chocolate Factory*,[30] five 'golden tickets' are concealed within Wonka's chocolate bars. For the children lucky enough to find them, a trip to the magical Wonka's Chocolate Factory (and, as it turns out, a great deal more) awaits. The hero, Charlie Bucket, lives in penury, and it is only with the greatest sacrifice that his family can afford even one chocolate bar. In contrast, the millionaire father of the spoilt Veruca Salt buys thousands of Wonka bars, and uses his enormous staff to search through them.

How do we feel towards Charlie and Veruca? While neither of them actually deserved their luck, we might feel that there was something unfair about Veruca's father skewing the odds so far in her favour. We might agree with Nozick that winners in the genetic lottery should be entitled to profit from their luck, *provided* that everyone had a roughly equal chance of emerging from that lottery as a winner. On the 'lottery ticket' model of justice, then, what would be unfair about a genetic supermarket is not that some people would emerge from it with unearned advantage – that, of course, happens anyway – but rather that some people had the odds stacked overwhelmingly in their favour from the beginning.

This view certainly has some intuitive appeal, but it is less clear that it stands up to rigorous scrutiny. Most obviously, it seems to rely on a notion of genetic inheritance that is somewhat questionable, as this description by Francis Fukuyama shows:

The genetic lottery is judged as inherently unfair by many because it

29 Though a cynic might point out that expecting final year law students – who are, almost by definition, academically talented, and about to enter lucrative jobs – to say otherwise would be akin to expecting turkeys to vote for Christmas!
30 Puffin Books, 2001.

condemns certain people to lesser intelligence, or bad looks, or disabilities of one sort or another. But in another sense it is profoundly egalitarian, since everyone, regardless of social class, race or ethnicity, has to play in it. The wealthiest man can and often does have a good-for-nothing son ... When the lottery is replaced by choice, we open up a new avenue along which human beings can compete, one that threatens to increase the disparity between the top and bottom of the social hierarchy.[31]

It is, of course, possible that the wealthiest man can have a 'good-for-nothing' son, just as it is possible that an elite athlete can have a frail and sickly child, or a philosophy professor a child with intellectual impairments. From this, though, Fukuyama seems to be drawing the altogether more questionable conclusion that the attributes our children inherit are wholly, or primarily, a matter of luck.

Yet if we assume that at least some of the qualities linked with success in sport, academia, business, etc. are to some extent genetic, then it simply is not true that every child has even a roughly equal chance of inheriting these qualities. Rather, our genomes are almost entirely (subject only to the rare effects of mutations) dependent on the genes our parents carry, both active and latent. (And of course, if we deny that these qualities are at least partly genetic, then we have no reason to think the genetic supermarket unfair, since it will make no difference to the children's chances of success!)

Far from being 'profoundly egalitarian', then, the genetic lottery in its present form is profoundly stacked in favour of those with genetically lucky parents; 'everyone, regardless of social class, race or ethnicity' might have to play in it, but not everyone starts off with the same number of tickets. As we saw in the previous chapter, any future child Shahana and Raj Hashmi may have has, without any technological intervention, a 1:4 chance of being affected by beta thalassaemia. Those of us with no genetic history of this condition, in contrast, have virtually no chance of having a similarly affected child.

More complex traits such as might be related to success in academia or business cannot be expressed in such simple percentage terms, but insofar as they are both rare and genetically inherited (and again, I take no position on the extent to which such traits are influenced by genetic factors), the unavoidable truth is that parents who already demonstrably possess those traits are more likely than most people to have similarly lucky children. There is, of course, no guarantee that they will pass on their advantageous traits, but to continue the metaphor, they start with a suitcase full of lottery tickets, or Wonka bars, while most of us have only one or two, or indeed, none at all.

31 Francis Fukuyama, *Our Posthuman Future: Consequences of the Biotechnology Revolution*, New York: Faber, Strauss and Giroux, 2002, p 157.

Viewed in this light, the 'lottery ticket' model of justice is more of an aspiration than a description of the status quo. Indeed, if anything, those who find the lottery ticket model appealing should be enthusiastic about GCTs, especially the more radical forms, affording as they do the opportunity to ensure that a profoundly skewed lottery could be rendered somewhat less unfair.[32]

Egalitarian models of justice

Both the 'so what?' and 'lottery ticket' models considered so far start with the assumption that our innate talents, while not deserved, pose no problems for distributive justice; any objections to using these talents or gaining from them must derive from the unfair means by which we came to have them. Egalitarian models of justice take a view that is altogether more sceptical of the assumption that justice has nothing to say about unearned advantage.

There is a long egalitarian tradition of challenging this assumed entitlement. While 'meritocrats' (like John Roemer) are concerned with ensuring that the most genuinely talented people are rewarded, and therefore that unfair obstacles to this – such as racism and sexism – are removed, egalitarians challenge the assumed fairness of a system that rewards undeserved talents. Thomas Scanlon has called this the 'brute luck' model approach to justice,[33] and its various incarnations share a conviction that mere luck should not determine the rewards we receive. As the authors of *From Chance to Choice* explain:

> the appeal of the brute luck view is simple and straightforward: To many people it seems unfair that some should have fewer opportunities as a result of factors over which they have no control – circumstances that did not result from their choices. . . . Whether an individual has certain abilities and talents may depend upon his or her luck in the natural lottery. Restricting our concern about equal opportunity to differences among those with the same talents and abilities seems arbitrary.[34]

Unsurprisingly, perhaps, this model has been popular among social reformers and socialists. The most radical approaches proclaim anything less than equality of outcome as unfair; such views count among the list of unfair advantages not only innate talent and inherited wealth, but also the *inclination*

---

32 Indeed, John Harris has proposed that an 'annual lottery' could be used to determine access to GCTs; see *Clones, Genes, and Immortality*, op. cit., fn 10, p 234.

33 Thomas Scanlon, *What We Owe to Each Other?* Cambridge, Mass.: Belknap Press of Harvard University Press, 1998.

34 Buchanan, Brock, Daniels and Wikler, *From Chance to Choice*, op. cit., fn 15, p 70.

to work at developing such abilities.[35] Clearly, such a view would pose interesting questions about free will and determinism. Nonetheless, if we accepted that neither the potential talents themselves, nor the psychological properties needed to develop those talents, were in any meaningful sense deserved or earned, then it is possible to understand the inclination that any disparity in rewards must be attributable to luck rather than fairness.

The strong egalitarian claim, then, regards both the innate talents we possess, and the inclination to develop those talents, as matters of luck.[36] The weaker egalitarian claim, which I will discuss later, makes no such deterministic claim about willingness to work, and indeed regards it as quite appropriate that we should be rewarded for sacrifice and toil, though not, of course, for innate talent. Where both differ from the 'so what?' and 'lottery ticket' models of justice, though, is in the further assumption that luck should not be allowed to determine the allocation of scarce resources. Where the other two models regard luck as carrying no necessary connotations of injustice, both strong and weak egalitarians seek to eliminate the relationship between luck – good and bad – and reward; where they differ, it is principally with regard to what should properly be regarded as a matter of luck, rather than of choice.

What would an egalitarian – strong or weak – make of the genetic supermarket? Certainly, in its laissez faire incarnation, it is a mechanism whereby the effects of luck can be replicated intergenerationally; parents who are themselves the beneficiaries of good luck will be able, to some extent, to pass that luck onto their offspring. The flip side of this set-up is equally unpalatable, with those having already suffered from bad luck – whether genetic or otherwise – being least able to afford GCTs.

If this is a valid concern for the principle of justice, how should we respond to it? Two obvious strategies suggest themselves. The state could intervene with the genetic supermarket to make GCTs available to those who could not otherwise afford them; or it could even out the perceived injustice by making sure that, if everyone cannot afford access, then no one can. The former approach, which I refer to as the 'subsidised supermarket' model, raises its own questions, and I will turn to these in due course. But it is the latter – the 'total ban' model – which would be most obviously impossible to reconcile with the pro-choice approach. There are, though, a number of reasons why it is an approach we should reject.

---

35 Of course, the choice is not really so stark as between 'choice' and 'no choice'; in fact, we could adopt any one of a number of positions along a wide spectrum, recognising that our opportunities to develop potential talents are *to varying degrees* matters of choice, depending on various factors, genetic and environmental.

36 It does not, of course, follow that the 'strong egalitarian' claim is *genetically* determinist. It would be quite compatible with this view to recognise that environmental factors, such as upbringing and education, also have a strong effect on our dispositions, because such factors are also likely to be unchosen and undeserved.

a. The pointlessness of prohibition

One reason why restrictions on access to GCTs are an inadequate response to egalitarian concerns lies in the impossibility of ensuring that such restrictions are universally applied. As James Hughes has observed:

> Bans on technologies are supposedly pointless since they will probably still be available somewhere. But if people have to fly to the South Pacific and pay tens of thousands of dollars for treatments that could have been available in their hometown for a fraction of the cost, that will significantly hamper the proliferation of that technology. They will only be available to the wealthy.[37]

Such predictions require no great feat of imagination. As we have seen in earlier chapters, when confronted by obstacles in their own country, both the Whitakers and the Mastertons simply travelled to less restrictive jurisdictions. And they are not alone. In 1997, Diane Blood successfully petitioned the courts to be allowed to take her late husband's sperm to Belgium, and there to become pregnant with it.[38] (The problem for Blood was that the sperm had been obtained and stored without her husband's written consent, in violation of the 1990 Act. Belgian law, however, was more liberal on this point.)

In other medico-legal contexts too, the ability to travel between jurisdictions has allowed people to circumvent domestic law. Faced with a criminal prohibition on assisted suicide, terminally ill British citizens like Reg Crew and Anne Turner have availed themselves of the more liberal regime in Switzerland.[39] And there is a long tradition of Irish women and girls – both from Northern Ireland and the Republic – travelling to the British mainland to obtain the abortions that are not permitted in their homelands.

Of course, this observation could be taken to ridiculous extremes. It certainly does not follow that there is no point in prohibiting any conduct that is permitted elsewhere. There may be a good reason to retain a ban on cannabis use, even though cheap flights to Amsterdam make the ban an inconvenience rather than an absolute obstacle; regardless of what happens elsewhere, British drug law ensures that the (alleged) socially disruptive effects of widespread cannabis use do not happen here, while simultaneously signalling

---

37 James Hughes, *Citizen Cyborg: Why Democratic Societies Must Respond to the Redesigned Human of the Future*, Westview Press, 2004, p 115.
38 *R v Human Fertilisation and Embryology Authority ex p Blood* [1997] 2 All ER 687. For commentary, see Derek Morgan and Robert Lee, 'In the name of the father? Ex parte Blood: dealing with Novelty and Anomaly', (1997) 60 *Modern Law Review* 840.
39 'Suicide doctor's final plea for right to die in Britain', *The Times*, 24 January 2006.

society's disapproval of recreational drug use.[40] But if our justification for regulating the genetic supermarket is to prevent it conferring unfair benefits on the already privileged, then the possibility of what has been dubbed 'reproductive tourism' must raise serious questions about whether any egalitarian purpose is served by prohibition.

b. The inevitability of inequality

There is another, perhaps deeper, reason why restricting access to the genetic supermarket will not satisfy the requirements of egalitarianism, and it derives from the recognition that inequality does not begin with germinal choice technologies. I argued earlier that the 'lottery ticket' model of justice is an inaccurate description of contemporary society, because it overlooks the degree to which the 'genetically fortunate' have a greater likelihood of passing on advantageous genetic traits. Even if inheritance did operate like a true lottery, though, producing winners and losers at random, this would not satisfy the egalitarian notion of justice; none of those winners and losers, after all, would *deserve* their genetic luck.

Both the 'true lottery' and 'stacked lottery' models, then, result in profoundly unegalitarian outcomes, in as much as they produce winners who do not deserve to win, and losers who do not deserve to lose. And this is true whether or not we accept the weak egalitarian claim that sacrifice and effort are chosen rather than determined. Venus and Serena Williams may not have come from economically privileged backgrounds, but they inherited 'natural assets' – physical strength, hand-eye co-ordination, balance – that no amount of dedication could have replicated. Miguel Indurain, the five times Tour de France winning cyclist, had a lung capacity around 60% bigger than the human average. And it is surely unlikely that any stars of the NBA would have been snapped up in any draft had they been 5'5 and disposed to a chubby physique. Even if we exclude the application and effort that were also indispensable ingredients in their success, a substantial measure of 'genetic luck' was clearly a causal prerequisite of the success of any elite athlete.

Furthermore, this is true whether or not those advantages were inherited in the context of a true lottery, a stacked lottery, a 'hard' genetic supermarket, or any other system that apportions natural assets unequally. The elite athlete, or academic genius, or imaginative artist, who inherits her talents courtesy of her parents' use of GCTs is no more, and no less, deserving of those

---

40 Of course, there are good reasons to believe that current UK drug law fails in both of these aims; despite its illegality, cannabis is widely available and widely consumed, while the perceived inconsistency with its treatment of alcohol and tobacco might be thought to blur any social message that the law is intended to convey. Nonetheless, the law has aims that are not rendered redundant by the ability to consume the drug elsewhere.

advantages than her contemporaries who inherited them through more traditional means. For the egalitarian, then, the most that could be said of the existence of a genetic supermarket is that it will produce *different* undeserving winners and losers. But while there are *any* undeserving winners and losers, the system will remain fundamentally unfair.

A subsidised supermarket

An incisive egalitarian, then, might recognise that the genetic supermarket is unlikely to cause a more unfair distribution of natural assets than that which already exists. If he is especially ambitious, he may go somewhat further, and ask whether GCTs could in fact be used to further egalitarian objectives. For there is no reason why the laissez faire or 'hard' model is the only possible kind of genetic supermarket. Instead of abandoning all genetic choice to the market, we could adopt a 'softer' model, in which the state provides access to such technologies for those who could not otherwise afford them.

Buchanan, Brock, et al have considered the extent to which a radical egalitarian approach may challenge our view of health and health care:

> If it becomes within our power to prevent what we now regard as the misfortune of a sickly constitution (a weak immune system) or the catastrophe (the natural disaster) of a degenerative disease such as Alzheimer's dementia, then we may no longer be able to regard it as a misfortune. Instead, we may come to view the person who suffers these disabilities as a victim of injustice. As our powers increase, the territory of the natural is annexed to the social realm, and the new-won territory is colonized by ideas of justice.[41]

Could such a project be reconciled with the pro-choice position? In one sense, this would be unproblematic. The state would simply provide access to GCTs free of charge (or at discounted rates) for those who could not otherwise afford them. Such a system, then, would involve no element of coercion. Indeed, by providing that which would otherwise have been out of reach, the role of the state would be in expanding rather than restricting choice.

James Hughes is an enthusiastic proponent of a 'subsidised supermarket' approach. His approach begins with a thorough rejection of the notion that fairness requires a total ban; in contrast, he argues that '[a]ny enhancement that promises to make people so dramatically superior in intelligence, longevity or health that it threatens social justice is an obvious candidate for subsidies and universal provision, not for a ban'.[42] In a similar vein, Ronald

---

41 Buchanan, Brock, Daniels and Wikler, *From Chance to Choice*, op. cit., fn 15, pp 83–4.
42 Hughes, *Citizen Cyborg*, op. cit., fn 37, p 233.

Dworkin has argued that '[t]he remedy for injustice is redistribution, not denial of benefits to some with no corresponding gain to others'.[43]

Examples of Dworkin's approach are not difficult to find. When it is established that a good diet is related to health and longevity, and further established that, in a given society, not everyone can afford a good diet, the efforts of egalitarians are not aimed at gratuitously denying good food to the wealthy but at ensuring that the underprivileged, too, have access to it. In relation to PGD, then, those concerned with justice should, according to Hughes and Dworkin, be concerned with ensuring that it is available to all, and not denied to those who can at present afford it.

The real problem, rather, might arise in finding a fair cut-off point. For unless we are to commit ourselves to funding *any* genetic choices, then a decision will be needed about which are cases deserving state support, and which are not. Hughes has acknowledged that '[w]e won't be able to, or want to, subsidize all enhancements, however; some will have to be left to be purchased "out of pocket" in the genetic marketplace'.[44] Such a requirement brings us back to the sort of line-drawing exercises that Jeremy Botkin thinks necessary. Hughes himself takes a fairly expansive view of what should be subsidised, according to which any genetic interventions that would increase a child's QALYs (quality adjusted life years)[45] should be provided by the state.

One advantage of Hughes's approach is that it dispenses with any need to draw lines between 'therapy' and 'enhancement', a distinction that has proved difficult for bioethicists. Rather, *any* genetic choice that would increase the length or improve the quality of a future child's life should be provided by the state. Those choices which would not produce more QALYs – such as '[s]electing a child's sex, sexual preference or skin color' – give rise to no obligation on the state, while those which would *decrease* QALYs should be 'strongly discouraged by society'.[46]

One problem with the Hughes approach derives from the difficulty presented by QALYs, and the inherent subjectivity of any judgment of which traits will enhance or diminish the quality of a life. We might agree that a life with Tay Sachs disease is blighted in a way that a 'normal' life is not, but what about the more controversial qualities encountered throughout this book? Is a decision to 'screen out' deafness or achondraplasia QALY-enhancing? What about testing for athletic ability or perfect pitch? Do natural athletes or musicians generally have a higher quality of life than less gifted mortals?

A somewhat less expansive view is suggested by Norman Daniels. Daniels

---

43 Ronald Dworkin, *Sovereign Virtue: The Theory and Practice of Equality*, Cambridge: London, Harvard University Press, 2000, p 440.
44 Hughes, *Citizen Cyborg*, op. cit., fn 37, p 234.
45 Or the number of QALYs in the world? Hughes is somewhat ambivalent as between person-affecting and non person-affecting models of utilitarianism.
46 Hughes, *Citizen Cyborg*, op. cit., fn 37, p 238.

sees health care as having 'one general function of overriding importance for purposes of justice: it maintains, restores, or compensates for the loss of . . . functioning that is normal for a member of our species'.[47] Rejecting the radical egalitarian aspiration of 'wherever possible eliminating all inequalities in the distribution of talents and skills or other capabilities',[48] Daniels argues only for a societal obligation to treat 'departures from species-typical normal functional organization or functioning'.[49]

On a 'normal functioning' model, then, the genetic supermarket would be subsidised to the extent that genetically based treatments or tests could ensure normal species functioning; if genetic therapy ever produced a cure for cystic fibrosis, Daniels' concept of justice would, it seems, require that the state provide such a treatment for all. Similarly, if a genetic test, such as that for phenylketunuria, allowed prophylactic measures to be taken early in a child's life that would spare this child later impairments, the state would again be required by the dictates of justice to provide this. There would, however, be no obligation to provide (arguably) QALY-producing enhancements for non-disabled people.

Daniels' view can be criticised for leading to arbitrary distinctions in how we respond to certain traits. As he himself acknowledges, it seems to require us to respond differently to two people with the same problem, if that problem has, for each of them, a different cause. Our response to an 11-year-old boy whose height is predicted not to exceed 160 cm would, as Daniels admits, depend on whether that child had a 'documented growth hormone deficiency', or just 'extremely short' parents; only in the former case is there a 'departure from species-normal functioning', so only in that case is 'treatment' required. Yet, from the point of view of justice, both children have acquired the same unearned disadvantages.[50]

Furthermore, both the Daniels and Hughes approaches risk falling foul of an objection that the laissez faire genetic supermarket model would avoid: the suggestion that when the state funds only some genetic choices, it sends out a negative 'expressivist' message to certain members of society. Hughes tries to avoid the twin charges of arbitrariness and offensiveness by throwing such decisions back to prospective parents:

> it is possible to imagine a universal, egalitarian health care system that makes enhancements widely available while accommodating radically

---

47 Norman Daniels, 'Individual differences and just health care', in Murphy and Lappé, (eds), *Justice and the Human Genome Project*, London: University of California Press, 1994, p 118.

48 Ibid, p 122.

49 Id.

50 Ibid, p 123. If the suggestion that such a height limitation would be disadvantageous is controversial, it should not be difficult to imagine other examples that illustrate the same point.

different values, and radically different calculations of QALY. The answer is to permit consumers to purchase health care from competing health plans with a voucher.

The appeal of such a scheme would lie in removing the expressivist taint from any decision about GCTs. The decision would be that of the prospective parents, and not the state, which funds parental choice in a non-judgmental fashion (although if the value to be upheld is really that of parental choice, we might begin to wonder if we would do better removing the QALY requirement from the equation altogether). The problem with such a 'subsid-ised supermarket' model, from an egalitarian perspective, is the same prob-lem that any such 'subsidised free market' scheme presents. Everyone would be allowed to buy *something* from the genetic supermarket, but those with more money would still be able to buy *more*. While most people might use up their voucher ensuring that their future children would be free from major genetic illnesses, the wealthy would be able to supplement this with tests for non-disease, 'enhancement' traits.

Even if the voucher scheme was generous, allowing everyone to remove the threats of diseases while leaving enough for a few non-disease tests, there will almost certainly always be other tests for other traits, tests that will only be available to those who can pay for them privately. Furthermore, we should expect that some people, perhaps for religious or other moral reasons, forego the opportunity to make use of GCTs; in much the same way as some parents decline to have their children immunised today, it is predictable that some people will prefer 'faith babies' even if the genetic supermarket were free to all. In short, it seems that as long as the supermarket model is retained, it will be open to the wealthy and willing to bestow genetic advantages on their children. A subsidised supermarket model may mitigate some of the most obviously unfair consequences – such as those that would see genetic diseases like cystic fibrosis become 'diseases of the poor' – but it seems unlikely to further any more ambitious egalitarian objective.

Neither, though, does it follow that it frustrates any such objective. GCTs are destined to be one more mechanism by which wealthy parents can pass on unearned advantage to their children, but is it really certain that selecting their children on the basis of their genotypes will prove a greater perpetuation of class division than the ability to provide 'private schools, culture in the home, a secure home environment, trips abroad, private lessons, an advan-taged peer group, and successful role models'?[51] Myriad ways already exist by which wealthy or well-connected parents can imbue their children with undeserved advantage, many of which may be far more influential on their

51 James Fishkin, *Justice, Equal Opportunity and the Family*, New Haven, Conn.: Yale University Press, 1983, p 52.

future prospects than PGD. Principles of distributive justice dictate that society should take cogniscence of all such advantages, and act to ensure that those who were, through no fault of their own, denied them do not suffer unnecessarily as a result.

Alternative egalitarian strategies

Throughout his life, John Rawls, one of the most renowned theorists in the field of distributive justice, repeatedly addressed the question of inequality of talent. In his most influential work, *A Theory of Justice*, Rawls proclaimed that 'No one deserves his greater natural capacity nor merits a more favourable starting place in society'.[52] Rawls later described the idea that we do not 'deserve' our natural endowments as a 'moral truism',[53] asking rhetorically:

> Who would deny it? Do people really think that they (morally) deserved to be born more gifted than others? Do they think that they (morally) deserved to be born a man rather than a woman, or vice versa? Do they think that they deserved to be born into a wealthier rather than into a poorer family?[54]

Of particular interest is how Rawls proposed that such an undeserved disparity of talent should be redressed. For acknowledging that such differences are undeserved does not lead Rawls to conclude that a just society must strive 'to ignore, much less to eliminate these distinctions'.[55] Rather, such differences can be accommodated within a fair society by ensuring that 'the basic structure can be arranged so that these contingencies work for the good of the least fortunate'.[56]

Much of the remainder of Rawls' work is dedicated to outlining what form such a structure might take. For present purposes, though, what is significant is his recognition that 'The natural distribution is neither just nor unjust . . . What is just and unjust is the way that institutions deal with these facts'.[57] Indeed, in other passages Rawls seems to suggest that a disparity of talents is something to be cherished rather than challenged:

52 John Rawls, *A Theory of Justice. Revised Edition.* Oxford: Oxford University Press, 1999, p 87. See also Thomas Nagel: 'to sever the connection between talent and income, if it could be done, would be fine. Those with useful talents do not naturally deserve more material benefits than those who lack them.' *Equality and Partiality*, Oxford: Oxford University Press, 1991, p 113.
53 John Rawls, *Justice as Fairness: A Restatement*, Cambridge, Mass.: London, Belknap Press of Harvard University Press, 2001, p 74.
54 Rawls, *Justice as Fairness*, op. cit., pp 74–5.
55 John Rawls, *A Theory of Justice*, op. cit., p 87.
56 Id.
57 Id.

The difference principle represents, in effect, an agreement to regard the distribution of natural talents as in some respects a common asset and to share in the greater social and economic benefits made possible by the complementarities of this distribution. Those who have been favoured by nature, whoever they are, may gain from their good fortune only on terms that improve the situation of those who have lost out.[58]

In a society devised along Rawlsian lines, then, the prospect of wealthy parents endowing their offspring with advantageous genes would not necessarily be incompatible with justice. This is so because (a) society would redress this imbalance by 'giv[ing] more attention to those with fewer native assets and to those born into the less favourable social positions';[59] (b) because '[t]hose who have been favoured by nature . . . may gain from their good fortune only on terms that improve the situation of those who have lost out';[60] and (c) because in any event, remuneration in such a society would be 'according to effort, or perhaps better, conscientious effort'[61] rather than 'rewarding people for that over which they had no control'.[62]

In a similar vein, Michael Albert, influential proponent of Participatory Economics, has advocated that a fair society would be one in which disparities in remuneration would exist only insofar as there were disparities in the degree to which individuals were willing to make sacrifices, in terms of their time or effort, but in terms of natural ability, the aggregate products of labour would be divided equally.[63] In a society modelled along such lines, the introduction of an uncommonly talented individual would not widen the gap between the already fortunate and the already unfortunate, but would raise (by however small a degree) the standard wage paid to all.

Such approaches recognise that inequalities of natural assets are probably inevitable, and concentrate instead in mitigating the *effects* of such inequalities. They recognise that, with or without GCTs, there will be people with competitive advantages in one or other arena; they do not, however, accept

---

58 See fn 55.

59 Ibid, p 86.

60 Ibid, p 87.

61 Ibid, p 274.

62 Id. This may make Rawls sound like a proponent of what I have called 'weak' egalitarianism. He goes on to note, however, 'that the effort a person is willing to make is influenced by his natural abilities and skills and the alternatives open to him'.

63 'In a parecon remuneration is for effort and sacrifice. Since parecons equilibrate jobs for quality of life implications, rewarding for effort and sacrifice conveniently means that you earn more only by virtue of working longer or working harder, and that you earn less only by virtue of working less long or less hard, assuming, of course, that you are doing socially valued labor that utilizes assets effectively.' Michael Albert, 'Revolution based on reason not faith or fantasy', 18 December 2003, available at http://www.zmag.org./ZNETTOPnoanimation.html.

that it is fair that our lives should be substantially determined by factors over which we had no control. Various strategies could be employed in pursuance of this egalitarian enterprise, including wealth redistribution by means of taxation, welfare schemes for those unable to attend to their basic needs, and some form of state health service to mitigate the effects of illness and disability. In all probability, these measures will never bring about an entirely egalitarian society. Even where incomes are equal, it is likely that talented people will continue to be admired, and physically beautiful people desired, and it is difficult to imagine what any government could do about that, however committed they might be to egalitarian ideals! But directing our attention to the most extreme rewards and punishments attendant to good and bad luck seems a more fruitful strategy for the egalitarian than the forlorn endeavour of seeking to eradicate genetic inequalities altogether.

Similarly, though, those whose success in life is due to innate athletic prowess, artistic creativity or physical attractiveness are scarcely more deserving of the rewards these bring (except insofar as they must be coupled with actual effort). Denying the wealthy access to the genetic supermarket will not bring about a Rawlsian utopia where reward follows effort. It will, at most, perpetuate the status quo, ensuring only that one undeserving elite benefits rather than another. If we are truly concerned with egalitarian justice, we must act so as to ensure that those who lack the attributes necessary to excel in business, sport, the arts, or whatever other area upon which our society chooses to lavish the greatest rewards, should not be abandoned to poverty-line drudgery. Whether the obstacles to their success were genetic or environmental, they were in any event not chosen or earned, and justice dictates that people should not be penalised for that which lies beyond their control. As the authors of one book on social class and justice have said: 'Luck *per se* may be ineliminable . . . But why should it be just to permit the fact that some are lucky and others unlucky to influence the distribution of rewards in society?'[64]

Those who regard the laissez faire approach to GCTs – what I have described as the 'hard' version of the genetic supermarket, and the version closest to what Nozick probably envisioned – as unjust are left with the problem of showing why it is any more unfair than the social arrangement we have today. The idea that it would stack a basically fair genetic lottery in favour of the wealthy is, I think, profoundly flawed, for two reasons. First, the 'lottery ticket' approach to justice, according to which winners in the lottery may enjoy the fruits of their good fortune provided only that everyone was provided with an equal chance of winning, seems an inaccurate description of our pre-genetic supermarket society, where those with 'golden genes' have

---

64 Gordon Marshall, Adam Swift and Stephen Roberts, *Against the Odds? Social Class and Social Justice in Industrial Societies*, Oxford: Clarendon Press, 1997, p 165.

a much higher chance of passing them onto their children. Second, even if we did, somehow, bring about a society modelled on a true genetic lottery, we may still dispute its fairness; winners, after all, would still reap the benefits of brute luck rather than of their own efforts or sacrifices. The genetic lottery contains more Veruca Salts than Charlie Buckets; but even Charlie Bucket does not *deserve* to inherit the Wonka chocolate empire, any more than the thousands of disappointed children who missed out.

There are various mechanisms by which society attempts to counter the unfair advantages that result from fortunate environmental factors. A substantial investment in comprehensive schools can help counteract the advantages bestowed by elite fee-paying schools. Inheritance tax can distribute what would have been unearned income accumulating in the hands of a small number of people. But even professed socialists seem reluctant to apply such measures to the inequalities borne of the genetic lottery.[65] For those concerned with egalitarian conceptions of justice, though, there can be no distinction in principle between unearned advantage of one sort or the other. George Monbiot is correct in claiming that whether parents bestow advantage genetically or environmentally is a matter of ethical indifference; yet he stops short of acknowledging that it is equally a matter of indifference whether one gains a genetic head-start through the deliberate efforts of one's parents, or through the chance outcomes of the existing genetic lottery.

Peter Wenz argues that some defences of genetic enhancement are flawed in that they presuppose the existence of an already fair society. The conclusion of *From Chance to Choice*, he argues:

> Supports only the conclusion that genetic enhancements may be deployed without impairing justice in a society that is already just and humane, by which they [the book's authors] mean a society that meets the justice requirements in John Rawls's theory of justice. The United States, however, does not meet these requirements.[66]

Rather, in real-life 21st century US society, 'more money is typically spent per capita to educate wealthy than poor children, even though the latter generally need extra educational resources to make up for socio-economic disadvantages'.[67]

I have my doubts as to whether this is an effective critique of *From Chance to Choice*, but I am fairly sure it does not address my argument from (in)justice. Far from relying on utopian fantasies of a fair society, my response to the egalitarian attack is that it is as valid for our real-life, 2006

---

65 See Alex Callinicos, *Equality*, Cambridge: Polity Press, 2000, pp 38–39 for some examples.
66 Peter Wenz, 'Engineering genetic injustice', *Bioethics* (2005); 19(1): 1–11, p 3.
67 Id.

society as it is for the society of the genetic supermarket. Egalitarianism holds that it is unfair that people benefit or lose according to factors they did not choose or deserve. Insofar as we find the egalitarian argument compelling, it is incumbent on us to compensate for the effects of lotteries, whether they be naturally occurring and relatively random, or stacked by wealthy and ambitious parents. The existence of a genetic supermarket will make little difference to such an ethical requirement, except perhaps in making it somewhat harder to ignore.

It is not at all obvious, then, that any of the leading views of distributive justice provide a compelling argument against a pro-choice attitude to GCTs, or at least to PGD. But if we are concerned with choice, with reproductive autonomy, rather than merely with liberty from state control, there may be a duty incumbent on the state to provide free or subsidised access to the genetic supermarket. Drawing a line between those genetic choices that are subsidised, and those that are merely available to those who can afford them, is a difficult business, not least because of the danger of straying into expressivist territory. Yet the expressivist message is surely less pronounced when we say that we will provide PGD for some purposes *but still allow it for others*, than when we prohibit the practice for all purposes other than excluding disease traits.

Nonetheless, there is no escaping the fact that this area brings two of the ethical principles I have identified into conflict. There is no way obvious to me that would both (a) satisfy the requirements of justice by being fair to those who risk having seriously sick or disabled children, but who could not afford PGD, and (b) satisfy the requirements of non-maleficence by avoiding offence to existing sick and disabled people. Yet for reasons I have shown, neither would abandoning the pro-choice approach satisfy either of these ends. Sick and disabled people would still be left wondering what their parents would have done had PGD been affordable. Wealthy prospective parents will still be able to travel to other, more liberal jurisdictions. And the inheritance of seriously disabling conditions, as well as advantageous and disadvantageous non-disease traits, would continue to see social goods distributed unequally and unfairly.

Discussion of how best to structure our approach to PGD and other GCTs, so as to reconcile the (sometimes competing) requirements of justice, autonomy and non-maleficence is only in its infancy, and I look forward to reading more imaginative solutions than I have probably managed here. But it seems that any such contributions must begin with a frank realisation that the genetic supermarket, at least in its softer forms, will not constitute an intrusion into some existing egalitarian utopia. The societies we inhabit are already profoundly unjust; the challenge we face is in deciding how, and how far, we can address that injustice without infringing on other important ethical principles.

Robert A Lindsay is one of the few authors to have acknowledged the inconsistency of those who complain about possible genetic injustice in the future, while remaining seemingly unperturbed by evident genetic injustice in the present. In his recent article in the *Kennedy Institute of Ethics Journal*, he makes this frank and incisive argument:

> Gaps in wealth (and income) are both a source and an object of concern. So why not deal with those disparities directly rather than indirectly through restriction of genetic interventions? And why not do something about those gaps now? Redistribution of wealth *prior* to the advent of genetic engineering will alleviate, if not eliminate, the problem of differential access to enhancements while allowing society to reap their benefits.[68]

Such an approach, Lindsay concludes, 'does not depend on speculation about the injustice of imagined social settings', but rather, 'addresses an injustice that is all too real presently'.[69] Although his argument relates to genetic modification rather than PGD, it holds equally true with regard to either technology.

The prospect that GCTs will be used only by the wealthy, then, poses questions about the shape of a future genetic supermarket, rather than a reason to reject it altogether. Respect for justice, though, poses certain other challenges to the pro-choice model, and it is to those that I now turn.

Immoral priorities

Even if it is possible to design our genetic supermarket in such a way as to ensure some approximation of equal access to it, and possible further to restructure our societies so that inborn inequalities – whether brought about by GCTs or 'naturally' – do not dictate how we live, another glaring example of injustice looms over the whole enterprise. For the sorts of genetic 'disorders' that GCTs would be likely to avoid, or address, are not, by a long way, the major causes of early death and human misery in the world. As Thomas Pogge has pointed out:

> One-third of all human deaths are due to poverty-related causes, such as starvation, diarrhea, pneumonia, tuberculosis, malaria, measles, and perinatal conditions; all of which could be prevented or cured cheaply through food, safe drinking water, vaccinations, rehydration packs or medicines.[70]

Malaria is one of the biggest preventable killers, claiming an estimated 1.5 million lives every year. Overwhelmingly, these occur in the undeveloped

---

68 Lindsay, 'Enhancements and justice', fn 10, p 33.
69 Id.
70 Thomas Pogge, *World Poverty and Human Rights*, Cambridge: Polity Press, 2002, p 98.

world. According to Roll Back Malaria, a body formed jointly by UNICEF and the WHO:

> The estimated cost for supporting the minimal set of malaria interventions required to effectively control malaria is around $3.2 billion per year for the 82 countries with the highest burden of malaria. . . . Only a fraction of this sum is available.[71]

Relative to GCTs, the technical requirements would be very modest: 'If every African child under five years slept under an [insecticide-treated net], costing only $4, nearly 500,000 child deaths could be prevented every year.'[72]

In contrast, the diseases that could be avoided by PGD are relatively rare. Cystic fibrosis is one of the more common single gene disorders, and its effects on life expectancy and quality are grave. But it affects only 50,000 people worldwide at any given time. In the genetics White Paper, 'Our inheritance, our future: Realising the potential of genetics in the NHS', the UK Government announced that £2.5 million would be made available for research into gene therapy for cystic fibrosis.[73] Meanwhile, the Cystic Fibrosis Trust has announced its commitment to 'raising a further £15 million over five years to fund pioneering research into gene therapy'.[74]

And CF research accounts for only a small percentage of genetic research. The Human Genome Project in total is estimated to have cost the UK Exchequer £200 million,[75] and the US taxpayer 'about $2.7 billion in FY 1991 dollars'.[76] Added together, these sums would just about add up to the sum identified by Roll Back Malaria 'to effectively control malaria'. The question for those concerned with justice, then, is stark: given that malaria kills many more than all the single-gene disorders combined, how can we justify such lavish expenditure on research into the latter, while neglecting the former? The answer, I suppose, is that we cannot and could not – if that were indeed the choice. The fact that cystic fibrosis predominantly affects Caucasian people, and is hence more common in Europe and North America, while malaria is predominantly a southern hemisphere disease, should not be allowed to dictate our spending priorities; both justice and beneficence require that the suffering and deaths of African and Asian people be accorded equal weight.

71 World Malaria Report 2005, available at http://rbm.who.int/wmr2005/html/exsummqary_en.htm.
72 http://www.unicef.org/mdg/disease.html.
73 Our Inheritance, Our Future, para 5.25. Available at http://www.dh.gov.uk/assetRoot/04/01/92/39/04019239.pdf.
74 http://www.cftrust.org.uk/cf2004/cf_trust/aims.htm.
75 The Guardian, 27 June 2000.
76 National Human Genome Research Institute, NIH, http://genome.gov/11006943.

This is the argument advanced by George Scialabba, who has argued that 'The best reason of all not to press forward into the posthuman future . . . [is] that the enormous resources required could be put to much better use helping the many people who do not now enjoy an human present'.[77] Scialabba plausibly cites clean water, food, housing, and health care as more pressing needs than genetic technologies: 'The UN estimates that all these needs could be met, at a basic level, for a yearly expenditure equal to 10 percent of the recently proposed US military budget – or slightly less than Americans and Europeans spend annually on pet food and ice cream.'[78]

For this to constitute a criticism of the subsidised genetic supermarket, though, it would need to follow that there was no other way to combat malaria than with the money presently earmarked for genetic research. There are, of course, numerous other savings that could be made and projects that could be abandoned. James Hughes, while agreeing with Scialabba's listing of priorities, questions the conclusion to which this leads him: 'If we agree that some sacrifices need to be made to correct these monstrous wrongs,' he suggests, 'surely our rights to pets or ice cream are more expendable than our rights to control our own bodies and reproduction.'[79]

There is no shortage of state-funded analogies with ice cream and pet food. The cost to London of hosting the Olympic Games in 2012 has been conservatively estimated at £2 billion, though Sports Minister Roger Caborn has warned that it may end up costing at least twice as much.[80] If he is right, this project – which may do a great deal for the prestige and morale of London, but is unlikely to save many lives – will cost more than establishing effective control of malaria. The rebuilt Wembley Stadium is currently estimated to cost £757 million,[81] while the infamous Scottish Parliament building is officially recognised as having cost £373.9 million.[82]

The UK Treasury presently pays an annual grant of £413 million to the Arts Council England;[83] we could agree wholeheartedly that the arts make a valuable contribution to our lives, while still wondering whether enriching some lives outweighs saving other lives. Most controversially of all, the invasion and continued occupation of Iraq has been claimed to have cost the UK £4.5 billion,[84] and the USA a staggering £320 billion.[85] Whatever the rights

---

77 George Scialabba, cited in Hughes, *Citizen Cyborg*, op. cit., fn 37, p 130.
78 Id.
79 Id.
80 *The Guardian*, 2 November 2002.
81 BBC Online, 31 March 2006.
82 http://www.holyroodinquiry.org/holyrood-history.htm.
83 *The Guardian*, 14 December 2004.
84 Iraq Analysis Group, 'The Rising Costs of the Iraq War', March 2006, http://www.iraqanalysis.org/publications/235.
85 *Washington Post*, 27 April 2006.

and wrongs of that project, not even its most robust supporters would claim that it will save the 1.5 million lives a year that would be spared by curing malaria. Stacked against such projects, £2.5 million for research into a cure for CF begins to look like a very decent bargain.

It is right that our fiscal priorities should be scrutinised through the lens of justice, and it is right that the 10/90 gap – whereby 'Only 10% of all medical research worldwide is devoted to medical problems that account for 90% of the global disease burden'[86] – is challenged. But it is wrong to posit a false choice between life-saving projects, when less urgent and – in terms of justice and beneficence – justified projects continue to be funded.

'Irresponsible reproduction'

In the introduction to this book, I stated that one interesting aspect of the pro-choice approach to GCTs is that it faces attack from two sides. We have already seen, in Chapter 3, that bioethicists like Harris and Savulescu believe there to be an ethical obligation to use GCTs when doing so would benefit the resulting children (and seen also how their definition of 'benefit' might be thought problematic). Another example of an attack on the pro-choice position from a pro-technology perspective arises in the context of justice and obligations to society.

The nature of this argument is expressed by Laura M Purdy:[87]

> Isn't it immoral to knowingly act so as to increase the demands on ... resources that could otherwise be used for projects such as feeding the starving or averting environmental disaster? Isn't attempting to avoid the birth of those who are likely to require extra resources, other things being equal, on a par with other attempts to share resources more equally?[88]

In a similar vein, Ingmar Persson has written of 'disabling diseases – perhaps like Down's syndrome' that 'may allow those afflicted, with some extra assistance, to lead lives that are reasonably good for them, but will rob them of the power to assist others much in return'.[89] If we assume that

---

86 Commission on Health Research for Development, 1990. *Health Research: Essential Link to Equity in Development*. Cited in Florencia Luna, 'Poverty and inequality: Challenges for the IAB: IAB Presidential Address', *Bioethics* (2005); 19(5–6): 451–9, p 458.
87 Although in truth, it is difficult to find professional bioethicists who actually adhere to this view.
88 Laura M Purdy, 'Loving future people', Joan C Callahan, (ed), *Reproduction, Ethics and the Law: Feminist Perspectives*, Bloomington: Indiana University Press, 1995, p 313.
89 Ingmar Persson, 'Equality and selection for existence', *Journal of Medical Ethics* (1999); 25: 130–6, p 131. See also Lee M Silver: 'Communitarians . . . may view the refusal to preselect against such medical conditions as inherently selfish. According to this point of view, such

certain genetic traits will make it possible to predict the extent to which someone will be able to make a societal contribution, does it follow that prospective parents are subject to an ethical duty to act in such a way as to maximise that potential? Or at very least to act so as to eliminate the possibility that their offspring will be so burdened by inherited disability as to be almost guaranteed to require expensive medical treatment or other support?

To assess this claim, we must assess three separate premises. First, does justice require that prospective parents avoid the birth of those with traits that will hinder their ability to assist others, or which make it likely that they will need expensive treatment or assistance? Second, can we identify, through preimplantation testing, which traits these are likely to be? And third, even if these questions can be answered in the affirmative, does this give rise to a duty upon prospective parents to make certain preimplantation choices? If each of these questions can be answered in the affirmative, then a fourth question necessarily arises concerning the relative weights of that interest and the parental interest in reproductive liberty.

Let us consider first the question of whether justice requires taking steps to avoid the birth of children who will be net 'takers from' rather than 'contributors to' the common pool of material resources.[90] John A Robertson is a renowned champion of a liberal approach to reproductive technologies, yet he has taken this possibility quite seriously:

> It may be that any additional child makes demands on societal resources, and incurs public subsidies to some extent. It may also be that only some children subsidized in this way repay those costs over their lifetime through their own contributions. . . . Persons who reproduce knowing that they will depend on the welfare system or the charity of others to support their children will be imposing costs on others.[91]

It is certainly intelligible to suggest that, for those whose interests make a demand upon a finite shared pool of available resources, those interests may to an extent be set back by the presence of other individuals who will be rivals for those resources. Thus, someone affected by cystic fibrosis who may very

refusal would – by necessity – force society to help the unfortunate children through the expenditure of large amounts of resources and money that would otherwise be available to promote the welfare of many more people.' *Remaking Eden. Cloning and Beyond in a Brave New World.* London: Weidenfeld and Nicolson, 1998, p 223.

90 It is, of course, the case that material resources account for only one way in which someone's life impacts on the world around them, but less tangible contributions being almost impossible to evaluate in the abstract, the present discussion must be confined to the material.

91 John A Robertson, *Children of Choice: Freedom and the New Reproductive Technologies*, Princeton, New Jersey: Princeton University Press, 1994, p 77.

well, in time, require a lung, heart-and-lung, or (due to the high incidence of secondary infection) kidney transplant may be said to have an interest in avoiding the birth of other CF sufferers who may, in time, become rivals for available organs.

This possibility is not one that can lightly be discounted. As I suggested earlier, finding the balance between the expressivist harms inherent in a policy of 'screening out' future similarly affected people, and the more objective harms arising from the presence of more competitors for scarce resources, is no simple task. This uncertainty as to which course of action would be the more harmful to people affected by similar conditions allowed me to propose, earlier in this chapter, that the wishes and interests of prospective parents should be accorded precedence, simply because of the impossibility of ascertaining precisely where those other interests lie.

While different disabled individuals and groups may have different, or even diametrically opposed, interests in relation to whether similarly disabled people are born in future, the same may not be true of the non-disabled population. Expressivist concerns, and interests in developing better treatments for the condition in question, will not be relevant to those who are rivals not for a particular resource or treatment, but rivals for resources from a larger shared pool, such as from the National Health Service, or the welfare state more generally.

The care and treatment of those affected by single gene disorders is said to cost the UK state around £2 billion every year.[92] Anyone who suffers from a shortage in NHS resources, considered at the macro or meso level, might be thought to have a grievance against those parents who, deliberately or 'negligently', gave birth to a child with expensive healthcare needs. Indeed, it might be thought that anyone who either pays into that shared resource pool, or in any sense requires to take from it, might complain that the choice of (or refusal to choose by – though this itself is, of course, a sort of choice) such parents is selfish or unfair. The taxpayer and the pensioner alike could claim to be harmed, to some extent, by such choices.

Earlier in this chapter, I argued for a version of justice that does not reward or punish us for what we did not choose or earn. Those born with genetic disorders or diseases, then, should not be penalised in any way for their conditions; indeed, it is incumbent on society to seek to compensate for any such disadvantages as accompany such undeserved traits. But what are we to say of those parents who could have avoided the birth of such children? Any additional burden that is placed on the pool of shared resources is, from their perspective, not a matter of chance, but of choice. They have, we might think,

---

92 *Our Inheritance, Our Future: Realising the Potential of Genetics in the NHS*, Cm 5791, June 2003, para 1.8.

acted in an ethically suspect manner by depriving others of needed resources, when it was possible to avoid doing so.

My third question will consider the possibility that such interests are too remote, too disparate and too minimal to outweigh the interest in reproductive liberty, but before turning to that, we must consider the second question. Can we, with any accuracy, identify traits through preimplantion screening that will allow us to designate embryos as likely 'givers' or 'takers'? In some cases, this will almost certainly be possible; those conditions almost universally agreed to be disastrous, such as Tay Sachs disease (considered in Chapter 3), will result in a child with expensive medical and caring needs who will never live long enough to make any sort of material contribution to the shared pool of resources.

Those conditions aside, though, what are we to say of conditions such as CF or Duchenne Muscular Dystrophy that will, predictably, affect individuals in a manner that places demands upon healthcare resources while, through physical infirmity and decreased life expectancy, limiting their ability to contribute? What of late-onset conditions such as Huntington's Disease? While there can be little doubt that exceptional individuals such as Woodie Guthrie made a positive contribution, those affected by HD might be thought to start life already owing a 'societal debt'; they will, should they live long enough for HD symptoms to manifest themselves phenotypically, inevitably require a substantial investment of resources to provide 24-hour care and very possibly medical treatment for attendant complications such as infections.

Yet the task of calculating the net balance of an individual's life – as well as being, for many, uncomfortably callous – is inherently difficult. Those with CF or HD will certainly require substantial resource investments during certain portions of their lives, but these will be preceded by or interspersed with periods of independence and reasonably robust health. Furthermore, the portions of their lives during which they will require intensive support, treatment or assistance may be relatively brief. How is this to be weighed against those without such rare conditions, whose 'normal' life expectancies see them live for decades after retirement, as net 'takers' from the resource pool? Indeed, given the extent to which the over-sixties and over-seventies place demands upon the welfare state,[93] it may well be that, over a lifetime, someone with Amyotrophic lateral sclerosis (ALS) whose 'resource dependent

---

93 'The NHS spent around 40% of its budget – £10 billion – on people over the age of 65 in 1998/99. In the same year social services spent nearly 50% of their budget on the over 65s, some £5.2 billion.' Department of Health, *National Service Framework for Older People*, March 2001, Chapter 1, para 2. Available online at http://www.dh.gov.uk/assetRoot/ 04/07/12/83/04071283.pdf. This is despite the fact that over-65s comprise only 16% of the UK population; National Statistics Online, available at http://www.statistics.gov.uk/cci/ nugget.asp?id=949.

period' will be brief though intense,[94] has a higher balance of contributions to, rather than demands upon, the common pool.

As I said, for many people, such a calculation is inherently callous or dehumanising, but for those who would seek to rely on the 'societal burden' argument against the pro choice approach, a far more sophisticated and informed analysis will be necessitated than a simple assumption that those with 'disabilities' are more burdensome, on balance, than those with 'normal' health.

The third question that must be addressed is whether, even if we concede some sort of societal interest in avoiding 'uneconomical' lives, and assume further that such lives can be identified in advance, this gives rise to an obligation on the part of prospective parents. That someone has an interest bound up with one's decision is not always enough to give rise to an ethical duty to further that interest, especially where competing interests (including one's own) must also be weighed in the balance. More specifically, the implications in recognising the existence of a reproductive 'duty to society' would, were it to be consistently applied, extend considerably beyond the area of PGD.

It is well documented that Europe faces a demographic problem arising from the coincidence of falling birth rates and increasing life expectancy,[95] such as may be thought to give rise to a non-trivial interest on the part of the present population that potential parents have more children than they are, if they follow the average, likely to. Does this impose an ethical duty on those potential parents – who may have no desire whatever to become actual parents – to reproduce? For if it does not, then it is difficult to see how they can be thought to be subject to duty to reproduce *in a certain, particularly beneficial manner*.

Perhaps it might be argued that, while no potential parents are required to act so as to positively contribute to pool of shared resources, all may be expected to act in such a way as to avoid (or minimise the chances of) making unnecessary demands of it. On such a view, we need not think them ethically required to create *any* child in order to think them ethically required to avoid creating a seriously disabled one. Yet this rests upon an assumed all-important distinction between positive and negative obligations that might be considered somewhat suspect. If the interests of their fellow citizens in receiving more generous pensions is the legitimate concern of potential parents, it

---

94 '[T]he mean survival time with ALS is three to five years'; ALS Association website, at http://www.alsa.org/als/symptoms.cfm?CFID=175234&CFTOKEN=39766255. It should be noted that the causes of ALS are still somewhat uncertain, although it is believed that at least *some* cases are genetic in origin.

95 'The current worker-pensioner ratio in Europe has fallen to about three workers for each pensioner, and it looks set to fall to a mere three workers for every two pensioners within thirty years.' 'Work longer, have more babies', leader column in *The Economist*, 27 September 2003.

should not matter whether they adversely affect those interests by their 'decisions to' or their 'decisions not to'; both action and inaction will have the same outcome.

I would suggest, then, that all three of the questions I have addressed pose problems for the 'irresponsible reproduction' objection to the pro-choice hypothesis. However, even were we to take the view that these questions could be answered in the affirmative, any such 'societal interest' or justice-based obligation must be shown to outweigh the interest the potential parents have in reproductive liberty. Inevitably, the business of balancing such radically different interests in any objective manner is a forlorn endeavour, but it may well be suggested that the immediate direct interest of the prospective parents in choosing what child they bring into existence weighs heavily against the relatively distant and trivial interests possessed by those whose investment in that decision amounts only to a tiny fraction of their present or future income, or to a miniscule reduction in their prospects of receiving healthcare treatment. As I suggested in Chapter 2, the outcome of reproductive decisions will have significant impacts on the future lives of the potential parents, and that gives rise to a strong pro tanto case that their choices should not lightly be interfered with. To quote Robertson again, since the 'reproductive interest is generally a strong one, only very compelling needs would justify overriding their fundamental right to procreate. Saving money and preventing offense ordinarily would not rise to the required level'.[96]

96 John Robertson, *Children of Choice*, op. cit., fn 91, p 85.

Chapter 8

Defending the genetic supermarket

I have argued, then, for a pro-choice approach to PGD, an approach that allows potential parents to avail themselves of any tests they choose, whether these are for what are commonly regarded as disease traits, for HLA compatibility, for embryonic sex, or for any other reason, including selecting for what are conventionally regarded as disabilities. In allowing them this choice, we respect and further their interest in reproductive liberty, and acknowledge that the outcome of that choice will impact more significantly upon their lives than on the lives of anyone else.

The contention that choice in reproductive matters is among our most powerful interests is a difficult one to prove empirically, but it is a view widely (if not unanimously) shared in the literature. Where my approach departs from that advocated by John Robertson or Joel Feinberg is in that I have not sought to impose artificial or arbitrary constraints on that interest. I have not, as Feinberg did, sought to designate certain interests as 'inherently immoral', and therefore outwith our sphere of ethical concern. Nor have I agreed with Robertson that only a reproductive choice that 'plausibly falls within societal understandings of parental needs and choice in reproducing and raising children'[1] should be protected.

Such approaches, I believe, are open to a charge of arbitrariness (who decides which interests are excluded, or which parental choices are sufficiently in keeping with societal expectations?) and may indeed surrender the Harm Principle of which Feinberg, and perhaps also Robertson, may be seen as champions, to the legal moralism, or 'tyranny of the majority', against which it is supposed to serve as a bulwark. Hence, even choices that may be seen as unorthodox, trivial or motivated by vanity or selfishness are bound up with the interest in reproductive choice, and require a substantial ethical counterweight if they are to be constrained.

If legal restraints on such exercises of reproductive autonomy are to be

---

1 John A Robertson, 'Extending preimplantation genetic diagnosis: medical and non-medical uses', comment in *Journal of Medical Ethics*, 2003 Aug; 29(4): 213–16, p 216.

justified, then it must be shown that some important ethical principles are threatened by the pro-choice approach. The principles I have considered do not constitute an exhaustive list of the sorts of concerns people may have about GCTs. Nor does my treatment of principles like autonomy, non-maleficence and justice constitute the last word on subjects; each of these principles has extensive bodies of dedicated literature, vastly more detailed than what I have been able to produce here.

What I have tried to show, though, is that it is not by any means obvious that the sorts of concerns to which GCTs give rise (a) always stand up to rigorous scrutiny, and, when they do (b) are better addressed by more state intervention. The most obvious examples of non-rigorous objections relate to future children – those whose lives have been prevented by PGD, as well as those created by it. The former, I have argued, are simply misplaced concerns. The fact that they have never had, and never will have, interests places them outside our sphere of ethical concern. Worrying about the putative people who might have existed, if only we had acted differently, is really no more than a waste of 'moral energy', akin to worrying about the fates of fictional characters in our favourite drama serials.

Concerns about the impact of reproductive choices on the children who actually come into existence is of a different nature, and it is legitimate – arguably, obligatory – to consider how our choices and actions will impact on their welfare in the future. Such concern, though, should be clear-headed, and should not selectively ignore or reject conclusions just because they challenge our prior intuitions. The Non-Identity Principle is certainly counter-intuitive. For some esteemed commentators, like Professor Margaret Brazier, it is simply too much to accept.[2]

Recent parliamentary debates on access to reproductive services also suggest that the notion is far from influencing the thinking of our political classes. Conservative MP Charles Walker, for example, referred to a same-sex couple of his acquaintance: 'Those two men are excellent parents and I am fond of them both, but that does not mean that I believe that children's best interests are served, in the main, by having two fathers.'[3] At no point does he explain how *this* child's best interests could be better served, perhaps because

2   'For several reasons, philosophical, theological and plain common sense, it is an analogy that sounds very good and, with the greatest of respect, means very little.' Margaret Brazier, oral evidence to Select Committee, Q880.
3   House of Commons Hansard Debates, 3 July 2006: Column 556, available at http://www. publications.parliament.uk/pa/cm200506/cmhansrd/cm060703/debtext/60703-0726.htm. Accessed: 4 July 2006. Similarly oblivious to non-identity issues was Labour MP Geraldine Smith, who argued that 'Most people in the country would think that it makes sense to start a child's life with a mother and a father. Of course, there are terrific single parents who do a wonderful job. If we are looking for a basis to create a child, however, surely it should start with two parents – a mother and a father' (ibid, at Column 542).

the only logical conclusion to his argument is that *this* child would have been better off never born at all.

In the two decades since Derek Parfit first wrote about his notional 14-year-old would-be mother, though, none of the array of commentators who have written about this has succeeded in showing why the girl is wrong to have the child now – at least from the perspective of the child, for whom the stark choice is between 'this life now' and 'no life'. The option of 'better life later' is simply not on the table for this child.[4]

Other prominent bioethicists, such as John Harris and Julian Savulescu, have accepted the Principle on its merits, but dispute that it addresses all our legitimate concerns. Instead, they have pointed to Non-Person-Affecting considerations, such as a concern for the amount of suffering or happiness in the world.

Recognising an ethical obligation to minimise overall suffering, though, seems to impose an obligation to refrain from having any children at all, while an ethical obligation to increase the happiness in the world, or the balance of happiness over suffering, seems to give rise to the equally unpalatable conclusion of a universal imperative to reproduce, at least up to the point where each additional child will no longer yield a marginal utility gain. Maybe, on this approach, it would be legitimate to demand that Sharon Duchesneau and Candy McCullough answer for their alleged failure to contribute more to the collective pot of human happiness. But if so, it is only fair that we all take our turn before the Utility Council, justifying our decisions not to stuff the world to bursting point with more and more (marginally) happy children.

The alternative to these utilitarian NPA approaches is to recognise that our ethical obligations should be limited to those interests that people (and, for that matter, sentient non-humans) actually have. This concern logically extends to those future people who will exist, but not to those who, as a consequence of our decisions, will never be more than potential future people.

When it comes to considering the actual, existing (or sure to exist) interests that could be adversely affected by PGD, there is no shortage of suggested candidates. The concern that a genetic supermarket will harm disabled people is far from fanciful, and it is incumbent on proponents of a pro-choice approach to PGD to engage with such concerns. My argument, though, has been that at least some of the harms referred to in this context may in fact be best addressed by a less, rather than more, restrictive approach. In particular, the expressivist objections so passionately voiced by writers like Marsha

---

4   The girl could, of course, freeze the embryo now, with a view to implanting it when she was more mature. Whether a genetically identical child born into (somewhat) different life circumstances should be considered a different child for the purposes of the Non-Identity Principle is an interesting question, raising some fascinating questions about identity, some of which I touch on in the Afterword.

Saxton seem more likely to be addressed by a state policy of neutrality with regard to PGD; the status quo, which allows its use only for the elimination of embryos likely to become disabled children (what Saxton deemed 'people like us'), is almost certain to convey an offensive message to disabled people who already feel devalued.

The alternative approach which I have proposed here would allow those parents – presumably the majority? – who wish to use PGD for screening out genetic disorders, but it would further allow it for those like the Mastertons, who wish to select their child's sex, like the Whitakers, who seek to ensure a tissue match, and any successors to Sharon Duchesneau and Candy McCullough, who wish to maximise the chances that their child shares their particular 'disability'. In so doing, society would send a message of support for parental choice, whatever form it may take, rather than for only *certain* selected parental choices. While this will not serve as a panacea for the painful feelings of rejection – or worries that they *would*, had the choice been available, have been rejected – spoken of by some disability activists, it will at least weaken the sense that 'society' is attempting to 'eliminate the disabled'.[5]

Such an approach, though, gives rise to further difficulties regarding the extent to which society should provide, rather than merely allow, access to PGD, and I readily concede that my conclusion with regard to this question is decidedly more tentative. I have suggested that the prospect of wealthy parents being able to further advantage their children with 'golden genes' (at least insofar as these were present in their own gametes) can perhaps be accommodated within a Rawlsian concept of distributive justice, according to which how we respond to disparities in unearned assets is more important than the fact that such disparities exist. Whether or not we allow the genetic supermarket to come about, wealthy parents will find ways to ensure that their children have 'unfair' advantages in life. And with or without the genetic supermarket, natural assets such as strength, dexterity and beauty will be 'unfairly' distributed. If we are concerned with justice, we should seek to devise a means to ensure that those blessed with such environmental or natural assets do not profit unfairly as a result. Curtailing access to PGD would be to address one, relatively minor symptom, rather than to address the underlying disease itself.

Yet a 'hard' version of the genetic supermarket seems at its most harsh and unfair when it abandons those less wealthy parents who know themselves to be carriers of some relatively serious genetic disability to the whims of the

---

5   A perception, it might be thought, that is likely to be strengthened by the UK Government's unambiguous and overwhelming enthusiasm for genetic screening for, inter alia, Down's syndrome, as recently expressed in the White Paper *Our Inheritance, Our Future: Realising the Potential of Genetics in the NHS*, Cm 5791, June 2003; see, in particular, para 3.28.

chromosomal lottery. Even were the sensible, and presumably non-offensive, concession to be made whereby PGD was provided for the avoidance of aneuploidy,[6] or slightly more controversially, for the avoidance of Worse Than Nothing (WTN) lives, this would still mean that less wealthy couples had no means available of avoiding a child affected with, for example, cystic fibrosis or muscular dystrophy, neither conditions that would plausibly render a life worse-than-non-existence, but both of which could impact significantly on the lives of these families.

A somewhat glib response would be to say that a Rawlsian policy of redistribution would reduce the divisions between rich and poor, such that no one would be unable to afford PGD. But such a noble aspiration is unlikely to offer much comfort to those who find themselves locked outside the genetic supermarket's doors. Maybe an analogous approach could be taken to that employed towards cosmetic surgery, according to which 'elective' procedures are at the individual's own expense, but 'remedial' work is provided at state expense. Yet this necessarily involves an exercise in line-drawing which would fall foul of the very expressivist objections I hoped the 'neutral' approach would avoid.

I have been unable to devise a solution to this problem that does not seem likely either to offend disabled people, or to abandon less wealthy couples to the reluctant parenthood of seriously (but not WTN) disabled children. There is probably no area of medical ethics that does not, in some cases, bring two or more ethical principles into potential conflict, and PGD is no exception. Nonetheless, it may be that a less restrictive approach, whereby PGD was still *provided* for relatively serious conditions, but was in addition *permitted* for all traits, might still be somewhat less offensive to disabled people than the status quo, where the choices of deaf or achondraplasiac couples to have similarly affected children would be prohibited outright.

Furthermore, it might be hoped that the questions of justice with which GCTs present us may lead us to challenge or revise some of our prior assumptions about fairness and desert. The 'lottery ticket' approach to distributive justice, according to which the winners are free to enjoy the fruits of their good fortune provided that everyone had a roughly equal chance of winning, is, I suggest, impossible to reconcile with the notion that we do not deserve that which was attributable neither to our choices or our efforts. The belief that rejecting the genetic supermarket involves rejecting the accumulation of genetic advantage in the hands of the wealthy overlooks the fact that genetic advantage, *whoever* possesses it, is by its very nature undeserved. Those concerned with just distribution of resources should, I think, be as

6   It being difficult to see how anyone could be offended by the screening out of an embryo that is unlikely to survive even until birth.

concerned with undeserved, inherited genetic advantage as with undeserved, inherited wealth.[7]

I began this argument with a 30-year-old vision of the future. Nozick's notion of a genetic supermarket, unconstrained by state interference, at first glance looks like one of the more outlandish approaches to PGD, on the outer borders of ultra-libertarianism. It may be, though, that a less restrictive approach to germinal choice might actually address some of the objections to PGD, while recognising and respecting the vastly important interest each of us possesses in planning our own reproductive future. The alternative is an approach that reduces democracy to majority rule, and that relegates respect for autonomy below popular distaste.

Perhaps the kinds of choices discussed in this book seem trivial compared with some of those for which Mill and Hart fought in the past. Perhaps they are less important than the battles for sexual freedom for same-sex or mixed-race couples. Perhaps choosing what *kind* of child to have just *is* less important than deciding whether or when to have children.

Perhaps. Somehow, though, I doubt that Michelle and Jayson Whitaker considered it trivial to have an unelected quango tell them that their quest to save Charlie's life was morally unacceptable. And I am fairly sure that Alan and Louise Masterton regarded it as no small matter to have their feelings for their past and future daughters dissected by a nation of armchair psychologists.

In any event, there is a wider principle at stake, a principle that underpins all of these choices. This principle reminds us that we do not need to like, or share, or agree with someone's choice in order to recognise that it *is* their choice. And it keeps in check the tendencies of the majority, or the state, to impose its values and tastes and preferences on minorities within its midst. In short, this principle says that those who want to take choice away from people – especially in the most important and intimate areas of their lives – owe those people a clear explanation; an explanation that derives from the consistent application of widely shared ethical values, such as non-maleficence, respect for autonomy or justice, and not merely from squeamishness in the face of the new possibilities that germinal choice technologies seem destined to offer us.

Unfortunately, the manner in which the genetic supermarket is currently regulated has no such solid ethical foundation. Rather, the history of regulation of PGD has thus far been deeply unsatisfactory and inconsistent. This is nowhere better exemplified than in the HFEA's treatment of tissue typing, an approach that saw it seek to synthesise various ethical principles (welfare, the Kantian imperative, perhaps some notion of virtue ethics) while doing justice to none. The result was a distinction that was highly questionable both on

---

7   A fact largely lost upon the unapologetic meritocrats of the current UK Government; see Alex Callinicos, *Equality*, Cambridge: Polity Press, 2000, pp 38–9.

ethical grounds – one child apparently condemned to die while another was denied an existence, and the parents deprived of both – and in terms of consistency. Although the HFEA has recently revised this policy, it has couched this about face in terms that offer little grounds for optimism in relation to future decisions.

In relation to sex selection, the current policy seems to derive from a hybrid of deference to public opinion, concern for demographic effects and a deep distaste for what is perceived as the inherent sexism in such choices. In relation to the first of these, the question of whether public opposition to a practice should justify its prohibition takes us back to the very origins of the Harm Principle, which, both in its Millian formation and as utilised by Hart in the 1950s, maintained that mere disapproval, however widely held, was an insufficient basis for criminalisation.[8] Anyone with the merest sympathy for the Harm Principle and the liberal sentiments underlying it will be unlikely to be impressed with an approach that makes individual liberty contingent on majority approval.

The demographic worries, I have shown, are challengeable on empirical grounds – there is simply not enough evidence to allow any sort of accurate prediction of how sex selection will be used, though such evidence as is available diminishes rather than enhances such concerns. For those who fear that a society dominated by one or other gender is both a realistic possibility and a worrying one, the consolation exists that this is not a 'stable door' issue where a failure to legislate immediately might see the damage ensue almost overnight – as might be thought to be the case with genetically modified organisms or xenotransplantation. Rather, the use of preimplantation sex selection could be monitored, with a view to imposing restrictions if and when a credible body of evidence showed that it was being used in harmful ways.

Perhaps most frustratingly, the repeated failure of the HFEA, the genetic supermarket's doormen, to acknowledge or engage with the Non-Identity Principle is an astonishing oversight, given the profound consequences this notion would have upon the Authority's decisions. And it may be that the conceptual confusion penetrates to a higher level still. The position adopted by the UK courts with regard to Worse Than Nothing lives in the context of selective non-treatment of neonates seems difficult to reconcile with the outright rejection by the Court of Appeal of wrongful life suits. The latter, though, is utterly impossible to reconcile with the apparent requirement in s 13(5) of the 1990 Act that reproductive service providers consider the welfare of any future child before assisting a woman to become pregnant.

Either it is possible to compare the quality of a life with non-existence, or it is not. A state of affairs that sees judges seek to avoid such a comparison on

---

8   See Chapter 2.

the grounds of its purported impossibility, while at the same time Parliament expressly requires medical professionals to undertake it, is simply untenable.

The approach I suggest would bring consistency to this area, interpreting s 13(5) so as to prevent the creation of WTN lives, while allowing wrongful life actions to be raised on behalf of those born into such lives. Furthermore, my approach also brings both areas of law into line with the Non-Identity Principle, by regarding any other sort of life (we might, I suppose, speak of Better Than Nothing lives, or even, in more cumbersome terms, of Lives Neither Better Nor Worse Than Nothing) as insulated by the Non-Identity Principle against both the prospective prohibition of s 13(5) or the retro-spective remedy of wrongful life. Children (and the adults they become) will continue to dream and grumble about the better lives 'they' might have led, if only their parents had acted differently. They are welcome to engage in such delusions, but it should not, I think, be for the law to indulge them.

As I write this conclusion, moves are afoot within the Department of Health to propose amendments to the 1990 Act, and to overhaul the Author-ity, perhaps incorporating it within a Human Tissue Authority with a broader remit. It would also be churlish not to acknowledge that the HFEA, under the guidance of present Chair Suzi Leather, has been both more consistent and more transparent in its decision-making than under her predecessor.[9] These are interesting times for the regulation of germinal choice technologies, and it could be that, a year from now, many of the concerns I have identified in this book will have been addressed.

Such an outcome, though, seems unlikely. The HFEA's report on sex selec-tion saw it ask for a *wider* remit, encompassing gametes as well as embryos. And the latter days of Tony Blair's government is unlikely to be an era renowned in the annals of British political history for its concern with indi-vidual rights and liberties. In a recent House of Commons debate on repro-ductive technologies, Dr Ian Gibson, MP, head of the Select Committee on Science and Technology, offered his memorable summary of the UK parlia-ment's approach to regulation: 'Sometimes we do nothing and sometimes we overreact, but I think that we in this country do nothing rather well.'[10] Unfortunately, one might add, in this area at least, they do not do nothing quite often enough.

Most of us do not have to answer to the government, to 'ethical watch-dogs', or to public opinion for our decisions about whether and when to have

---

9 In May 2006, the Authority announced that PGD will now be available for the avoidance of late-onset disorders, such as genetically linked cancers; still a long way from the pro-choice approach advocated here, but progress nonetheless. See Press Release at http:// 212.49.193.187/cps/rde/xchg/SID–3F57D79B–192F530A/hfea/hs.xsl/1124.html. Accessed: 21 June 2006.

10 *Hansard*, 3 July 2006: Column 553. Available at http://www.publications.parliament.uk/pa/ cm200506/cmhansrd/cm060703/debtext/60703–0725.htm. Accessed: 4 July 2006.

children. The fact that, for some people, such decisions sometimes involve technological rather than 'natural' means does not invalidate their claim to autonomy or privacy. As more radical technological breakthroughs occur, and more unexpected choices are made, tough decisions will inevitably have to be made about which of these choices our society should permit, and which it should provide. But while other people's germinal choices might see some of us spluttering indignation over our morning coffee, we should try to remember that those choices mean a good deal more to them. If we are to deprive them of these choices, we at least owe them a good explanation for doing so, an explanation that weighs their important interest in reproductive choice against other important ethical principles.

If we can find no such principles that are threatened by their choices, or if the balancing of those competing principles fails to provide a justification for intrusion, then it will inevitably fall to us to do that apparently hardest of things for governments, religious leaders, tabloid editors and neighbourhood gossips: to recognise that sometimes, what other people choose is their concern, and none of ours.

Afterword: a frank admission

Philosophers may revel in paradox and uncertainty, but we lawyers are trained to argue for clear outcomes. One recognised tactic in building a case is to omit any evidence unfavourable to the interests of one's clients – and to hope that the other party has overlooked it too. To the perceptive reader, it may seem as though I have attempted a similar trick in this book. Having set out my stall to discuss germinal choice technologies in general, I have proceeded to construct an argument around one particular example of such technologies, preimplantation genetic diagnosis. Even if my pro-choice arguments in relation to PGD are convincing, it does not follow that they would be equally successful in relation to other GCTs. In particular, genetic modification (GM) may be thought to present possible problems that are of a different nature to those I have attempted to address.

1. One obviously distinct feature of GM that may give us cause for concern is that it opens a range of technological possibilities that PGD does not. I showed in Chapter 1 that PGD offers prospective parents only a choice between those genetic possibilities that are permitted by their gametes. Thus, the prospects of a physically homogenous population of blond-haired, blue-eyed children is not a serious possibility, any more than the average couple – however wealthy – being able to guarantee that their offspring are naturally gifted athletes or musicians.

GM is not limited in this way. Rather than merely allowing a choice between embryos, it affords the possibility of altering the genetic content of those embryos, thereby widening by a considerable margin the range of choices available to ambitious parents. If the gene sequence responsible for, say, fast twitch muscle could be identified and replicated, there is no obvious reason why this could not be inserted into otherwise physically average embryos. Suddenly, the modest range of possibilities afforded by currently available GCTs begins to look altogether wider.[1]

---

1 Some of the more ambitious possibilities have been discussed – with some enthusiasm! – in a range of recent books celebrating 'enhancement' technologies: see Gregory Stock,

Should this be of concern to advocates of the pro-choice position? It might be thought that several of the ethical principles I discussed would face somewhat different challenges from this technology. In relation to justice, we might be concerned about the extra ability of the wealthy to bestow advantages on their children. I argued in Chapter 7 that innate competitive advantage is invariably undeserved, and that therefore attempts by wealthy parents to ensure their children enjoyed elite status brought about a state of affairs no more and no less 'unfair' than the present arrangement; a truly fair society could not be achieved by closing down the genetic supermarket. GM, however, opens up other possibilities. Some writers have, for example, considered that it may some day be possible, through this or related means, to extend – possibly even quite dramatically – human life expectancy.

Writers like Bill McKibben have disputed the benefit of extra longevity,[2] but it is at least possible to see how it could be seen as a different sort of advantage to those made possible by PGD. Whereas bestowing competitive advantage on one's offspring merely means that *different* people will be at the top of the (sporting, academic, business) heap, shuffling details within a basically unfair system, leaving longevity to the genetic supermarket risks introducing a different kind of unfairness: one that sees children without wealthy parents denied the benefits of a non-competitive advantage, a 'natural primary good'. There is at least a plausible case for thinking that *all* the recipients of the longevity gene would benefit as a result – by having extra time to pursue life projects and be with people they love – without other people losing out as a result.

Does it therefore follow that the dictates of justice would require state provision of such a benefit? Or to put it another way, would a system wherein only the children of rich parents enjoy such advantages be unfair? Within a society like the UK or USA, the answer may be similar to that I offered up in Chapter 7: allowing life-extension technology only to the wealthy would of course be unfair, but it would be hypocritical to express shock at this while regarding the status quo as satisfactory. Our economic circumstances already dictate, to a significant extent, how long we will live. Amartya Sen has shown that the poorest strata of US society tend to die younger than their equivalents in much of the Third World, despite enduring less absolute poverty.[3] The

---

Redesigning Humans, London: Profile Books, 2002; James Hughes, *Citizen Cyborg*, Westview Press, 2004; Ronald Bailey, *Liberation Biology*, New York: Prometheus Books, 2005; Ramez Naam, *More Than Human*, New York: Broadway Books, 2005.

2   'If time stretched out forever before you,' McKibben has suggested, 'then you'd never need to really choose', before giving the rather strange warning that 'your satisfactions would be the satisfactions of a slow-motion orgy, not of love'. Bill McKibben, *Enough: Staying Human in an Engineered Age*, New York: Times Books, 2003, p 159.

3   Amartya Sen, *Development As Freedom*, Oxford: Oxford University Press, 1998.

inhabitants of Kensington and Chelsea already live an average of 11.5 years longer than inhabitants of my home town of Glasgow.[4]

Longevity is therefore already distributed on a supermarket model; if we find that objectionable (as of course we should), then a frank appraisal of the shortcomings of our current socio-economic arrangements is unavoidable. Making a scapegoat of GM technology may appease our consciences, but it would not discharge our moral obligations.

In fact, if the visions of science fiction authors are to be believed, it may be that the availability of radical life extension technologies, but only for the super rich, would precipitate a radical – even revolutionary – response.[5] Present inequalities in longevity are widely documented in academic publications, but they rarely feature prominently in election campaigns or tabloid headlines. A pill or potion that would grant a hundred extra years of life could not be other than a major news story, and it is difficult to imagine that the majority of the populations of developed societies would simply tolerate being denied access to it.

The more troubling problems for justice posed by life extension technologies might be of a somewhat different nature. Citizens of developed societies like those of the EC and USA already consume a far higher share of the world's scarce resources than those of poor countries.[6] A technology that allowed them to prolong their lives by decades, or perhaps even longer,[7] would undoubtedly place an even greater burden on those resources, with profound implications for both international and inter-generational justice, with attendant acceleration of climate change. Could the environment tolerate the populations of the USA and UK living twice as long?

The choice, though, may not be as stark as between environmental devastation on the one hand, and banning life extension on the other. To date, the governments of the developed world have avoided any sort of radical environmental policies. But curbing petrol or electricity consumption – even very severely – may come to be thought a worthwhile compromise in return for the gains of life extension technologies. Certainly, it seems incumbent on our governments at least to consider, perhaps, a ban on private cars, or power 'brown-outs' in the evenings, before embracing the more draconian measure of denying their populations 20 or 30 years of life.

2. Perhaps the greatest ethical disparity between PGD and genetic modification relates to the non-identity considerations I set out in Chapter 4. There,

---

4   National Statistics, 'Inequalities in life expectancy persist across the UK', 10 November 2005, available at http://www.statistics.gov.uk/pdfdir/lifexp1105.pdf.

5   See, for example, John Wyndham's *Trouble with Lychen* and Nancy Kress's *Beggars in Spain*.

6   See Peter Singer, *One World: The Ethics of Globalisation*, Yale University Press, 2002.

7   Aubrey De Grey, a biomedical gerontologist from Cambridge University, has predicted that life expectancy could come to exceed 1,000 years; see 'Scientists at odds over longevity', BBC Online, Tuesday, 28 March 2006.

I showed that the nature of PGD renders almost any 'harm to the child' arguments philosophically tenuous; since the technique involves selecting one embryo over others, the resulting child cannot really complain about his or her life circumstances without expressing a preference for non-existence. Can the same, though, be said of GM? I have deliberately avoided specifying the details of such technologies, because it is likely that by the time GM proves possible, the precise techniques will have moved on from those currently available or foreseen. But GM by its nature involves alteration rather than selection; not *choosing*, but *changing* embryos. This raises the possibility of a child growing up with a valid complaint about his parents' choices. Instead of the adolescent existentialist cry that he would rather never have been born, he might – perhaps more legitimately – protest that he would rather have been born without his parents imposing certain genetic traits on him.

The possibility of GM poses considerable difficulties for the Non-Identity Principle. It seems to me that it *is* coherent to speak of some degree of embryonic modification being consistent with continuity of identity; had my parents made some adjustment to ensure that I shared my father's brown rather than my mother's blue eyes, I think it would be reasonable to think of myself as 'the same person', with only a modest superficial change (although my relationship with my parents would presumably have been very different had they been the sort of people to care about such trivialities). It follows, then, that a child genetically modified for deafness, or short height – or whose parents elected *not* to modify them to be free of cystic fibrosis or the like – might have a legitimate complaint that *they*, and not some alternative child, could have been born with hearing or normal height or properly functioning lungs.

If this is so, then GM poses questions more akin to those raised by 'conventional' medical therapies. When considering modifying an embryo, parents might legitimately be required to justify such modification in terms of the best interests of the child who will result. At very least, modifications likely to frustrate the child's predicted interests should be prohibited – which inevitably brings us back to difficult questions about which traits are 'disabling'. If Duchesneau and McCullough really had been trying to make a baby deaf, rather than a deaf baby, is that the sort of intervention the law should allow? There seems no way to answer this without confronting the question of whether deafness is a good, bad, or neutral trait.[8]

But there must, I think, come a point when the degree of genetic alteration

---

8   We might also wonder how to accommodate within the 'best interest' paradigm a modification that seeks to change the interests which that child will possess! An attempt to 'correct' a gene for severe cognitive impairment seeks to alter the resulting child by bestowing upon it capacities that the unaltered, impaired child will not understand or care about. Would such a modification be beneficial? And to whom?

is such as to come up against the Non-Identity Principle. If the extent of genetic modification was so great that the majority of an embryo's genome had been changed, it might begin to make sense to talk about having replaced, rather than altered that embryo. Indeed, altering 50% of that embryo's genes would mean that it had no more genetic similarity with the original embryo than (on average) with its siblings. Even a lesser degree of alteration, in genetic terms, could have dramatic results for the NIP, if the genes altered are 'identity defining'. As Walter Glannon points out, 'correcting' a gene that would cause severe cognitive impairment would radically alter the values, priorities and capabilities of the person who would result. Insofar as these are the sorts of elements that define identity, 'curing' severe cognitive impairment actually amounts to replacing the severely cognitively impaired person with a different person.[9] The prospect of GM, then, forces us – or those of us who consider the non-identity principle to be important – to face up to difficult questions about identity. Then again, so do other, already existing therapies and medical choices. As I showed in Chapter 4, worries already exist about the importance of continuity of identity in relation to advance medical directives. Furthermore, neuropharmaceuticals can have profound impacts on the mental states of those who consume them – indeed, that is precisely their purpose. As the range of 'conditions' for which such drugs are prescribed continues to expand, some bioethicists have begun to worry that we are witnessing the 'medicalisation' of what we used to view as normal (if statistically deviant) human behaviour.[10] But does a 'treatment' for autism, or hyperactivity, or bipolar disorder raise questions about continuity of identity? Certainly, the post-treatment person may be happier, more stable, better able to function in their society. But are they the *same* person?

How many of our behaviour traits must change before it stops making sense to talk about continuity of the person? How many of our values, our relationships, our memories? These questions seem to me at least as valid as asking 'how many genes must change?' Until we can attempt some sort of answer to this question, it is impossible to say where the point occurs when genetic modification becomes more like PGD than like regular therapies.

These are enormously profound questions, and not, as I said, only for genetic technologies. Continuity of identity seems destined to become one of the most challenging questions for bioethics in the 21st century. But to say that the philosophy of identity throws up hard questions is not to say that all

9 Walter Glannon, *Genes and Future People: Philosophical Issues in Human Genetics*, Oxford: Westview Press, 2001, p 91.
10 See Fukuyama, *Our Posthuman Future: Consequences of the Biotechnology Revolution*, New York: Faber, Strauss and Giroux, 2002, Chapters 2 and 3; Carl Elliott, *A Philosophical Disease: Bioethics, Culture and Identity*, London: Routledge, 1999.

questions of identity are hard. If my analysis in Chapter 4 is even roughly valid, then it seems that the identity questions posed by preimplantation genetic diagnosis are actually quite easily answered. Modifying an embryo at the genetic level might, at some point, involve changing the identity of the resulting child, but replacing it with a different embryo always will. We can, and should, think about how to respond to genetic modification if and when it becomes a real concern, but such consideration should not prevent us from treating PGD on its own merits.

Bibliography

Case reports

Re A (Children) (Conjoined Twins: Surgical Separation) [2001] 57 BMLR 1

Re B (a Minor) (Wardship: Medical Treatment) (1981) 3 All ER 927

Re J (a Minor) (Wardship: Medical Treatment) [1991] Fam 33

McKay v Essex Area Health Authority [1982] QB 1166

R (on the application of Quintavalle) v Secretary of State for Health (2002) 63 BMLR 167, (2003) 71 BMLR 209

R (on the application of Quintavalle) v Human Fertilisation and Embryology Authority [2003] 3 All ER 257

Re Y (Mental Incapacity: Bone Marrow Transplant) [1997] Fam 110, (1996) 35 BMLR 111

Reports, consultation documents and press releases

Comment on Reproductive Ethics, press release, 'Tissue-typing hearing tomorrow', 31 March 2003. Available at: http://corethics.tiscali-business.it/document.asp?id= CPR310303.htm&se=2&st=4 (accessed 9 July 2006)

Committee on Homosexual Offenses and Prostitution, *Report of the Committee on Homosexual Offenses and Prostitution*, London: Her Majesty's Stationery Office, 1957

Department of Health, *Our Inheritance, Our Future: Realising the Potential of Genetics in the NHS*, June 2003, Cm 5791. Available at: http://www.dh.gov.uk/Publications AndStatistics/Publications/PublicationsPolicyAndGuidance/PublicationsPolicy AndGuidanceArticle/fs/en?CONTENT_ID=4006538&chk=enskFb (accessed 9 July 2006)

Ethics Committee of the Human Fertilisation and Embryology Authority, *Ethical Issues in the Creation and Selection of Preimplantation Embryos to Produce Tissue Donors*, 22 November 2001. Available at: http://66.249.93.104/search?q=cache: 0N6Rr0k_qwYJ:www.hfea.gov.uk/PressOffice/PressReleasesbysubject/PGDand tissuetyping/Ethics%2520Cttee%2520PGD%2520November%   25202001.pdf+% 22Ethical+Issues+in+the+Creation+and+Selection+of+Preimplantation+ Embryos+to+Produce+Tissue+Donors%22&hl=en&ct=clnk&cd=1 (accessed 9 July 2006)

House of Commons Select Committee on Science and Technology, Fourth Report,

18 July 2002. Available at: http://www.parliament.the-stationery-office.co.uk/pa/cm200102/cmselect/cmsctech/791/79103.htm (accessed 9 July 2006)

Human Fertilisation and Embryology Authority, *Code of Practice*, sixth edn, 2003

Human Genetics Commission, *Choosing the Future: Genetics and Reproductive Decision Making*, July 2004. Available at: http://www.hgc.gov.uk/UploadDocs/DocPub/Document/ChooseFuturefull.pdf (accessed 9 July 2006)

—— *Making Babies: Reproductive Decisions and Genetic Technologies*, January 2006. Available at: http://www.hgc.gov.uk/UploadDocs/DocPub/Document/Making%20Babies%20Report%20-%20final%20pdf.pdf (accessed 9 July 2006)

Joint Working Group of the HFEA and Human Genetics Commission, *Outcome of the Public Consultation on Preimplantation Genetic Diagnosis*, November 2001

Monographs, chapters and articles

Albert, Bill, 'The new genetics and disability rights', presentation to EU Conference 'Human genetic testing: what implications?', Brussels, 6 May 2004. Available at: http://www.dpi.org/en/resources/topics/bioethics/05–10–04_balbert.htm (accessed 9 July 2006)

Albert, Michael, 'Revolution based on reason not faith or fantasy', 18 December 2003. Available through http://www.zmag.org./ZNETTOPnoanimation.html

Almond, Brenda, 'Rights', in Singer, P (ed), *A Companion to Ethics*, Oxford: Blackwell Publishers Ltd, 1991

Andrews, Lori B, 'Torts and the double helix: Malpractice liability for failure to warn of genetic risks', *Houston Law Review* (1992); 29(1): 149–84

Anstey, K W, 'Are attempts to have impaired children justifiable?' *Journal of Medical Ethics* (2002); 28: 286–8

Ao, Asangla, 'Preimplantation genetic diagnosis of inherited disease', *Indian Journal of Experimental Biology* (1996); 34: 1177–82

Ashcroft, R, 'Bach to the future: response to: Extending preimplantation genetic diagnosis: medical and non-medical uses', *Journal of Medical Ethics* (2003); 29(4): 213–16

Ayer, A J, 'Happiness as satisfaction of desires', in Glover, J (ed), *Utilitarianism and its Critics*, New York: Macmillan Publishing Company, 1990

Baily, Mary Ann, 'Why I had amniocentesis', in Parens and Asch (eds), *Prenatal Testing and Disability Rights*, Washington, DC: Georgetown University Press

Barrow, Robin, *Utilitarianism: A Contemporary Statement*, Aldershot: Edward Elgar, 1991

Bayles, Michael, *Reproductive Ethics*, New Jersey: Prentice-Hall, Inc, 1984

—— 'Harm to the unconceived', *Philosophy and Public Affairs* (1976); 5(3): 292–304

Baylis, Françoise and Robert, Jason Scott, 'The inevitability of genetic enhancement technologies', *Bioethics* (2004); 18(1): 1–26

Beauchamp, Tom L and Childress, James F, *Principles of Medical Ethics*, fifth edn, New York: Oxford University Press, 2001

Beaumont, Patricia M A, 'Wrongful life and wrongful birth', in Sheila A M McLean (ed), *Contemporary Issues in Law, Medicine and Ethics*, Aldershot: Dartmouth, 1996

Bentham, Jeremy, *An Introduction to the Principles of Morals and Legislation*, in Mary Warnock (ed), *Utilitarianism*, Collins Fount Paperbacks, 1979

Berkowitz, Jonathan M, Snyder, Jack W, 'Racism and sexism in medically assisted conception', *Bioethics* (1998); 12(1): 25–44

Berlin, Isaiah, *Four Essays on Liberty*, Oxford: Oxford University Press, 1969

Beyleveld, Deryck, 'Is embryo research and preimplantation genetic diagnosis ethical?' *Forensic Science International* (2000); 113(1–3): 461–75

Botkin, Jeffrey R, 'Fetal privacy and confidentiality', *Hastings Center Report* (1995); 25(5): 32–9

—— 'Line drawing: developing professional standards for prenatal diagnostic services', in Parens and Asch (eds), *Prenatal Testing and Disability Rights*, Washington DC: Georgetown University Press, 2000

—— 'Prenatal diagnosis and the selection of children', *Florida State University Law Review* (2003); 30: 265–93

Brandt, R B, *Morality, Utilitarianism, and Rights*, Cambridge, New York: Cambridge University Press, 1992

Brock, Dan, 'The non-identity problem and genetic harms: The case of wrongful handicaps', *Bioethics* (1995); 9(3/4): 269–75

Buchanan, Allen, 'Choosing who will be disabled: genetic intervention and the morality of inclusion', *Social Philosophy & Policy* (1996); 13(1): 18–46

——, Brock, Dan W, Daniels, Norman and Wikler, Daniel, *From Chance to Choice: Genetics and Justice*, New York: Cambridge University Press, 2000

Burgess, J A and Tawia, S A, 'When did you first begin to feel it? Locating the beginning of human consciousness', *Bioethics* (1996); 10(1): 1–26

Callahan, Daniel, 'The genetic revolution', *Hastings Law Journal* (1994); 45: 1435–1526

Callinicos, Alex, *Equality*, Cambridge: Polity Press, 2000

Cameron, C, Williamson, R, 'Is there an ethical difference between preimplantation genetic diagnosis and abortion?' *Journal of Medical Ethics* (2003); 29(2): 90–2

Chadwick, Ruth, 'Having children: Introduction', in her collection *Ethics, Reproduction and Genetic Control*, London: Routledge, 1990

—— and Ngwena, Charles, 'The development of a normative standard in counselling for genetic disease: Ethics and law', *Journal of Social Welfare and Family Law* (1992) 276–95

Charlesworth, Max, *Bioethics in a Liberal Society*, Cambridge: Cambridge University Press, 1993

Chung, Kay, *Designer Myths: The Science, Law and Ethics of Preimplantation Genetic Diagnosis*. Progress Educational Trust (Briefings in Bioethics: Vol 1), 1999

Clarke, Angus, 'Response to: "What counts as success in genetic counselling?" ', *Journal of Medical Ethics* (1993); 19: 47–9

Dahl, E, Beutel, M, Brosig, B, and Hinsch, K-D, 'Preconception sex selection for non-medical reasons: a representative survey from Germany', *Human Reproduction*, (2003); 18(10): 2231–34

——, Hinsch, K-D, Beutel, M and Brosig, B, 'Preconception sex selection for non-medical reasons: a representative survey from the UK', *Human Reproduction* (2003); 18(10): 2238–9.

Degener, Theresa, 'Female self-determination between feminist claims and "voluntary" eugenics, between "rights" and ethics', *Issues in Reproductive and Genetic Engineering* (1990); 3(2): 87–99

Delatycki, M B, 'Commentary on Spriggs: genetically selected baby free of inherited predisposition to early onset Alzheimer's disease' *Journal of Medical Ethics* (2003); 29(2): 120

Devlin, Patrick, *The Enforcement of Morals*, London: Oxford University Press, 1965

Dobson, R, ' "Saviour sibling" is born after embryo selection in the United States', *British Medical Journal* (2003); 326: 1416 (28 June)

Donagan, Alan, *The Theory of Morality*, Chicago: University of Chicago Press, 1977

Duster, Troy, *Backdoor to Eugenics*, London: Routledge, 1990

Dworkin, Gerald (ed), *Morality, Harm and the Law*, Colorado: Westview Press Inc, 1994

—— 'Paternalism' and 'Paternalism: Some second thoughts', in Feinberg and Gross (eds), *Philosophy of Law*, Wadsworth Publishing Company, 1995

Dworkin, Ronald, *Taking Rights Seriously*, London: Duckworth, 1977

—— *Life's Dominion*, London: HarperCollins, 1993

—— *Sovereign Virtue: The Theory and Practice of Equality*, Cambridge, London: Harvard University Press, 2000

Dyer, C, 'Watchdog approves embryo selection to treat 3 year old child', *British Medical Journal* (2002); 324: 503

Edwards, S D, 'Prevention of disability on grounds of suffering', *Journal of Medical Ethics* (2001); 27: 380–2

—— 'Disability, identity and the "expressivist objection" ', *Journal of Medical Ethics* (2004); 30: 418–20

Feinberg, Joel, 'The rights of animals and unborn generations', in his collection *Rights, Justice, and the Bounds of Liberty*, Princeton University Press, 1980

—— 'The child's right to an open future', in W Aitken and H LaFollette (eds), *Whose Child? Children's Rights, Parental Authority, and State Power*, Totowa, NJ: Rowman & Littlefield, 1980

—— *Harm to Others*, New York: Oxford University Press, 1994

Fine, Michelle and Asch, Adrienne (eds), *Women with Disabilities: Essays in Psychology, Culture and Politics*, Philadelphia: Temple University Press, 1988

Finger, Anne, 'Claiming *all* of our bodies: Reproductive rights and disability', in Rita Arditti, Renate Duelli Klein, and Shelley Minden (eds), *Test-Tube Women: What Future for Motherhood?*, Boston: Pandora Press, 1984

Fishkin, James, *Justice, Equal Opportunity and the Family*, New Haven, Conn: Yale University Press, 1983

Fukuyama, Francis, *Our Posthuman Future: Consequences of the Biotechnology Revolution*, New York: Faber, Strauss and Giroux, 2002

Gavaghan, Colin, 'Deregulating the genetic supermarket: Pre-implantation screening, future people and the harm principle', *Cambridge Quarterly of Healthcare Ethics* (2000); 9(2): 242–61

—— 'Use of preimplantation diagnosis to produce tissue donors: An irreconcilable dichotomy?' *Human Fertility* (2003); 6, 23–5

—— ' "Designer donors"?: Tissue-typing and the regulation of pre-implantation genetic diagnosis', [2004] 3 *Web Journal of Current Legal Issues*

George, Robert P, *Making Men Moral: Civil Liberties and Public Morality*, Oxford: Clarendon Press, 1993

Glannon, Walter, *Genes and Future People: Philosophical Issues in Human Genetics*, Oxford: Westview Press, 2001

Glover, Jonathan, *What Sort Of People Should There Be?* London: Penguin, 1984
—— *Causing Death and Saving Lives*, London: Penguin Books, 1990
—— 'Future people, disability, and screening', in John Harris (ed), *Bioethics*, Oxford: Oxford University Press, 2001
Goodin, Robert E, 'Utility and the good', in Singer, P (ed), *A Companion to Ethics*, Oxford: Blackwell Publishers Ltd, 1991.
Green, Ronald M, 'Parental autonomy and the obligation not to harm one's child genetically', *Journal of Law, Medicine & Ethics* (1997); 25: 5–15
Griffin, James, 'A sophisticated version of the desire account', in Jonathan Glover (ed), *Utilitarianism and its Critics*, New York: Macmillan Publishing Company, 1990
Habermas, Jürgen, *The Future of Human Nature*, Cambridge: Polity Press, 2003
Hall, C, 'Two cases have similarities and vital differences', *The Daily Telegraph*, 3 August 2002
Hamer, Dean, and Copeland, Peter, *Living With Our Genes*, London: Pan Books, 2000
Hanson, C, Hamberger, L, and Janson, P O, 'Is any form of gender selection ethical?' *Journal of Assisted Reproduction and Genetics* (2002); 19: 431–2.
Harcourt, Bernard E, 'The collapse of the harm principle', *The Journal of Criminal Law and Criminology* (1999); 90(1): 109–57
Hare, R M, 'Abortion and the Golden Rule', *Philosophy and Public Affairs* (1975); 4(3): 201–22
—— *Moral Thinking: Its Levels, Method and Point*, Oxford: Clarendon Press, 1981.
Harris, John, *Wonderwoman and Superman: The Ethics of Human Biotechnology*, Oxford: Oxford University Press, 1992
—— 'One principle and three fallacies of disability studies', *Journal of Medical Ethics* (2001); 27: 383–7
Hart, H L A, *Law, Liberty and Morality*, Oxford: Oxford University Press, 1963
—— *Essays on Bentham: Jurisprudence and Political Theory*, Oxford: Clarendon Press, 1982
Häyry, Heta, *Individual Liberty and Medical Control*, Aldershot: Ashgate, 1998
Häyry, Matti, *Liberal Utilitarianism and Applied Ethics*, London: Routledge, 1994
Herissone-Kelly, P, 'Bioethics in the United Kingdom: Genetic screening, disability rights, and the erosion of trust', *Cambridge Quarterly of Healthcare Ethics* (2003); 12(3): 235–41.
Heyd, David, *Genethics: Moral Issues in the Creation of People*, Berkeley: University of California Press, 1992
Holm, Søren, 'Ethical issues in preimplantation diagnosis', in Harris and Holm (eds), *The Future of Human Reproduction: Ethics, Choice, and Regulation*, Oxford: Clarendon Press, 1998
Holmes, Helen Bequaert, 'Choosing children's sex: Challenges to feminist ethics', in Joan C Callahan (ed), *Reproduction, Ethics and the Law: Feminist Perspectives*, Indiana University Press, 1995
Holtug, Nils, 'Altering humans: The case for and against human gene therapy', *Cambridge Quarterly of Healthcare Ethics* (1997); 6: 157–74
—— 'On the value of coming into existence', *The Journal of Ethics* (2001); 5: 361–84
—— 'The harm principle', *Ethical Theory and Moral Practice* (2002); 5: 357–89
Hubbard, Ruth and Wald, Elijah, *Exploding the Gene Myth*, Boston: Beacon Press, 1993

Kagan, Shelly, 'The argument from liberty', in Coleman and Buchanan (eds), *In Harm's Way*, Cambridge University Press, 1994

Kant, Immanuel, *Groundwork of the Metaphysics of Morals*, 1785, translated and edited by Mary Gregor, Cambridge: Cambridge University Press, 1998

Kavka, Gregory S, 'The paradox of future individuals', *Philosophy and Public Affairs* (1981); 11(2): 93–122

Kent, Deborah, 'Somewhere a mockingbird', in Parens and Asch (eds), *Prenatal Testing and Disability Rights*, Washington DC: Georgetown University Press, 2000

Kitcher, Philip, *The Lives To Come*, London: Allen Lane: The Penguin Press, 1996

Kuljis, Rodrigo O, 'Development of the human brain: The emergence of the neural substrate for pain perception and conscious experience', in Beller and Weir (eds), *The Beginning of Human Life*, Dordrecht, Boston, London: Kluwer Academic Publishers, 1994

Lafolette, Hugh, 'Licensing parents', *Philosophy and Public Affairs* (1980); 9(2): 182–97

Lee, Robert, 'To be or not to be: is that the question? The claim of wrongful life', in Lee and Morgan (eds), *Birthrights: Law and Ethics at the Beginnings of Life*, London: Routledge, 1989

—— and Morgan, Derek, *Human Fertilisation and Embryology: Regulating the Reproductive Revolution*, London: Blackstone Press Limited, 2001

Leiser, Burton M, *Liberty, Justice, and Morals: Contemporary Value Conflicts*, second edn, New York: Macmillan Publishing Co, Inc, 1979

Lennard, A L, Jackson, G H, 'Stem cell transplantation', *British Medical Journal* (2000); 321: 433–7

Lindsay, Ronald A, 'Enhancements and justice: Problems in determining the requirements of justice in a genetically transformed society', *Kennedy Institute of Ethics Journal* (2005); 15(1): 3–38

Lippman, Abby, 'The genetic construction of prenatal testing: Choice, consent, or conformity for women?', in Rothenberg and Thomson (eds), *Women and Prenatal Testing: Facing the Challenges of Genetic Technology*, Ohio State University Press, 1994

—— 'Prenatal genetic testing and screening: constructing needs and reinforcing inequalities', in Angus Clarke (ed), *Genetic Counselling: Principles and Practice*, London: Routledge, 1994

Liu, J, Lissens, W, Devroey, P, Liebaers, I and van Steirteghem, A, 'Cystic fibrosis, Duchenne muscular dystrophy and preimplantation genetic diagnosis', *Human Reproduction Update* (1996); 2(6): 531–9

Liu, P and Rose, G A, 'Social aspects of > 800 couples coming forward for gender selection of their children', *Human Reproduction* (1995); 10(4): 968–71

Lucarelli, G, Andreani, M, Angelucci, E, 'The cure of thalassemia with bone marrow transplantation', *Bone Marrow Transplantation* (2001); 28: S11–3.

Macklin, Ruth, *Against Relativism: Cultural Diversity and the Search for Ethical Universals in Medicine*, Oxford: Oxford University Press, 1999

MacLean, Anne, *The Elimination of Morality: Reflections on Utilitarianism and Bioethics*, London: Routledge, 1993

Mahoney, John, 'The ethics of sex selection', in Peter Byrne (ed), *Medicine, Medical Ethics and the Value of Life*, Chichester: Wiley, 1990

Marshall, Gordon, Swift, Adam, and Roberts, Stephen, *Against the Odds? Social Class and Social Justice in Industrial Societies*, Oxford: Clarendon Press, 1997

McCormick, Richard A, 'Abortion: The unexplored middle ground', in John F Monagle and David C Thomasma (eds), *Health Care Ethics: Critical Issues*, Aspen Publishers Inc, 1994

McKibben, Bill, *Enough: Staying Human in an Engineered Age*, New York: Times Books, 2003

McLean, Sheila, 'Abortion law: Is consensual reform possible?', *Journal of Law and Society*, 1990, 17(1); 106–23

—— 'The right to reproduce', in Tom Campbell (ed), *Human Rights: From Rhetoric to Reality*, Oxford: Blackwell, 1986

Mill, J S, 'On liberty' and 'Utilitarianism', in Mary Warnock (ed), *Utilitarianism*, Collins Fount Paperbacks, 1979

Monbiot, George, 'Rock-a-bye baby with the perfect genes', *The Guardian*, 18 February 1997

Morgan, Derek and Lee, Robert, *Blackstone's Guide to the Human Fertilisation & Embryology Act 1990*, London: Blackstone Press, 1991

Morris, Anne and Saintier, Severine, 'To be or not to be: Is that the question? Wrongful life and misconceptions', *Medical Law Review* (2003); 11: 167–93

Morris, Jenny, 'Tyrannies of perfection', *New Internationalist*, July 1992

Munthe, Christian, 'The argument from transfer', *Bioethics* (1996); 10(1); 26–42

Nagel, Thomas, *Equality and Partiality*, Oxford: Oxford University Press, 1991

Narveson, Jan, *Morality and Utility*, Baltimore, Maryland: Johns Hopkins Press, 1967

Nelson, James Lindemann, 'Prenatal diagnosis, personal identity, and disability', *Kennedy Institute of Ethics Journal* (2000); 10(3): 213–28

Nippert, I, Edler, B, Schmidt-Herterich, C, '40 years later: the health related quality of life of women affected by thalidomide', *Community Genetics* (2002); 5(4): 209–16.

Norton, Vicki G, 'Unnatural selection: Nontherapeutic preimplantation genetic screening and proposed regulation', *UCLA Law Review* (1994); 41: 1581–1650

Nozick, Robert, *Anarchy, State, and Utopia*, Oxford: Basil Blackwell, 1974, 1986 edn

Overall, Christine, (ed) *The Future of Human Reproduction*, Toronto: The Women's Press, 1989

—— 'Do new reproductive technologies benefit or harm children?', in Dickenson, D L (ed), *Ethical Issues in Maternal-Fetal Medicine*, Cambridge: Cambridge University Press, 2002

Parens, Erik and Asch, Adrienne, 'The disability rights critique of prenatal testing: reflections and recommendations', in Parens and Asch (eds), *Prenatal Testing and Disability Rights*, Washington DC: Georgetown University Press, 2000

Parfit, Derek, *Reasons and Persons*, Oxford: Clarendon Press, 1984

Pennings, G, Schots, R and Liebaers, I, 'Ethical considerations on preimplantation genetic diagnosis for HLA typing to match a future child as a donor of haematopoietic stem cells to a sibling', *Human Reproduction* (2002); 17(3): 534–8

Persson, Ingmar, 'Equality and selection for existence', *Journal of Medical Ethics* (1999); 25: 130–6

Peters, Philip J, 'Harming future persons: Obligations to the children of reproductive technology', *Southern California Interdisciplinary Law Journal* (1999); 8: 375–400

Pettit, Philip, 'Consequentialism', in Peter Singer (ed), *A Companion to Ethics*, Oxford: Blackwell, 1991

Purdy, Laura M, 'Loving future people', in Joan C Callahan (ed), *Reproduction, Ethics and the Law: Feminist Perspectives*, Bloomington: Indiana University Press, 1995

Rachels, Stuart, 'Is it good to make happy people?', *Bioethics* (1998) 12(2): 93–110

Rawls, John, *A Theory of Justice: Revised Edition*, Oxford: Oxford University Press, 1999

—— *Justice as Fairness: A Restatement*, Cambridge, Mass., London: The Belknap Press of Harvard University Press, 2001

Raz, Joseph, *The Morality of Freedom*, Oxford: Clarendon Press, 1986

—— 'Autonomy, toleration, and the Harm Principle', in Ruth Gavison (ed), *Issues in Contemporary Legal Philosophy: The Influence of H L A Hart*, Oxford: Clarendon Press, 1987, pp 313–34.

Regan, Tom, 'Feinberg on what sorts of beings can have rights', *The Southern Journal of Philosophy* (1976); 14: 485–98

Reinders, Hans S, *The Future of the Disabled in Liberal Society: An Ethical Analysis*, Notre Dame, Indiana: University of Notre Dame Press, 2000.

Roberts, Melinda A, 'Present duties and future persons: When are existence-inducing acts wrong?' *Law and Philosophy* (1995); 14(3/4): 297–327

—— *Child Versus Childmaker: Future Persons and Present Duties in Ethics and the Law*, Maryland: Rowman and Littlefield, 1998

Robertson, John A, 'Ethical and legal issues in preimplantation genetic screening', *Fertility and Sterility* (1992); 57(1): 1–11

—— *Children of Choice: Freedom and the New Reproductive Technologies*, Princeton, New Jersey: Princeton University Press, 1994

—— 'Genetic selection of offspring characteristics', *Boston University Law Review* (1996); 76(3): 421–82

—— 'Preconception gender selection', *The American Journal of Bioethics Online* (2001); 1(1): 2–9

—— 'PGD: New ethical challenges', *Nature Reviews Genetics* (2003); 4(1): 6

—— 'Extending preimplantation genetic diagnosis: medical and non-medical uses', *Journal of Medical Ethics* (2003); 29(4): 213–16

Roth, William, 'Handicap as a social construct', *Society*, March/April 1983, 56–61.

Rowland, Robyn, 'Motherhood, patriarchal power, alienation and the issue of "choice" in sex preselection', in Gena Corea et al (eds), *Man-Made Women: How New Reproductive Technologies Affect Women*, Bloomington: Indiana University Press, 1987

Sanchez, Julian, 'Wronged possibilities: The Non-Identity Problem and harms to future persons', unpublished but available at the author's own website at http://www.juliansanchez.com/wrongposs.html

Savulescu, Julian, 'Sex selection: the case for', *Medical Journal of Australia* (1999); 171(7): 373–5

—— 'Procreative beneficence: Why we should select the best children', *Bioethics* (2001); 15 (5/6): 414–26

—— and Dahl, Edgar, 'Sex selection and preimplantation diagnosis': A response to the Ethics Committee of the American Society of Reproductive Medicine', *Human Reproduction* (2000); 15(9): 1879–80

Saxton, Marsha, 'Born and unborn: the implications of reproductive technologies for people with disabilities', in Rita Arditti, Renate Duelli-Klein, Shelley Minden (eds), *Test-Tube Women: What Future for Motherhood?*, Boston: Pandora Press, 1984

—— 'Disability rights and selective abortion', in Rickie Solinger, (ed), *Abortion Wars: A Half Century of Struggle*, Berkeley: University of California Press, 1998

Sermon, Karen, Van Steirteghem, André, Liebaers, Inge, 'Preimplantation genetic diagnosis', *The Lancet* (2004); 363(9421): 1633–41

Shakespeare, Tom, 'Back to the future? New genetics and disabled people', *Critical Social Policy* (1995); 15 (2/3): 22–35

Sheldon, Sally and Wilkinson, Stephen, 'Hashmi and Whitaker: An unjustifiable and misguided distinction?' *Medical Law Review* (2004); 12: 137–63

Shepherd, Lois, 'Protecting parents' freedom to have children with genetic differences', *University of Illinois Law Review* (1995); 4: 761–812

Singer, Peter, *Practical Ethics*, second edn, Cambridge: Cambridge University Press, 1993

—— and Wells, Diane, *The Reproductive Revolution*, Oxford: Oxford University Press, 1994

Smart, JJC and Williams, Bernard, *Utilitarianism: For and Against*, Cambridge: Cambridge University Press, 1973

Smith, Patricia, 'The metamorphosis of motherhood', in Joan C Callahan (ed), *Reproduction, Ethics, and the Law: Feminist Perspectives*, Bloomington: Indiana University Press, 1995

Spriggs, M, 'Lesbian couple creates a child whom is deaf like them', *Journal of Medical Ethics*, Online eCurrent Controversies, 2 May 2002

Stacey, Meg, 'The new genetics: a feminist view', in Theresa Marteau and Martin Richards (eds), *The Troubled Helix*, Cambridge: Cambridge University Press, 1996

Statham, Helen, Green, Josephine, Snowdon, Claire, France-Dawson, Merry, 'Choice of baby's sex', *The Lancet* (1993); 341(8844): 564–5

Steinbacher, Roberta and Holmes, Helen B, 'Sex choice: survival and sisterhood', from G Corea et al, *Man-Made Women*, op. cit., p 230.

Steinbock, Bonnie, 'The moral status of extracorporeal embryos', in Dyson and Harris (eds), *Ethics and Biotechnology*, London: Routledge, 1994

—— *Life Before Birth: The Moral and Legal Status of Embryos and Fetuses*, New York: Oxford University Press, 1992

—— 'Disability, prenatal testing, and selective abortion', in Parens and Asch (eds), *Prenatal Testing and Disability Rights*, Washington DC: Georgetown University Press, 2000

Steiner, Hillel, 'Silver spoons and golden genes: Talent differentials and distributive justice', in Justine Burley (ed), *The Genetic Revolution and Human Rights*, Oxford: Oxford University Press, 1999

Stock, Gregory, *Redesigning Humans: Choosing Our Children's Genes*, London: Profile Books, 2002

Taverne, Dick, *The March of Unreason: Science, Democracy, and the New Fundamentalism*, Oxford: Oxford University Press, 2005

Thornton, Neil, *The Problem of Liberalism in the Thought of John Stuart Mill*, London: Garland, 1987

Tizzard, Juliet, 'Why is PGD for tissue typing only not allowed?', *BioNews*, No 169, Week 29/7/2002–4/8/2002

Tooley, Michael, 'Value, obligation and the asymmetry question', *Bioethics* (1998); 12(2): 111–25

Ulmer, Todd, 'A child's claim of wrongful life: A preference for nonexistence', *Medical Trial Technique Quarterly Annual* (1992); 38: 225–39

Vehmas, Simo, 'Is it wrong to deliberately conceive or give birth to a child with mental retardation?' *Journal of Medicine and Philosophy* (2002); 27(1): 47–63

Warren, Mary Anne, *Gendercide: The Implications of Sex Selection*, New Jersey: Rowman and Allanheld, 1985

—— *Moral Status: Obligations to Persons and Other Living Things*, Oxford: Oxford University Press, 1997

Wells, Dagan, 'Advances in preimplantation genetic diagnosis', *European Journal of Obstetrics and Gynaecology and Reproductive Biology* (2004); Vol 115, Supplement 1: S97–S101

Wendell, Susan, *The Rejected Body: Feminist Philosophical Reflections on Disability*, London: Routledge, 1996

Wenz, Peter, 'Engineering genetic injustice', *Bioethics* (2005); 19(1): 1–11

Wertz, Dorothy C and Fletcher, John C, 'Fatal knowledge? Prenatal diagnosis and sex selection', *Hastings Center Report*, May/June 1989, 21–7

—— and Fletcher, John C, 'A critique of some feminist challenges to prenatal diagnosis', *Journal of Women's Health* (1993); 2(2): 173–88

Williams, Bernard, 'Who might I have been?' in *Human Genetic Information: Science, Law and Ethics (Ciba Foundation Symposium 149)*, Chichester: John Wiley & Sons, 1990

Wolff, Jonathan, 'Tin genes and compensation', in Justine Burley (ed), *The Genetic Revolution and Human Rights*, Oxford: Oxford University Press, 1999

Woodward, James, 'The Non-Identity Problem', *Ethics* (1986); 96: 804–31

Index